Living with Confidence in a Chaotic World

Living with Confidence in a Chaotic World

What on Earth Should We Do Now?

David Jeremiah

THOMAS NELSON
Since 1798

NASHVILLE   DALLAS   MEXICO CITY   RIO DE JANEIRO   BEIJING

Published in Nashville, Tennessee, by Thomas Nelson. Thomas Nelson is a registered trademark of Thomas Nelson, Inc.

Published in association with Yates & Yates, LLP, www.yates2.com.

Thomas Nelson, Inc. titles may be purchased in bulk for educational, business, fund-raising, or sales promotional use. For information, please e-mail SpecialMarkets@ThomasNelson.com.

Unless otherwise noted, Scripture quotations are taken from the New King James Version®. © 1982 by Thomas Nelson, Inc. Used by permission. All rights reserved.

Scripture quotations marked KJV are from the King James Version.

Scripture quotations marked MSG are from *The Message* by Eugene H. Peterson. © 1993, 1994, 1995, 1996, 2000. Used by permission of NavPress Publishing Group. All rights reserved.

Scripture quotations marked NASB are from the New American Standard Bible®, © The Lockman Foundation 1960, 1962, 1963, 1968, 1971, 1972, 1973, 1975, 1977, 1995. Used by permission.

Scripture quotations marked NIV are from the Holy Bible: New International Version®. © 1973, 1978, 1984 by International Bible Society. Used by permission of Zondervan Publishing House. All rights reserved.

Scripture quotations marked NLT are from the Holy Bible, New Living Translation. © 1996. Used by permission of Tyndale House Publishers, Inc., Wheaton, Illinois 60189. All rights reserved.

ISBN 978-0-8499-4677-7 (IE)

Library of Congress Cataloging-in-Publication Data

Jeremiah, David.
  Living with confidence in a chaotic world : what on earth should we do now? / David Jeremiah.
    p. cm.
  Includes bibliographical references.
  ISBN 978-0-8499-1962-6 (hardcover)
  1. Christian life. 2. Hope—Religious aspects—Christianity. 3. Eschatology. I. Title.
BV4501.3.J467 2009
248.4—dc22

2009028477

Printed in the United States of America
1 2 3 4 5 6 QW 09 10 11 12

To Marvin L. "Buzz" Oates

whose love for God and His Word has touched all of us at *Turning Point* and will, from this day forward, help us touch the rest of the world with the unchanging message of God's Word

Contents

Acknowledgments

EVERY DAY OF MY LIFE I HAVE THE PRIVILEGE OF DEVOTING MY time and energy to the only two things in the whole world that are eternal: the Word of God and people. I am so blessed to be surrounded by a team that is deeply committed to these two priorities.

At the center of that team is my wife, Donna, whose office is right next to mine and whose heart has been next to mine for forty-six years. Together we have dreamed and planned and worked toward the goal of influencing our world for Christ. More than ever before, we have been seeing our dreams come true. Like every book I have written, this one has Donna's fingerprints all over it.

Our son, David Michael, is our managing partner at *Turning Point Ministries*. His role continues to expand each year, and it is because he has taken so much off of my administrative plate that I am able to produce books such as the one you are about to read.

Diane Sutherland is my administrative assistant at our media center, and she coordinates my schedule, my travel, my partnerships . . . basically my life! All of us at *Turning Point* wonder how we ever got along without Diane.

Cathy Lord is the coordinator of research and editing. She not only provides considerable research herself, but she works with our team to assure that our information is timely and accurate. Cathy is a stickler for details and a sleuth when it comes to locating original sources.

Rob Morgan and William Kruidenier have worked with me at *Turning Point* to enrich my work. These have to be two of the most well-read men in America. I am constantly amazed at the helpful insights they bring to our writing projects. Rob Suggs is the gifted wordsmith who adds his artistry to the final product.

For the last three years, *Turning Point* has been aggressively involved in the marketing of our books. Our creative department, led by Paul Joiner, has developed some of the finest marketing strategies I have ever seen. Everyone who has seen Paul's work agrees with my assessment. Paul Joiner is one of God's best gifts to *Turning Point*.

The people of the Shadow Mountain Community Church hear what you are reading long before it is written, and they often send me notes which say, "This is going to be a book, isn't it?" Their notes are passed to me through the office of Barbara Boucher, who has been my administrative helper at Shadow Mountain for seven years. Thank you, Barbara, for your faithfulness.

Once again, as with all my other writing projects, I am represented by Sealy Yates of Yates and Yates. I am convinced that no one understands the publishing world like Sealy. He is my agent, my attorney, the chairman of our board, and, most of all, my friend.

None of us deserve to have our name on the same page with the name of our Lord and Savior, Jesus Christ. Together we all want to say,

This is really all about Him. This is His Message! We are His people!
Whatever glory comes from this endeavor belongs to Him and Him alone.
He is the only One who is worthy!

INTRODUCTION

Knowing the Signs

HOW ON EARTH DID WE GET INTO THIS MESS?

Sure, we realized the good times couldn't last forever. Everybody knows that economies move through seasons and cycles, just like everything else. What goes up must come down—just basic common sense, right?

Still, those realizations didn't quite prepare us for the reality. It was as if the United States of America went to the doctor's office for its annual checkup. The nurse said, "This will hurt just a little bit," then picked up a mallet and smashed us a good one on the head! There was a bad financial story in the headlines, then another, and the hits just kept coming. As the late Senator Everett Dirksen is credited with saying, "A billion here, a billion there, and sooner or later it adds up to some real money."[1]

For months, the pundits had been tossing around what they called "the R word"—*Recession*. Then, almost overnight, they were talking about "the D word"—*Depression*. And sure enough, we were all a little depressed.

The numbers tell the story in their cold, hard fashion. By the end of the year 2008, American investors had lost $6.9 trillion in the stock market. (One sign of the times in this grave new world, by the way, is that we find ourselves talking in numbers usually reserved for those astronomers who watch distant galaxies. *Trillions!* Can you wrap your mind around such sums of money?)

Here is a number that fits my level of comprehension: *one half.* That's the portion of the total wealth of the United States and, in fact, of the entire world that did a vanishing act in just months—fifty cents of every dollar; half of every yen, pound, mark, shekel, or whatever is used for money in your corner of the world. We've seen the illusionist make the rabbit disappear, but we always know it's merely sleight of hand; the rabbit always makes a return appearance.[2]

If only that could happen today. If only one of these brainy economists could walk onto the world stage and pull half the world's wealth out of his top hat. So many of our friends would have their jobs back. Young couples wouldn't lose their homes. We can only dream.

Wealth is a fluid thing. If all this capital vanished in a cloud of collapse and selling off, it can reappear in a cloud of demand and buying. But the experts tell us that is unlikely, at least in the near future. The buyers are presently nursing their wounds. This economic tsunami has been a sign before them, written in glaring red letters that read, "Let the buyer beware!" Economies boom in an atmosphere of confidence, when people go to market with the assurance that buying and selling are safe options. Toxic credit has poisoned the well on Wall Street; bad mortgages have left a trail of disaster; and banks have collapsed like a series of dominoes.

Forbes magazine compiles an annual list of the world's billionaires. These lists tend to resemble exclusive clubs, with the membership carrying over from one year to the next. At least they did so in the past. In the 2009 list, 30 percent of the 2008 membership dropped off the list, billionaires no more. Those members had lost an accumulated two trillion dollars—in one year! The best of times had become the worst of times.[3]

The cynic will say, "How sad about those poor, suffering billionaires! Now that they're only *millionaires,* how will they pay their water and power bills?" But you see, we're all interconnected. No man is a financial island in this world economy. The truth is that the net worth of US households fell by $11.2 trillion in 2008. We've seen the steepest decline in the housing market since 1951, and in stocks since 1946. The total nonfinancial household debt in the US is now $13.8 trillion.[4]

Throwing the word *trillions* around makes me dizzy. So let's talk about unemployment. At this writing, the national figure stands at 14.5 million or 9.4 percent of the workforce, the highest in more than two decades.[5] People who don't hold jobs don't make mortgage payments; therefore, it's not surprising that foreclosures climbed 30 percent in a single, horrible month.[6] What could be sadder than all those empty houses being sold by the banks? Our beautiful Southern California avenues are cluttered with them. I drive by them on my way to our church and shake my head; but when I look across the congregation and see the sad faces of those without jobs and homes, the truth of it really touches home. *How did we get here, Lord? How could we have not foreseen that this storm was coming?*

World leaders are meeting, working desperately to put aside political and cultural differences to find ways to stop the bleeding. Everyone looks to the United States for leadership, (also for blame—it goes with the territory). The US Congress passed a stimulus package and a $787 billion recovery plan to inject some life into a very sick economy. The new US Treasury Secretary has indicated that "as much as $2 trillion could be plowed into the financial system to jump-start lending."[7] Is it too much, too soon? Too little, too late? We hear every kind of answer, every variety of opinion. The truth is that no one really knows. We hope and pray that our economic experts are applying the right remedies, but none of them saw the crash coming—so what qualifies them as experts?

Meanwhile, across the sea, the European Central Bank has cut interest rates to a new ten-year low. There, too, the effort is to infuse more money to stimulate the economy of the European continent. Germany expects the global economy to shrink "at the worst rate since the Great Depression." Switzerland's National Bank has been negatively impacted despite its safe haven status. Obviously there is no such thing as a safe haven.[8]

In Australia, unemployment is rampant even as the government injects billions of dollars into the country's financial system. China tries its own hand at a stimulus package to fill the gap left by the loss of its export markets. As many as twenty million Chinese are out of work.

Forty heads of state met at the World Economic Forum in Switzerland. Chinese Premier Wen Jiabao urged "greater cooperation . . . in tackling the global crisis and building a new world economic order." Russian Prime Minister Vladimir Putin declared the world economic crisis to be a "perfect storm." He voiced his nation's willingness to join with other nations to address the crisis. And not surprisingly, the tensions began to rise. Mr. Putin exploited the opportunity to disparage American delegates who, the previous year, had declared "the US economy's fundamental stability."[9] Economic crises may come and go, but political bitterness is forever.

Nor was Russia the only nation to complicate an already horrendous

problem by taking jabs at the United States. In a series of provocative and dangerous maneuvers, Chinese ships harassed two US naval
vessels in open seas, coming within twenty-five feet of the USNS
Impeccable.

More ominously, North Korea has again expelled UN nuclear
inspectors from its Yongbyon nuclear plant,[10] conducted an underground nuclear test and launched six short-range rockets (all in the
space of one week), and appears poised to launch a long range ICBM,
all in direct violation of UN Security Council Resolutions.[11]

In the Middle East, tension is the status quo. Iran's Ahmadinejad
continues to blame the West for the global economic situation and
declared that "the capitalist system is on the brink of disintegration."[12]
Meanwhile, his government continues to push forward with its
nuclear program, threatening others with disintegration. The launch
of a multistage rocket early this year now enables the Iranians to place
satellites in the Earth's orbit, adding to concerns over a nuclear-armed
Iran's ability to wreak havoc in the world.

Had enough? Me too. Say what you want about this past year, but
you have to say it hasn't been dull. I actually made a point to compile
a list of global crises that have occurred during the last twelve months,
and I came up with one or more for every letter of our alphabet. How
that will come in handy, I have no clue.

Think about this. You and I have lived through some tumultuous
times. The twentieth century is surely the most remarkable hundred
years in the history of our planet. There will be some readers who
remember Pearl Harbor, D-Day, the atomic bomb, the advent of television, the revolutions of the 1960s, Neil Armstrong's walk on the
moon, the end of the Berlin Wall, the arrival of personal computers
and the Internet. Some of us have parents who can tell us about the

Great Depression of the 1930s. But I would suggest that there's never been a time like this one in our collective memory. Even that earlier depression, though it had an international scope, came before the age of the "global village." Today we are more interconnected than ever as passengers on the voyage of Spaceship Earth.

Some of you may have read my previous book, entitled *What in the World Is Going On?* In that book I summarized ten world events and related them to the prophetic Word of God. Among other things, we talked about the rebirth of Israel as a nation, the redistribution of wealth through oil, the realignment of Europe, the rise of radical Islam, and the resurgence of Russia. You know how rapidly the world landscape can change these days. Just as the book was finished and ready to hit the bookstores, along came the reversal of the financial markets. Any one of these events by itself might not cause us a concern, but all of them, taken together, present a frightening picture.

Now I wish to paint for you a separate picture. It couldn't create a starker contrast with the one we've just described, the landscape of current events. Yet this other picture is every bit as real, every bit as true. It simply lies in the future rather than the present.

We serve a loving heavenly Father who wants us to know that this world and its troubles will not last forever. In His inspired Word, He offers us a preview of a time that is so wonderful, so blessed, that the tribulations of any historic era—whether this present hour, the Hebrew captivity in Babylon, Rome's persecution of the young church, or any other you might name—would seem like a swiftly fading headache. Just before Jesus Christ returns to earth, keeping the promise He made to His disciples, this troubling time will finally arrive. And, my friends, it's quite possible that we have entered the early stages of those events.

In Paul's first letter to the Thessalonians, we are told: "But concerning the times and the seasons, brethren, you have no need that I should write to you. For you yourselves know perfectly that the day of the Lord so comes as a thief in the night. For when they say, 'Peace and safety!' then sudden destruction comes upon them, as labor pains upon a pregnant woman. And they shall not escape" (1 Thessalonians 5:1–3).

As I think about that passage, I find myself observing how that metaphor, about labor pains, perfectly fits the headlines I'm reading. An expectant mother endures quite a trial as she prepares for the birth of her child. She has morning sickness, she goes through all kinds of other drastic bodily changes, and then the labor pains arrive. As that child is preparing to enter the world, the mother's discomfort is amplified—it's a message that God doesn't want her to miss. *Rejoice! Your child is on the way!*

Similarly, our world is in pain even now. When the time comes for the blessed event that awaits all of creation, we will feel it as the nations quake. *Rejoice! Your Redemption draweth nigh!* This pain, this confusion, this anxiety is only for a little while longer.

What about these *catastrophes*? That's a word that seems to be recurring more frequently in the news media. Financial, societal, even natural catastrophes are rending this globe and all of its occupants. It's an odd four-syllable word, isn't it? The word *catastrophe* represents the union of two Greek words, *cata*, meaning "over," and *strophe*, meaning "to turn." The full picture is one of overthrow, of everything turning over in sudden and violent change.

Ask any Californian about sudden and violent changes. Living on or near various fault lines, we take these things in stride. During the most recent week, for example, we had more than seven hundred earthquakes in our region, or so I'm informed from the latest Southern California Earthquake Data Center Web site.[13] Nonchalant as we may appear, we all have that identical thought in the back of our minds: *the big one*. The ground could open up any second now. "It's California," someone will tell you. "Deal with it! You don't like it, move!" Then, just as he finishes those words, that familiar tremble of the foundations may begin. Even quakeproof buildings are suddenly doing that frightening dance. And the fellow who told you to "deal with it" is doing so himself, with a frantic dash toward the exit.

All of us are brave while we're under the impression that the coast is clear. However, here's one more statistic: Did you know that there has been a 42.8-percent spike in earthquakes measured worldwide between 2000 and 2008?[14]

Labor pains or simple geology? You make the call.

We could just as well talk about the terrible tsunami that hit Asia, or the unprecedented storms that hit the Gulf Coast, or any number of increasingly violent storms that are now becoming a fixture in the daily news. Tornadoes, hurricanes, ice storms, blizzards, floods, extremes of heat and cold. The Weather Channel has a growing audience and a show entitled *Storm Stories*.

We could also discuss eruptions in the spiritual world. We are seeing an outpouring of pure, unrestrained evil such as we would never have thought possible even a few years ago. It's the clear symptom of a culture in disintegration. I don't need to say much here; you need only turn on your television set to agree that too much freedom of a certain kind can lead to the worst enslavement. Our society has lost its moorings, so that reports of mass shootings, many involving someone's own family, are no longer particularly shocking to us. We read of fathers imprisoning their own children for immoral purposes and mothers selling their young children to representatives of the sickest underbelly of a lost culture.

Clergy misconduct, I'm sad to say, is never far from the headlines. And we've read of the monumental fraud of Bernard Madoff, which represented friendships exploited into the loss of billions of dollars. Our newspapers, ironically in their own death throes at a time when there is more news than ever before, look more and more like supermarket tabloids. Current events are just that appalling.

If even churches, families, and friendships no longer provide a safe haven, what does that suggest about the future of humanity? Could we really be approaching the terminal point of the human experience? In plain terms, something's got to give.

A year ago my question was, "What in the world is going on?" Today there can be but one question: "Is there any way for us to live with confidence in a chaotic world?" You see, we no longer have the luxury of sitting back in our recliners, stroking our chins, and examining this spectacle from some distance. Now we are all players in world events. If you have not lost a job or a home, you undoubtedly know someone who has. By this time, virtually every American has been affected by the cultural fallout that has been highlighted by our economic system. If you and I are up to our ears in this, then, what on earth can we do? We need a plan, and we need one as quickly as possible.

In our last book we examined the passages that describe the future return of Jesus Christ to this earth. But what if I told you that those same texts contain clues for how we are to live in the meantime? In scouring the books of the New Testament, I discovered ten practical strategies to help us live with confidence in a chaotic world. We *can* know what on earth to be doing when our challenges exceed our courage.

As we face the uncertainty of our troubled generation, we cannot afford to turn away from the priceless counsel of the Word of God. We need it more than ever because it provides a firm foundation even when the world seems in the grip of quicksand's undertow.

As I feel the anxiety of these times, I draw profound peace from the promise that Jesus gave to His disciples—that includes you and me—in the Upper Room. He told them that He would never leave them without comfort: "The Helper, the Holy Spirit whom the Father will send in my name, will teach you all things, and bring to your remembrance all things that I said to you. Peace I leave with you, My peace I give to you; not as the world gives do I give to you. Let not your heart be troubled, neither let it be afraid" (John 14:25–27).

In those words I can hear Jesus speaking to our generation. He assures us that we need never live in fear, no matter what the newspaper says. Jobs can be lost, homes can be lost, but the love of Christ is forever. Understanding that calms our spirits and allows us to begin thinking—really thinking—about the new world around us. As we work through the ten chapters of this book together, I pray that you will see your own circumstances with new eyes; and that you will look within, finding new courage not in your own strength or skills, but in the unlimited resources of Christ, in whom we can do all things. Then, as we finish these pages, we will smile in the midst of it all and agree: in the power and love of Almighty God, we *can* live with confidence in an age of chaos.

—David Jeremiah
San Diego, CA
June 2009

ONE

Stay Calm

FUNNY HOW IT NEVER RAINS IN BEIJING WHEN AMERICAN PRESI-dents arrive for high-profile visits. It's no coincidence. Military meteorologists in China seed the clouds and empty them of their moisture in advance.[1] The weather is tailor-made for the occasion. That's why the skies were picture-perfect for the opening ceremonies of Beijing summer Olympics in 2008. Using an arsenal of rockets, artillery, and aircraft, Chinese scientists blasted the clouds right out of the sky. "We can turn a cloudy day into a dry and sunny one," boasted Miam Donglian of the Beijing weather bureau.[2]

That's nothing to what's coming. Weather modification is a rapidly developing technology, spurred on by billion-dollar investments in climate change and global warming. It's the new science, and its ramifications aren't lost on military planners. Secret laboratories in military installations around the globe are developing what may be the most underreported arms race on earth: weather warfare.

Many military and environmental scientists believe we can learn to use powerful chemicals and electromagnetic scalar waves to manipulate and control short-term weather patterns in ways that can alter the world's balance of power. According to some reports, the US Air Force is determined to "own the weather" by 2025; but other nations and terrorist states have timetables of their own.[3]

Former Secretary of Defense William Cohen warned that military manipulation of the biosphere is a frightening threat, saying that some countries are engaging "in an eco-type terrorism whereby they can alter the climate, set off earthquakes and volcanoes remotely through the use of electromagnetic waves." He said, "There are plenty of ingenious minds out there that are at work finding ways in which they can wreak terror upon other nations. It's real . . ."[4]

I don't know if it's real or not; but if some doomsdayers are right, technology is being developed that could trigger earthquakes by well-placed underground nuclear explosions, or by earth-penetrating electromagnetic waves, or by injecting superfluids into major fault zones. Blizzards could be pulled down. Volcanoes could be cooked up. Typhoons and tsunamis could be triggered and aimed against unfriendly coasts. Communications could be disrupted by heated plumes of supercharged particles altering the atmosphere.

Writing in *The Ecologist*, Michel Chossudovsky of the University of Ottawa warned that "the world's weather can now be modified as part of a new generation of sophisticated electromagnet weapons. Both the US and Russia have developed capabilities to manipulate the climate for military use . . . Weather manipulation is the pre-emptive weapon par excellence. It can be directed against enemy countries or 'friendly nations' without their knowledge, used to destabilize economies, ecosystems and agriculture. It can also trigger havoc in financial and commodity markets."[5]

When we read what's coming, we feel like we're either hurtling into the age of science fiction or stepping into the pages of the book of Revelation. The last book of the Bible indicates that catastrophic disruptions in earth's meteorological patterns will wreak havoc on the world during the Great Tribulation.

But here's what I want you to know: as we await the Lord's return, the atmospherics of your heart and mine should be calm. The Bible says we have a God who calms the storm and a Savior who rebukes the wind and waves so they are calm (Psalm 107:29; Luke 8:24). The writer of Psalm 131 said, "Surely I have calmed and quieted my soul." Proverbs 17:27 tells us that a person of understanding has a calm spirit; and in Isaiah 7:4 (NIV), the Lord tells us, "Be careful, keep calm, and don't be afraid. Do not lose heart."

Calm is an interesting word that is known more for what it is not: agitation, fear, or turbulence. But "calm" does require some kind of storm or we would never notice it. The weather world gave us the word in the first place. It means wind that is moving one mile per hour or less. The Beaufort Scale has "Calm" at one end and "Hurricane" at the other—extreme opposites.

Take a moment and evaluate your own life. As you attempt to move through these chaotic days, where would the Beaufort Scale register the winds of your soul?

A September 2008 American Psychological Association poll indicated that 80 percent of us were under significant stress because of the economic mess. That figure represented a rise of fourteen percentage points in only five months. And we don't even have the numbers for early 2009, when the unemployment epidemic really cut a swathe through the American workplace. If you haven't lost your job, your home, or your savings, you're probably worried that it could happen, and you're concerned for those of your friends who have been so devastated.

One industry is actually doing very well: pharmaceutical medicines for anxiety. I've read claims that fifteen million Americans suffer from enough anxiety to need medication.[6] While this may represent a wise option in cases of clinical stress, there are deeper causes for panic attacks and anxiety that medication will never penetrate.

Perhaps this is a good time to remember why I wrote this book and why you have chosen to read it. We are trying to determine what on earth we should be doing in these stressful times. And we have discovered that God has given us solid answers to our questions in the very passages that tell us of His Son's return to earth.

In this chapter, and in every chapter that follows it, I have identified instruction for living life while we are looking for the Savior. I can find no better resource for our troubled days. Jesus, for example, spoke to His disciples about His purposes after leaving earth. Here is how He began: "Let not your heart be troubled" (John 14:1). He would not have said these calming words unless His followers needed them. Their hearts were troubled; He knows that ours are too. Each one of us has a different "anxiety quotient."

Some people believe that when they accept Christ, they will receive a *Get Out of Stress Free* card and live a life of uninterrupted bliss. To be honest, when I became a believer, I picked up a few new problems I hadn't had before. Jesus never offered a false promise. At every point, He warned us that troubles would follow our path and that obedience to Him would actually increase our persecution. But He is also the one who said, "These things I have spoken to you, that in Me *you may have peace.* In the world you will have tribulation; but be of good cheer, I have overcome the world" (John 16:33, emphasis added).

Jesus Himself felt pressure. He was distressed as He watched Mary weep over the death of her brother Lazarus. He "groaned in the spirit and was troubled" (John 11:33). As He contemplated the cross, He felt genuine anxiety (John 12:27). As He waited for Judas to betray Him, He was troubled (John 13:21). He is a high priest who can "sympathize with our weaknesses" (Hebrews 4:15).

As the death of our Lord Jesus nears, His disciples begin to be anxious about their life situations, and Jesus comforts them with these words:

> "Let not your heart be troubled; you believe in God, believe also in Me. In My Father's house are many mansions; if it were not so, I would have told you. I go to prepare a place for you. And if I go and prepare a place for you, I will come again and receive you to Myself; that where I am, there you may be also. And where I go you know, and the way you know." Thomas said to Him, "Lord, we do not know where You are going, and how can we know the way?" Jesus said to him, "I am the way, the truth, and the life. No one comes to the Father except through Me." (John 14:1–6)

The Ultimate in Comfort

We need to return to this passage whenever we are besieged by worry. Remember, Jesus didn't say these words as He stood beside a Galilean stream on a sunny day, without a care in the world. He said them as He stood near the jaws of hell itself. He didn't speak from the all-protective shelter of His Father's arms. He sat with His frightened disciples in the Upper Room, preparing for the worst of humanity and the silence of heaven. His words were, "Let not your heart be troubled."

It encourages me to realize that He faced what He did, felt the worst of what we would feel, and still drew enough strength to comfort others. He looked at His friends and felt compassion for them. These were men He had asked to follow Him. For three years He had been their life. Then He had begun to speak of leaving them. In John 13, He had told them that the time was drawing near for Him to leave, and that this time they would not be able to follow Him. Peter asked Him exactly where He was going. Jesus told him again that it was a place to which he could not come until sometime in the future (John 13:36).

This conversation would have been terribly upsetting for the disciples who had depended upon Jesus for everything. Our Lord's words of encouragement to His close friends were preserved by the apostle John, so that they are available to give comfort to us as well. Jesus gave His disciples some things to believe, things to hold onto. He asked them to put their trust in four things that He promised would provide courage and renewed strength for their troubled hearts. I think you will discover as you read the following pages that these timeless truths are just what you and I need in these chaotic days.

Jesus Asks Us to Believe in a Person

When a child is afraid during the night, who but a parent can provide comfort? The child will cling to Mommy or Daddy and begin to feel calm. That's how it is with Jesus. His comfort begins with His very identity. "Let not your heart be troubled," He tells us. "You believe in God, believe also in Me" (John 14:1).

The people of Judea believed in one God. The center of their faith was expressed in the *Shema*: "Hear, O Israel: The LORD our God, the

LORD is one! You shall love the LORD your God with all your heart, with all your soul, and with all your strength" (Deuteronomy 6:4–5). These Jewish followers of Jesus had been trained since infancy to love God exclusively. Now Jesus was telling them something shocking; He wanted them to believe in Him in the exact same way—because He was God's Son. If the divine nature of Jesus is difficult for us to understand, you can imagine how the disciples would have struggled to wrap their minds around such an idea. In fact, it wasn't until after His resurrection that they began to process what He was telling them.

Jesus was asking men who had been schooled in the Hebrew Scripture to expand their faith in their heavenly Father to include His Son, their earthly teacher. Calling upon His full authority as the Lord of heaven and earth, He said, "I and the Father are one" (John 10:30 NIV). To believe in what I say, you must believe in who I am.

Jesus Asks Us to Believe in a Place

Now Jesus tells His disciples, "In My Father's house are many mansions; if it were not so, I would have told you. I go to prepare a place for you" (John 14:2).

A man takes a new job in another city. He is in the process of moving his family to a brand new home there, but he must travel ahead of them and start his work earlier. His child cries because he will be gone for a week, but the father stoops, pulls him into an embrace, and says, "I'll be there getting your new room ready. You're going to have a place to ride your bicycle, and I'll be starting on that tree house we're going to build." The tears dry as the child sees all this in his mind. That's a picture of what Jesus is doing here. He encourages His disciples to think of the wonderful future He is planning for them.

The Scriptures include many synonyms for heaven. We know it is vast, we know it is beautiful and wonderful beyond all imagining. We know it is a country, one about which our most gorgeous earthly landscapes are only rough drafts. It is, in another way, a magnificent city, built and perfected by the architect of this universe. Then we can think of it is as a kingdom, the realm of the powerful king. Heaven is also called *paradise*, a word suggesting its supreme beauty.

Those metaphors are beautiful pictures of our future home, but Jesus' description of heaven is my favorite: "My Father's house." We know what that means. Many of us had favorite grandparents we visited. We think, "This is where Dad was a little boy. This is my father's house!" It holds a special charm and wonder for us, associated with Christmas, joy, and laughter. I like to think of heaven that way.

There was a special house where I grew up. My parents, as they grew older, finally moved away from it, and that was hard for me to take. I hadn't lived there for some time, but the house symbolized my whole past, my first memories, my childlike innocence and security. It was part of me. Praise God, He never decides to move to a smaller home. There is ultimate security in the eternal nature of heaven. Author Thomas Wolfe wrote a book called *You Can't Go Home Again*, but there is one home we can never lose or leave. Christ has gone there to prepare it for us, and that gives us comfort.

Heaven is real. Cloud-and-golden-gate–laden cartoons, movies, and jokes have reduced heaven to a stereotype. We need to realize just what is being stolen from the sanctified imagination when this precious image is made trivial to us. We are not yet in heaven, but it has power for us right now. It extends its hope to us. It guides our aspirations. It soothes our hearts when we lose a loved one. And when we think of its eventuality, we realize there is nothing mundane or insignificant about any of us—we are children of the kingdom; we are bound for heaven! It is real, and it is home.

About Those Mansions

Many of us are familiar with the phrase "many mansions," as we learned it in our King James Bibles. Newer translations substitute something like "many rooms" or "many dwelling places." The explanation is that this word, now associated with the homes of millionaires, originally meant a simple dwelling place. Jesus is actually saying, "In my Father's house are many rooms." But please don't think we'll all be tenants of a large boarding house, with cramped quarters and a shared bathroom down the hall. Heaven is the infinite expanse of God's glory; it is perfection, and the idea of a mansion is more than appropriate.

This language of an ultimate home is a powerful balm to the heart. Home means something different to every person, but it's a longing we all share. Home, no matter how humble, is the place where we begin life. It is the place we must inevitably leave to build an adult life. And the yearning to recapture that basic security and sense of belonging remains in us. Ecclesiastes 3:11 says that God has set eternity in our hearts, and that's heaven, our ultimate home.

On one occasion, Dr. Paul Tournier, the brilliant Swiss Christian medical doctor, counseled a young man from a troubled home situation. "Basically, I'm always looking for a place—for somewhere to be," said the man. Tournier explained that each of us long for a true home.[7]

You can see this longing through history. The first thing men do upon becoming substantially wealthy is to build the "dream home." In some cases they've become consumed by this quest. In the nineteenth century, King Ludwig II of Bavaria nearly bankrupted his German nation by building palace after palace. He had to be removed from power, and his greatest castle remained incomplete.[8]

In the United States, two palatial houses qualify as "castles." North Carolina has the Biltmore House while California has its Hearst Mansion. The Biltmore House has over 250 rooms, including 35 bedrooms and 43 bathrooms. George Washington Vanderbilt nearly depleted his incredible fortune in completing the estate, then died after only a few years of enjoying it. The home of William Randolph Hearst has a mere 165 rooms, with 127 acres of gardens, terraces, pools, and walkways. Again, a heart attack took the founder before he could enjoy the fruit of his labor. In both cases, tourists have come out as the true winners.

Today we have every kind of television show about homes and making them perfect. The yearning never dies. But no matter how luxurious a palace we build, no matter how much we spend, we can't take it with us, nor will any moat or drawbridge keep death from the front door. These architectural obsessions simply prove our longing for the one and only home that will be enjoyed throughout eternity. Can you imagine living in the Biltmore House or Hearst Mansion? Beside the home Jesus is preparing, either would seem like a run-down tool shed.

What Makes a Home?

There will be some readers who have lost their homes, or come close to it, in the recent mortgage crisis. I realize this subject is a sensitive one for you, and I don't wish to cheapen the loss you've experienced with trite assurances. Even so, I truly believe that God can help you experience the reality of your eternal home, and in that way give you comfort and reassurance. We must remember that a house is not a home, any more than the church is a building. A true home is an intangible thing, composed of love, relationships, and peace. Heaven may be like a mansion or a billion mansions—but no ornamentation or architecture will make it precious to us. Only the presence of our Lord will do that.

As we continue to explore what on earth we should be doing now, let us not forget about our Lord's words concerning heaven.

None of us know what the future holds for our own crisis. My prayer for you is that you come through your crisis strong. This can be a time of maturity for all of us, helping us to understand that we are not citizens of this world, and that we cannot place our faith in any of its establishments or institutions. As we await His return, we trust Him to care for our every need, and we remember that Jesus himself said, "Foxes have holes and birds of the air have nests, but the Son of Man has nowhere to lay His head" (Matthew 8:20).

Do we really long for that ultimate and eternal home, rather than simply a place to lay our heads? C. S. Lewis writes that sometimes it seems as if we have no desire for heaven at all; other times, it seems to him we've never desired anything else. In truth, he says, our yearning for heaven is "the secret signature of each soul." It is the thing we have desired all along and will continue to desire, even when we don't realize it's the thing we most want.[9]

Jesus Asks Us to Believe in a Promise

A particularly wonderful aspect of the Bible is its many promises. When God makes a promise, it is our rock. Jesus comforts us with this promise: "And if I go and prepare a place for you, I will come again and receive you to Myself; that where I am, there you may be also" (John 14:3).

Some interpret this as a description of what happens when we die. The problem is that we have no specific scriptural support for the idea of Christ returning for each believer at death. Luke 16:22 suggests that the angels handle that task. No, this verse is certainly a description of the triumphant return of Christ. Our comfort is in looking forward to His return, when He will take us away from all the problems and heartbreaks of this life.

What I have just said is certainly nothing that hasn't been said countless times before. I doubt it's the first time it's been expressed to you in similar wording. And yet it is the most profound statement in all of history. Here is the very heart of Jesus' message to His troubled disciples. The deepest, most far-reaching truth in the entire universe is not expressed in any of Einstein's laws but in a children's song that goes, "Jesus loves me, this I know, for the Bible tells me so." It's nothing new, but it's the best news you'll ever hear. How much different would our lives be if we could only begin to embrace the truth that the God of heaven desires to spend eternity with us? Listen to our Lord as He puts this desire into prayer: "Father, I desire that they also whom You gave Me may be with Me where I am, that they may behold My glory which You have given Me; for You loved Me before the foundation of the world" (John 17:24).

We need our Lord's promise as we continue to walk the uncharted roads of our current crisis. We might lose our jobs or our homes; the devil may win the battle—but Christ has already won the war.

In the darkest days of the Second World War, as defeated US troops in Bataan awaited promised reinforcements, President Roosevelt ordered the ignominious General Douglas MacArthur to leave the

Philippines for Australia—virtually deserting his men. Upon his arrival in Australia, he made a speech promising those troops and the Filipinos, "I shall return." US government officials asked him to change the line to, "*We* shall return," but he stood firm.[10] His promise, therefore, became a personal one that he fulfilled four years later when he triumphantly reappeared in that part of the world to retake the lost ground and free the captives. By the way, MacArthur understood the concepts we're discussing. On April 9, 1942, in a tribute to the troops of Bataan, he stated, "To the weeping mothers of its dead, I can only say that the sacrifice and halo of Jesus of Nazareth has descended upon their sons, and that God will take them unto Himself."[11]

If a general can keep his promise to return, how much more certain is the covenant of that same Jesus of Nazareth? He will come back to take *all* of us unto Himself. And even now, He has ascended into heaven, and is preparing our place. That's how much He loves us! Can we begin living like it?

Winning the Battle

There is hope in trusting a future that Jesus has guaranteed, but there is still the daily battle. I don't want you to feel that I would attempt to minimize the anxiety or hardship you may be experiencing. This world's problems are real. But we need to fully grasp that God's solutions are too. When Jesus says, "Let not your heart be troubled," He means it. And not just for the men who were in that room with Him two thousand years ago; He means it for every troubled time and every troubled person.

We can master anxiety. But we can't do it with a fatalistic attitude about problems—that loses the battle before the first shot is fired.

When we believe in the victorious Christ, and trust Him to guide us forward toward positive solutions, we will begin to live with supreme confidence.

Jesus says, "Believe in me. Believe in the reality of my home. Then believe my promise. *Believe*." For some, believing can be difficult to accept because the problems of this world are visible and tangible, but the hope and power come from an invisible reality. Our only bond to that world is our faith—our decision to *believe*. When we do that, we are declaring victory over this world's problems before they occur, in the name of Jesus, who is the object of our faith. We will still have sorrow and setbacks, but we stubbornly view them only in the much larger context of eternity—today's tears making tomorrow's joy sweeter.

Our growth over the years helps us with this perspective. After forty years as a pastor, I can testify that I see problems in a different light than I once did. There are disappointments that would have knocked me down years ago. Today I have more readiness to chalk them up to the challenges of my profession, and to simply move on. By now I've had enough opportunities to see what the Lord does with the worst of circumstances. He has more than won my trust, so it will take a far greater blow than it took yesterday to knock me down today.

Jesus Asks Us to Believe in a Plan

Finally, Jesus has a plan for us to trust. It is revealed in John 14:5–6. Thomas, always uncertain, asks Jesus, "Lord, we do not know where You are going, and how can we know the way?"

Jesus answers him: "I am the way, the truth, and the life. No one comes to the Father except through Me."

If Jesus was leaving, Thomas wanted a map. Global Positioning

System (GPS) receivers were not available. Thomas was asking, "Can't you even leave a forwarding address?"

Jesus' answer is surely not what Thomas is expecting to hear. Jesus says that He *is* the map. He is the Global Positioning Savior. He shows the way to heaven, takes us there, and ultimately is the journey Himself.

Now imagine you're on a business trip and stop at a convenience store to ask directions. The cashier gets that all the time, so he fires the turns at you in rapid succession: first right, third traffic light, dog-leg left, straight at the Methodist church, then go through four or five intersections, if you see the Jiffy Burger you've gone too far, what you want is the second left past the old gas station . . .

All of this was spewed out before you could get the cap off your pen, and there's a look of abject despair on your face. So the cashier glances at his watch and says, "Know what? I get off in three minutes, and it's on my way home. I'll lead you right there myself."

Now you're smiling. That cashier has become the way. He not only has the directions but is the means for getting there. He is your new best friend. William Barclay says that this is what Jesus does for us. "He does not tell us about the way; He is the Way."[12]

I'm told that in many of the "big box" stores today, employees are trained to become the way when someone asks where something is—to walk the customer there. That level of service is sacrificial and well appreciated. And it's the way of Jesus.

But Jesus says something else that many people would rather skip over or explain away. Jesus says not only that He will take us to heaven, but that He is the only one who can: "No one comes to the Father except through Me."

Those who remember their grammar lessons know the difference between a definite and indefinite article. The former signifies "the one and only"; not just *a* restaurant but *the* restaurant. A restaurant is indefinite; we could be talking about any eating establishment. When Jesus says He is "the way," He uses the definite article, and He is definitely clear about it. He never said He was *a* way, but *the* way. Then, to clinch the issue, He added that no one could come to the Father "except through Me."

Today we have decided that this ancient, inspired, and specific article of Christian doctrine is no longer politically correct. It is, we are told, bigoted and intolerant. According to some recent polls, a majority of Americans—70 percent—think some non-Christian religions also provide paths to salvation. Pollsters at Pew Research Center were amazed to find how many respondents accredited more than one way to heaven. Fifty-seven percent of evangelicals said they believed *many* religions can lead to eternal life. In other words, nearly half of American evangelicals were left in the category of believing Jesus is not the exclusive way to heaven.[13]

Respondents to an online poll by the evangelical periodical *Christianity Today* indicated a similar belief pattern. Forty-one percent believe there is more than one way to heaven.[14]

What part of John 14:6 do we not understand?

Overwhelming Evidence

This last year I had the privilege of meeting Billy Graham's grandson, Will, and to hear him preach. He gave me an idea of what it was like to be the grandson of Billy Graham. "Everybody wants to meet you," he said. "Then, as soon as they meet you, you discover they don't really want to meet you, but they want you to help them to meet your grandfather." He shared his humorous response for dealing with that inevitable question: "The Bible says the way to the father is through the son, not through the grandson."

Jesus' words in John 14:6 clearly teach the exclusive, one-way nature of salvation. But this truth is not isolated to one text, as the following references demonstrate.

- "Enter by the narrow gate; for wide is the gate and broad is the way that leads to destruction, and there are many who go in by it." (Matthew 7:13) Narrow gate or narrow mind? You be the judge.
- "Therefore I said to you that you will die in your sins; for if you do not believe that I am He, you will die in your sins." (John 8:24)
- "Nor is there salvation in any other, for there is no other name under heaven given among men by which we must be saved." (Acts 4:12)
- "For there is one God and one Mediator between God and men, the Man Christ Jesus." (1 Timothy 2:5)

The Scriptures are remarkably clear on this issue. Jesus is the one and only way, the one and only truth, and the one and only life. If that is narrow-minded, so be it. I'm happy to be narrow-minded if that's what God is because this is His truth, not mine.

What about the other religions? Again the Bible says, "There is a way that seems right to a man, but its end is the way of death" (Proverbs 14:12). It's not about what seems right that counts; it's about what *is* right. The various world religions are neither different versions of the same story nor parallel steps leading skyward on some pyramid of truth where all the differences melt away. Other religions teach starkly different versions of reality. Life is either a circle, as Eastern religions have it, or time is linear with a beginning and end, as the Word of God has it. There is either endless reincarnation as those religions insist, or it is given to man but once to live, once to die, as the Bible teaches in Hebrews 9:27.

Most scientists would agree with me that there is only one law of gravity, and that we don't get a vote on it. Science, mathematics—neither of these disciplines is democratic. Neither has a "choose your own truth" policy. Why should the spiritual realm be any different?

Let's not build up false charges of narrow-mindedness when the obvious character of Jesus is one of love, forgiveness, and total sacrifice. He wants to take us to heaven—all of us. But He is the only way. He invites us to come to Him—to be saved by grace, received through our faith as it responds to Him. He demands no sacrifice, no achievement, nothing other than a sincere *yes* from the human will.

Then He wants to enter our hearts and give us joy and wisdom for the rest of this life, and His glorious presence in the next. He has written that invitation in the blood of His own hands. And when we accept His invitation, He has promised to write our name in the Lamb's Book of Life.

Dr. Ruthanna Metzgar is not your general run-of-the-mill church wedding singer. She is a professional. Her résumé is impressive. She has sung in the United States, Canada, Europe, and Japan. She is world-renowned as an instructor, lecturer, and conductor of both choirs and orchestras.

She also has an impressive repertoire. Her versatile soprano voice has performed everything from classical, sacred, musical theater to contemporary gospel. She is also a gifted communicator about her personal faith in Christ. It is in that context that I first came across her story.

Anyone who has taken voice lessons, sung in a top-notch college choir, or played in an adult orchestra knows the penchant directors and conductors have for detail. They leave nothing to chance. They almost obsess over every difficult passage, making sure it is practiced and polished and performance ready. They don't like surprises at an important presentation.

Well, Ruthanna must have been very preoccupied because she missed a very important detail. It isn't often that even a professional singer is asked to sing at the wedding of a millionaire. Ruthanna was. The wedding took place in the tallest skyscraper in Seattle—on the top two floors! She described the "atmosphere as one of grace and sophistication." From that vantage point the view of Puget Sound and both the Cascade and the Olympic Mountains was spectacular.

After the ceremony, "the bride and groom approached a beautiful glass and brass staircase that led to the top floor." They ceremoniously cut the satin ribbon that had subtly acted as a lustrous boundary and invited their guests to follow them up to the reception. Just one more detail and Ruthanna and her husband, Roy, would be among the honored guests at the gala dinner.

At the top of the stairs stood a tuxedoed gentleman with an ornately bound book, who asked, "May I have your name please?" Ruthanna gave him their names and expected to be ushered directly into the party. But, as hard as he looked, as carefully as she spelled her last name, he firmly announced, "I'm sorry, but your name is not here. Without your name in this book, you cannot attend this banquet."[15]

Ruthanna explained to him there must be a mistake; she had just sung at the wedding. With a hundred or so guests waiting on the steps below her, he simply replied: "It doesn't matter who you are or what you did, without your name in the book, you cannot attend this banquet." He promptly signaled for them to be escorted to the service elevator and taken to the parking garage.

Roy Metzgar wisely waited until they were well on their way home before he asked what had happened. In tears, Ruthanna replied, "When the invitation arrived for the reception I was very busy and I never bothered to return the RSVP . . . Besides, I was the singer, surely I could go to the reception without returning the RSVP!"

There was no shrimp, smoked salmon, no luscious hors d'oeuvres, no exotic beverages for her that night. Rather there was only the sad realization of the overwhelming evidence against her. She had failed to follow the only plan that would get her into that banquet. She didn't mean to refuse the invitation; she merely let the opportunity slip away. It was really a decision to take no action.

Fortunately, Ruthanna's inaction held only a temporary consequence. You have a similar opportunity to make a decision. You have been issued an invitation with eternal consequences. There is just one plan. I urge you to make take the action that leads to eternal life in heaven. A confirmed reservation for a joyous eternity is the evidence that provides the settled calm that can carry us through any storm.

Mark Twain once quipped, "Everybody talks about the weather, but nobody does anything about it."[16] Well, no longer. As we step into the era of designer skies and weather weaponry, let's keep our eyes on the master of earth and skies, knowing He controls all the elements of our future.

Because of Christ, we have a better forecast and a cloudless future.

TWO

Stay Compassionate

ARIEL, THE MODERN CITY, IS LOCATED LESS THAN FORTY MILES due north of Jerusalem in the "occupied territories." Its ancient olive trees belie the establishment of the city just thirty years ago. The gospels relate Jesus' journeys and ministry in this area known then, as now, as Samaria. I love the way the King James puts it: "and [Jesus] must needs go through Samaria" (John 4:4). Samaria was definitely on Jesus' radar screen! He loved the people of Samaria.

Today, David Ortiz is the pastor of a small congregation of mostly Palestinian Christ-followers. However, there are some in the town of Ariel who loathe Christians. Ironically, the Ortiz family learned the depths of this hatred on the joyous holiday of Purim in 2008. Gifts of food and drink are sent to friends, and gifts are made to charity to celebrate the preservation of the Jews from the total extinction that had been planned for them by Haman (Esther 9:18–32).

As if in celebration of the holiday, a gift basket was delivered to the Ortiz home. Fifteen-year-old Ami was home alone, and he tore into the package with the anticipation of some candy or some other sweet treat. He certainly did not anticipate the explosion that ripped into his young body. Hundreds of shards, including pieces of metal, safety pins, and screws, pierced him and left him in critical condition. He was blinded by the shrapnel imbedded in his eyes, and both eardrums were punctured, leaving him with a significant loss of hearing.

Ami spent five months in the hospital, lost some toes through amputation, and endured nearly a year in a pressure suit to assist in his healing from his severe burns. More than a year later, he still faces several more surgeries. In a recent television interview in Israel, he told a reporter, "It was a shock. I didn't know what to do. Just to find out you're missing parts of your body. It's kind of hard."

Israeli television anchorwoman Ilana Dayan described Ami as "probably the Israeli who has been injured the worst by Jewish terror."[1] You read that correctly. After viewing the real-time video of the attacker dressed in an Israeli Defense Forces (IDF) uniform placing the basket at the door, police believe that the bomb was the work of radical Jews. The man has not yet been arrested.

No one would blame Ami for hating these neighbors and for desiring to seek revenge. But when Ami was questioned by the reporter about his attitude toward those who did this evil to him, he replied: "I don't feel hate. I don't see a reason for it. I could say they're blinded by their hate. They think it's the right thing. You can't blame a blind person for running over you, so I don't see [how I could blame them]. It's just not there. It wasn't there from the beginning. I don't even know how to explain it, but it's just not there. No hate at all."

Ami knows what is like to be blinded. Thankfully, several successful surgeries have restored his sight. Perhaps his physical blindness explains his compassion on the spiritual blindness of those who do not know Christ.

The antithesis of hate is compassionate love. Ami and his family seek to demonstrate Christ's compassion to their neighbors, knowing that at any time, any place, they might again become targets. Instead of retreating into their fear, every Thursday Ami and his family help out at a soup kitchen that also provides a small medical clinic and clothes to those in need. Recently, his mother Leah wrote, "It is an important and vital work being done in the name of *Yeshua*. I never have realized before how much the Lord wants us to be His eyes, hands, and feet in these last days."[2]

Thankfully, most of us will never have our capacity for compassion tested at such a heinous level. But in these chaotic days, we are being tested to decide if we will be self-centered takers or compassionate givers. One such decisive moment happened in Sacramento a few months ago.

The drink was a Grande Gingersnap Latte. Nothing too special, except that it created a small, public statement about the power of kindness.

It was the Monday of Thanksgiving week, and a woman was at the Starbucks drive-through window, picking up her morning beverage. As she reached for her pocketbook, some inspirational quirk inspired her to do something extravagant: she paid for the customer behind her—someone she didn't know.

That driver, needless to say, was startled—and sufficiently moved to follow suit. He paid for the driver behind him. In the end, one hundred nine people had gotten in on the fun and paid for the next customer's coffee. An employee told the local TV station that those working the windows caught the fever too. "We're all in this economy thing together," she said.[3]

A popular movie from a few years ago helped spread the "pay it forward" principle, but the idea can be traced back as far as 1784, when Benjamin Franklin advocated progressive kindness. He received what used to be called a "begging letter" from a man in financial need. Franklin responded, "I do not pretend to give such a sum; I only lend it to you . . . When you meet with another honest man in similar distress, you must pay me by lending this sum to him . . . I hope it may thus go thro' many hands before it meets with a knave that will stop its progress."[4]

Being part of a good works chain is rewarding.

When the bottom falls out of our economy, as it has recently done, we see two equal and opposite reactions. One is the hardening of the heart, fueled by cynicism and despair. "Time to take care of my own," says this type of person. "The rest of you are on your own. Me, I'm locking the door and hunkering down. Wake me when the recession is over; I'll be sleeping with my wallet under my pillow."

Of course, there's an alternative response. It's the behavior we would expect from children of God's kingdom, who try to live in a way that will please him and minister to a hurting world. During that nightmarish week, when global stock markets declined by seven trillion dollars, *Time* magazine asked Christian author Philip Yancey for his take on how Christians should pray at such times. Yancey said the first part is simple: Cry, "Help!" He said that he had stopped editing his prayers for sophistication and the ring of maturity because God wants us to be ourselves.

Then, he explained, the second stage was that of listening to God in meditation and reflection. The question here would be, "What can we learn from this catastrophe?" One possible lesson would be that we're foolish when we place our ultimate trust in governments and economies.

The third stage, Yancey told the magazine, was to ask God for help in taking our eyes off our own problems "in order to look with compassion on the truly desperate." He concluded, "What a testimony it would be if, in 2009, Christians resolved to increase their giving to build houses for the poor, combat AIDS in Africa, and announce kingdom values to a decadent, celebrity-driven culture. Such a response defies all logic and common sense—unless, of course, we take seriously the moral of Jesus' simple tale about building houses on a sure foundation."[5]

Yes, it's clear that our next step forward in tough times is to protect and even extend our spirit of compassion. The apostle Paul wanted the church at Thessalonica to understand that during its own rough period. As Paul wrote them a letter, he broke into prayer: "Now may our God and Father Himself, and our Lord Jesus Christ, direct our way to you. And may the Lord make you increase and abound in love to one another and to all, just as we do to you, so that He may establish your hearts blameless in holiness before our God and Father at the coming of our Lord Jesus Christ with all of His saints" (1 Thessalonians 3:11–13).

Concerning that last phrase, the New Testament teaches us that Jesus will return. That is a 100 percent biblical certainty, and it could happen any day. It's Paul's context for the instruction he gives here. So does he advise the Thessalonians to shut everything down, put on their Sunday best, and sit patiently in their pews until the wonderful day? Not in the least. He consistently commands believers to be busy in the interim period, doing kingdom business—our hands busy with the earth, our hearts occupied with heaven.

This particular letter to the Thessalonians, perhaps the second of all his letters (the first being Galatians), is one of the essential documents pertaining to our Lord's return. Paul wanted to visit Thessalonica and help the believers work through some problems. But it was evidently not God's will for him to do so. Make no mistake; this was not a rejection slip from Paul to one more congregation competing for his time ("We regret that present scheduling will not allow for a visit from the apostle"). His language in this letter betrays his intense personal desire to be with his friends.

The problem was that "Satan hindered us" (1 Thessalonians 2:17–18). That's a common occurrence. The devil will present obstacles to God's work whenever he can—though God, who uses all things for His glory and our good, turns the worst crises to His own advantage. Here is how God did it in this situation: if Paul had gone to the city as he wanted, you could erase the amazing letters to the Thessalonians from your Bible. We wouldn't have the invaluable teachings we've enjoyed for twenty centuries. The devil, you see, has a way of winning the battle but losing the war. Now we have two incredible letters to the Thessalonians that tell us what we need to know about the return of Christ and what on earth we should be doing as we wait.

Paul couldn't see how God would use his letter; seldom do we live long enough to see the ultimate fruit of our service to God. That's something to remember when we feel discouraged. Paul couldn't have dreamed that his private correspondence would bless untold billions of people in the future. From his perspective, the church at Thessalonica was a group of his friends who were suffering—persecuted for loving Christ—struggling just to get by. They were experiencing hard times not too different from the ones that inspired this book. So how did they handle it? Did they pull in their heads, give in to self-pity, and harden their hearts, as some might do? How are you responding? Always remember that what life does to us depends upon what life finds within us. In school, you perform on a test based on how you studied for that test. If you fail, don't blame life or the school—you had every opportunity for preparation. You perform in life's testing, too, based on how you've readied yourself. Paul knew these people of Thessalonica. He realized they could be strong under trial, but he sensed they were overmatched.

Paul understands their discouragement, but he wants to bolster his friends, keep them from giving in to self-pity, and motivate them to serve God with deeper resolve. He wants to offer them a prayer, but what do you pray for people under intense pressure? Would you ask God for protection? Courage? Perhaps removal of the problem? Paul doesn't take any of those roads. He asks God to teach the Thessalonians to be more loving and compassionate toward one another. It seems counterintuitive, doesn't it?

Have you stopped and considered that the real purpose of your struggles, at a given moment, might be the heart of compassion that God is building within you? Smooth sailing doesn't develop such a thing, you know. Trials develop our humility, and humility opens our eyes to the needs of others. If we look to do His service during tough times, we will come out better rather than bitter. That's Paul's prayer for the struggling church at Thessalonica.

The Essence of Compassion

The world is cold and cruel in the best of times; on tough days, things only get worse. In this present crisis, we expect a new age of cynicism and the hardening of hearts. While cutting our own budgets back, or even worrying about the loss of a career, the temptation is to shut out the problems of those who have it worse than we do. Yet this is the very time when the world needs us most of all. What's the use of a sunny-day Christian? We need devoted followers of Christ who are at their best when the clouds come out.

Someone will say, "That's all fine and good, but I'm just not feeling it. At this moment, my heart is not 'abounding and overflowing with love.'" That's to be expected. Don't worry, the heart of God overflows so magnificently that we need only stand under it and catch the spray. And a little of that is enough for a miracle. It's His love the world really needs, after all. "The LORD is gracious and righteous; our God is full of compassion" (Psalm 116:5 NIV). We also read that "His compassions fail not" (Lamentations 3:22). Notice, by the way, that the latter verse comes from a book of lamentations, of all things. Sad times are good times for realizing God's goodness.

No matter what we face, the abounding love and compassion of God are more than sufficient for us to enjoy ourselves and to share with someone else—and when I say "no matter what," I mean it. In *Campus Life* magazine, author Shannon Ethridge remembers a terrible day from her eleventh grade year. Attempting to apply lipstick while driving on a bumpy country road, she struck and killed a bicyclist. That was the beginning of her nightmare. What stunned her most was what the victim's husband said, upon being told he had lost his wife. His first question was, "How is the girl? Was she hurt?"

It was inconceivable to Ethridge that anyone could take such a devastating blow and have immediate concern for the author of the tragedy. The night before the funeral, she forced herself to visit the bereaved husband. "As I entered the house," she writes, "I looked down the entry corridor to see a big, burly middle-aged man coming toward me, not with animosity in his eyes, but with his arms opened wide."

The man was a Wycliffe Bible Translator named Gary Jarstfer. He gave her a large, compassionate embrace, and she dissolved into tears.

Over and over she wept the words, "I'm sorry, I'm sorry!" Jarstfer gently spoke to Ethridge about the life and legacy of his beloved wife. He added, "God wants to strengthen you through this. He wants to use you. As a matter of fact, I am passing Marjorie's legacy of being a godly woman on to you. I want you to love Jesus without limits, just like Marjorie did."

Gary Jarstfer insisted that all charges against the distraught eleventh grader be dropped. Then he began to look out for her and encourage her in the development of her life. Ethridge writes, "Gary's merciful actions—along with his challenging words to me that night before Marjorie's funeral—would be my source of strength and comfort for years to come."[6]

The logic of such behavior is never found in the world but only in the Word. The love capable of such abounding compassion is never found within ourselves but only as we are in Christ. Human nature dictates that we act very differently when things go wrong. The flesh (in Paul's terminology) encourages us to go inward and look to self. The Spirit encourages us to go outward and become all the more loving and forgiving—including forgiving oneself.

Therefore, when the men and women of Thessalonica are being treated terribly simply for loving and worshiping the one true God, Paul doesn't pray that they will be stronger in fighting evil. He doesn't ask God to strike down the oppressors. His prayer is that the people will be abounding in love and compassion. As Jesus said, "Love your enemies, bless those who curse you, do good to those who hate you, and pray for those who spitefully use you and persecute you, that you may be sons of your Father in heaven" (Matthew 5:44–45a).

The essence of identifying with someone else is the Incarnation —God wrapping Himself in flesh and becoming a man, then taking on our sins at the cross. All that we do in this world should be an echo of what Christ has done on the cross. We love. We are compassionate. We identify with others and their problems, and we take up their crosses for them. Gary Jarstfer is a perfect example. He had his own grief to handle, but he identified with the very person who would have been the object of anyone else's bitterness. He empathized with Shannon Ethridge, felt her pain even as he had plenty of his own, and took up her cross, making sure that her tragedy could be turned to triumph.

Don't you think the world needs more of that kind of love? What would happen if we replaced the here-today-gone-tomorrow love of contemporary marriage with the ironclad, unconditional love of 1 Corinthians 13? What would happen if every Christian in America went to work tomorrow after making a granite-solid personal covenant to love everyone at the office in the way God loves them? Can you imagine what would happen to our society?

God and only God can give us this love. Left to ourselves, we would make a hopeless mess of any difficult relationship. This is why we can't be too upset at our nonbelieving friends who don't love us unconditionally. Just as we wouldn't be angry with a blind man for stepping on our toes, we should be nothing but compassionate to people who don't know Christ.

Sometimes I listen to the news, hear the griping, the complaining, and the whining, and have to stop and remember that these people don't know the Jesus we know. There is so much anger, so little forgiveness; so many demands, so little service. I think Longfellow had it right when he wrote, "If we could only read the secret history of our enemies, we should find in each man's life sorrow and suffering enough to disarm all hostility."[7] It takes godly compassion to live with that outlook.

What God wants from us in the midst of this crisis is compassion—broken-heart compassion that sees the hurts of those around us as an invitation to express God's love in meaningful acts of kindness.

The Expression of Compassion

Let's think about the focus of all this compassion. It is expressed "to one another and to all" (1 Thessalonians 3:12). That pretty much covers everyone you can think of, doesn't it?

There is a basic standard for love, as John describes it: "If someone says, 'I love God,' and hates his brother, he is a liar; for he who does not love his brother whom he has seen, how can he love God whom he has not seen? And this commandment we have from Him: that he who loves God must love his brother also" (1 John 4:20–21).

Jesus set forth this standard to His disciples in the Upper Room, only hours before He was arrested: "By this all will know that you are My disciples, if you have love for one another" (John 13:35).

An e-mail circulated recently, telling the story of one of those angry drivers who was tailgating everyone, sitting on his horn, honking when people stopped for a yellow light, and so on. Then, in his rearview mirror, he saw the blue, revolving light. Soon the police officer was asking the man to exit the car with his hands up.

He took the driver to the station and had him searched, fingerprinted, photographed, and placed in a holding cell. Finally the staffers came for him, brought him back to the booking desk, and returned his personal effects. The arresting officer was very apologetic. "I made a mistake," he explained. "I was behind you in traffic while you were blowing your horn, making hand gestures, and cursing at the guy in front of you. When I saw the *What Would Jesus Do?* bumper sticker and the chrome-plated Christian fish emblem on the trunk, I assumed you had stolen the car."

People are watching, and they watch more closely when they know we are people of faith. It has been said that we are the only Bible some people will ever study. They have the right to expect our walk to reasonably match our talk even though consistent love and compassion don't come easy. Henri J. M. Nouwen expresses it this way: "Compassion is hard because it requires the inner disposition to go with others to the place where they are weak, vulnerable, lonely, and broken. But this is not our spontaneous response to suffering. What we desire most is to do away with suffering by fleeing from it or finding a quick cure for it."[8]

Dionysius, a second-century bishop in the city of Corinth, wrote letters describing how Christians behaved in the grip of a rampant plague:

> Most of our brethren showed love and loyalty in not sparing themselves while helping one another, tending to the sick with no thought of danger and gladly departing this life with them after becoming infected with their disease. Many who nursed others to health died themselves, thus transferring their death to themselves . . . The heathen were the exact opposite. They pushed away those with the first signs of the disease and fled from their dearest. They even threw them half dead into the roads and treated unburied corpses like refuse in hopes of avoiding the plague of death, which, for all their efforts, was difficult to escape.[9]

The world is watching how we treat each other. Will they see a difference?

The biblical standard is simply to love one another. But now we come to the difficult part. If we stayed with the basic standard to love each other, our faith would be little different than any belief system in this world. But there is a higher standard of love, and Jesus came to give it the definitive expression through His life and teachings. In the words of Eugene Peterson's paraphrase, he said, "If all you do is love the lovable, do you expect a bonus? Anybody, can do that" (Matthew 5:46 MSG). Paul is referring to the basic standard when he uses the phrase "one another" and the higher standard when he adds, "and to all."

Loving our loved ones is a good start. If we can't do that, we definitely have a problem. The higher standard, on the other hand, sends a strong, clear message that we, the people of Christ, are not your average, everyday human beings. Those who are watching us don't weigh the size of the Bibles we carry. They don't keep a calendar for totaling the number of Bible study meetings we attend, nor do they give us a test on mastery of biblical trivia. But they watch with intense interest to see how we treat others: first, those close to us and then—the championship round—everyone else. Paul writes, "May the Lord make you increase and abound in love to one another *and to all*" (1 Thessalonians 3:12). Those final three words are the tricky part.

For the Thessalonians, *all* was a difficult word. *All* constituted certain people who were abusing and persecuting them. "As you abound and increase in love," Paul is saying, "Don't forget these!" We don't like that at first because we know we can't individually get it done. Just as Jesus said, we can love our families, our buddies, and our friendlier neighbors all by ourselves. So can those who don't know God. But if we're going to love beyond those comfortable boundaries, if we're going to advance this love into hostile territory—well, we're going to need to rely on a greater source. We're going to need the power of the Holy Spirit. And of course, once we realize that, He has us right where He wants us.

C. S. Lewis helps us with this in one of his writings. He says that an unbeliever makes his choice as to whom he will show kindness, but a Christian has a different secret. He writes that we shouldn't waste our time worrying about whether we love our neighbors—just act as if we did. The difference between worldly people and Christians is that the worldly treat people kindly when they like them; Christians try treating everyone kindly and thus find themselves liking more people—including some they'd never have expected to like![10]

Christians, in other words, let their actions lead and their feelings follow. Human nature feels its way into acting (which can be a long wait). Christ-centered faith acts its way into feeling (which is quick, powerful, and liberating). To put it simply, we followers of Christ are realists. We understand that, naturally speaking, we're never going to like certain people. We know we're not prone to doing the right thing when left to our own devices. But for the sake of Christ, we're going to walk in the Spirit and treat others well because it's the very nature of who Jesus is. Therefore (if we're living as we ought to), we treat our enemies as benevolently as our friends and soon enough discover we have no enemies anymore.

Think about that person you simply don't like. You keep your distance and harbor ill feelings. What do ill feelings do when we give them free reign? They grow more ill; they are never self-healing. But what happens if you ignore the ill feelings and put your best foot (the "Christ" foot, if you will) forward? You find that friendliness with that person isn't as bad as you thought. Much of the time, that person (sensing or outright knowing your dislike) is surprised, shamed, or hopefully inspired into returning the friendliness. This is what Paul, quoting Proverbs, calls "heaping hot coals on someone's head" (Romans 12:20). And in the next verse of Romans, Paul adds, "Do not be overcome by evil, but overcome evil with good." That's leading with actions and letting the feelings follow, and when we do it, we begin to look an awful lot like Jesus.

Some call it the "As If" principle. If you act as if you feel a certain way, you'll find you really do soon enough. You're becoming your own self-fulfilling prophecy. Call it what you will, but it's really walking by faith, being obedient and trusting God to make you the person you haven't yet become. Sometimes the growth in us is what God's agenda has been all along. He wants to see how we'll respond to difficult personalities and whether we'll be obedient when it demands sacrifice on our part. It's the only way we can grow and become transformed to the image of Christ. Living and loving by faith is one of the great adventures of life.

The Example of Compassion

The essence of compassion is that we increase and abound in love for one another. The expression of it is acting out our love for others, including those difficult to love. What about the example of compassion? Paul completes the thought: "May the Lord make you increase and abound in love to one another and to all, just as we do to you" (1 Thessalonians 3:12).

Paul is saying, "I'll lead. You follow." He has established a consistent model, and that gives him the luxury of saying not only "Do as I say," but also "Do as I do." The New Testament implies that when Paul first visited Thessalonica, he wasn't initially accepted. But he persisted, kept putting his "Christ" foot forward, and let his love for them increase and abound. The evidence is in plain view, all throughout this letter. Here are a few of the ways he demonstrated his love for the people of this city:

- *He thanked God for them.* "We give thanks to God always for you" (1 Thessalonians 1:2*a*). He offered his gratitude to God, a perfect strategy for building love in our hearts for someone.
- *He prayed for them.* "Making mention of you in our prayers" (1:2*b*). How else do we grow a sturdy love for another person? We pray for their needs. The end result of that is always compassion as we are given God's heart for the person.
- *He preached the Gospel to them.* He writes: "But even after we had suffered before and were spitefully treated at Philippi, as you know, we were bold in our God to speak to you the gospel of God in much conflict" (2:2). People don't always appreciate having the gospel preached to them, but that's our work, and it is the greatest evidence of our love.
- *He was gentle, kind, and considerate toward them.* "But we were gentle among you, just as a nursing mother cherishes her own children. So, affectionately longing for you, we were well pleased to impart to you not only the gospel of God, but also our own lives, because you had become dear to us" (vv. 7–8). This is precisely what compassion looks like.
- *He sacrificed for them.* "For you remember, brethren, our labor and toil; for laboring night and day, that we might not be a burden to any of you, we preached to you the Gospel of God (v. 9). This is the ultimate proof of compassion.

What is Paul talking about in that ninth verse? As he was building his relationship with the church at Thessalonica, he refused to let these friends pay for his preaching service. Instead, he worked an extra job as a tentmaker. You may remember that was his "practical" craft. In order to preach for his brothers and sisters in Christ at no cost, he supported himself with his hands. Now you can see how Paul is able to say, "Follow my example."

Read that list of five proofs of compassion again, but this time substitute the name of Jesus for Paul. Did Christ not do each of those things for us? Does He not call us to imitate Him? I challenge you to think of one person you know who is in need. Then, systematically follow the procedure Paul has laid out: Thank God for him. Pray for him. Talk to him about Christ and what He has done for you. Suffer for him in helping him. Be gentle, kind, and considerate. Then, however necessary, sacrifice yourself in some way in behalf of that person.

A woman once asked me, "How do I minister to somebody who won't even let me talk about Jesus? I want her to go to heaven, but she simply isn't open to hearing about the Lord. How do I witness to someone like that?"

My reply was, "You have to be Jesus to her."

She wanted me to explain my comment. I said, "You have to love her well. If she rejects your love, be resolute and keep on loving. Don't worry about what to say because words aren't necessary in cases like this. She's not listening to anything but your actions. Words can be refuted, but actions overwhelm every defense. That's how Jesus did it for us; that's what the cross is all about. So love her as Jesus loves you."

Paul, the author of this Thessalonian letter, was not born loving. He was a hater and hunter of Christians. He approvingly watched the death of Stephen, the first Christian martyr. He knew all the words that made up the law, but when he met Jesus on the road to Damascus, he experienced something far more powerful than words.

A more recent persecutor of Christians in the Middle East is named Tass Saada. They called him "Butcher." He was a PLO sniper, and one of Yasser Arafat's bodyguards. Like Paul, he had an encounter with the living Christ. By the power of the Holy Spirit, he was transformed into a brand-new person. The Butcher became a man of love and compassion. But that made him very unpopular with his family, and some wanted to kill him because of his conversion.

Today Tass and his American wife, Karen, have a compassion ministry to those living in miserable poverty and daily danger in Gaza and the West Bank. It was there that Joel Rosenberg and his wife traveled to meet the Saadas not long ago. They were there to visit a hospital that treated victims of the border clashes, both Jew and Arab. The Israeli doctors couldn't believe Saada's stories about the man he had once been—a PLO killer capable of murdering all the Jews to whom he was presently speaking. Now he was a man helping to finance a hospital, rather than putting people in one.

How on earth, he was asked, had such a change come about? It wasn't a matter of earth but heaven. Taas gave the credit to Christ and the glory to God. His heart, he said, was completely transformed so that he had a deep love for the Jewish people. As a matter of fact, Taas said, he now had something to ask. He wanted each member of the hospital staff to forgive him. The moment was transcendent. A man of hatred had become an ambassador of God's love for all humanity.[11]

If God could do this for killers such as Paul and Taas, do you have any doubt that He can fill your heart with abounding love?

The Effect of Compassion

What is the effect of compassion? "That He may establish your hearts blameless in holiness . . ."

This is a purpose clause. It shows exactly why we are to be loving others. The purpose of all those years of school is to have an education and be knowledgeable. The purpose of going to work forty hours a week is to earn a living. What is the purpose of loving others? It is to develop holy, blameless hearts.

Christian means "little Christ." We want to be just like Him, to imitate Him in every way possible so that we could be mistaken for Him. How do we do it? By following His lead; by doing what He did.

Some people believe they can become Christ-like by reciting numerous Scripture verses. Some believe they can do it by mastering the spiritual lingo and delivering the most impressive spoken prayers. Some of those things are good, some are worthless; none make us like Jesus.

And how did Jesus live? He loved people everywhere He went. He touched lepers, befriended social pariahs, cured sick people, cherished children, and had compassion for everyone in His path. His last acts were to pray for the forgiveness of His murderers, and then to look beside Him and feel compassion for a dying thief, whom He encouraged and assured of salvation. In His deepest hours of agony, never for a moment did He take a break from loving others. In the Upper Room, He told His disciples that their main work would be to love one another. The more difficult His life became, the more crowded He was by the demands of people, and the closer to a torturous death—the more loving, compassionate, and forgiving He became.

"Who could follow that act?" you ask with reasonable incredulity. "Who could have such a heart?"

That's irrelevant when you're at the starting line of loving someone. Just do it and worry about motives later. Love, as Paul describes it in this chapter, is a living thing. It starts from the tiny seed of obedience and blooms as we water it with our actions. Go love and serve, and you will find a miracle happening within yourself: a holy and blameless heart.

The Exercise of Compassion

There are so many fringe benefits to living the way God wants us to live. Here is another one: showing compassion has measurable therapeutic value for our lives.

Allan Luks was the executive director of the Big Brothers and Big Sisters charity for eighteen years leading up to his retirement. In his book *The Healing Power of Doing Good,* he describes a study of three thousand volunteers of all ages throughout the country. The results of a computerized questionnaire demonstrated a clear cause-and-effect relationship between helping others and good health. He concluded that helping contributes to the maintenance of good health, even diminishing the effect of diseases and disorders: serious and minor, psychological and physical.

Doing good for others does good for us. It reverses the destructive process of self-absorption, moves us into the healthy arena of seeing the needs of others, and ultimately opens us up to the reality of God and His destiny for us.

William Booth, the founder of the Salvation Army, was passionate about showing compassion, especially for the downtrodden of the London slums. One day his son Bramwell entered the room early and found his father furiously brushing his hair, brushes in both hands, as he frantically finished dressing for the day. No time for "Good morning"; Booth looked at his son and cried, "Bramwell! Did you know there are men sleeping outdoors all night under the bridges?" He'd been in London late the preceding night, and this had been a shocking sight on his way home.

"Well, yes," said Bramwell. "A lot of poor fellows, I suppose."

"Then you ought to be ashamed of yourself for having known it and done nothing for them," answered William Booth.

Bramwell began constructing elaborate excuses. He could never add such a complex project to all the things he had going on in his life, which he now began to name. His plate was full.

His father simply barked, "Go and do something!"

That moment of resolve was the beginning of the Salvation Army Shelters, a special ministry that changed the lives of hundreds of homeless men during the early days of the Salvation Army work in London.[12]

Have you ever had a Booth moment, when suddenly you saw some person or situation through God's eyes and developed a fiery determination to see it change?

Roy Anthony Borges had a moment like that in prison. Having become a Christian, he had to begin unlearning everything life had taught him—particularly everything prison had taught him. Hate, they taught, was the thing that made you survive. And every inmate had far more enemies than friends.

A typical enemy for Borges was Rodney, who stole his radio and headphones one day while Borges was playing volleyball in the prison yard. It was an expensive radio, a gift from his mother. The earphones had been a Christmas present from his sister. In a prison cell, such a thing is a treasure to cherish. Borges was angry and his heart went directly to the possibility of revenge. But he was wise enough to pray, and he began to feel in doing so that God was testing him.

The anger was not so easily removed. Every day he had the impulse to jump Rodney, to wipe the arrogant grin off his face. But there was a Bible verse that wouldn't get out of his mind. It was Romans 12:20–21, Paul's instruction to forget about vengeance, to leave all that to God. Finally Borges actually began to see his enemy from a perspective he'd never had: God's view. He began praying for the man, and expecting something miraculous to happen in the life of the man who had stolen his radio.

It got even stranger. Before he knew it, Borges was helping his enemy, talking to him about Jesus, entirely forgetting to hate Rodney. One day he saw the miracle. Rodney was kneeling next to his bunk, reading the Bible on his own. He said, "I knew [then] that good had overcome evil."[13]

In these difficult days, there will be stress and tension. You will be more prone than usual to give in to bitterness. It will be an easy time to nurture a potent grudge against someone else. Maybe you'll give in to those impulses. You can rationalize it by saying you've had a hard time, that you'll get back to being Christ-like when times are better, and that God will understand. But that vaults you onto the sad, downhill slope toward living in the hopelessness of this world, where people's happiness is based solely upon circumstances. In this world, it will never be convenient to be godly on those terms.

There is another way, and that's the way of responding to crisis by doubling down on patience, kindness, longsuffering, and compassion. Let your love increase and then abound. The result will be a joy that transcends these circumstances. And if enough of us get in on that, then even the circumstances cannot hold out. The love of God is the one thing that can and will turn this world upside down. Let's get to work.

THREE

Stay Constructive

ATHEISM HAS TAKEN OVER THE BUSES. IN NEW YORK, THEY'RE chugging past the Empire State Building bearing twelve-foot long signs announcing: *You Don't Have to Believe in God.* Thousands of people in Chicago are getting on and off buses emblazoned with a similar message: *In the Beginning Man Created God.* In Indiana, the bus banners say: *You Can Be Good Without God.*

In other American cities, the buses are wrapped in this message: *Why believe in a god? Just be good for goodness' sake!* Another slogan gives this bit of atheistic reassurance: *Don't Believe in God? You're Not Alone.*

Riders in Genoa, Italy, are bouncing around in vehicles that declare: *The Bad News Is that God Does Not Exist. The Good News Is that You Do Not Need Him.*

(Let me get that straight. The atheists are admitting their core teaching is *Bad News?*)

And then there's the slogan of the original atheistic bus campaign in London. It said: *There's Probably No God. Now Stop Worrying and Enjoy Your Life.*

Let me rephrase that.

- There's Probably No God. So Your Life Has No Ultimate Meaning.
- There's Probably No God. So You Came From Sludge and Are Returning to Dust.
- There's Probably No God. So You Can Never Be Forgiven of Your Sins.
- There's Probably No God. So Good Luck Dealing with Your Problems.
- There's Probably No God. So You'll Never See Your Loved Ones in Heaven.
- There's Probably No God. So Live for Fun and Die in Despair.
- There's Probably No God. So There's No Hope, No Life, No Grace, No Heaven.

I don't know who'd want to believe that message, let alone advertise it. For that matter, I've never met anyone who could actually prove that God doesn't exist. There are no true atheists. Nevertheless, a new, aggressive, in-your-face brand of atheism is gaining millions of adherents in these last days.

Atheists are ready to come out of the closet, and they're itching for a fight. They've gotten a boost from President Barack Obama, who included a reference to "nonbelievers" in his inaugural address. *USA Today* said that Obama's inaugural address represents the first time in inaugural history that an American president has explicitly acknowledged atheists and atheism.[1]

Atheism is finding its voice because our culture has become

totally secularized, and secularization is not neutral; it's inherently anti-Christian.

But there's nothing constructive about secularization or atheism. Look at what the twentieth century's most famous atheists did to the world: Lenin, Stalin, Hitler, and Mao Zedong. Without God, we can only tear down. With Christ, we're in the business of building up.

As Christians face these perilous times, our message is fresh, positive, exciting, energetic, and eminently constructive.

In the Old Testament there is a beautiful passage about the shifting seasons of life. One of its statements is, "There is a time to tear down, and a time to build up" (Ecclesiastes 3:3b NASB). Within living memory, we've seen generations dedicated to both.

Half a century ago, there was a time to build up. The late author Stephen Ambrose wrote extensively about the Second World War and the generation of young men who returned from it. Ambrose's father came home from the war, put up a backboard, and a whole squad of ex-GIs from the neighborhood came over regularly to play basketball. Ambrose never remembered their last names, but he remembered the scars on their arms and chests. As he reflected on their accomplishments he wrote:

> But in fact these were the men who built modern America. They had learned to work together in the armed services in World War II. They had seen enough destruction; they wanted to construct. They built the interstate highway system, the St. Lawrence Seaway, the suburbs (so scorned by the sociologists, so successful with the people), and more. They had seen enough killing; they wanted to save lives. They licked polio and made other revolutionary advances in medicine. They had learned in the armed forces the virtues of solid organization and

teamwork, and the value of individual initiative, inventiveness, and responsibility. They developed the modern corporation while inaugurating revolutionary advances in science and technology, education and public policy.[2]

They labored, they filled their station wagons and ranch-style homes with children, and they retired. Perhaps they really are the "Greatest Generation."

Then came the time to tear down. You've lived through that time, and so have I—decades of national division. Future generations will look back and see this as a season of wanton destruction. From top leadership on down to the man on the street, we've been about the business of demolition rather than construction. We've become adept at poisoning the wells of culture, politics, business, spirituality, the family, and every other sphere. For reasons unknown, we've begun tearing down everything between ourselves and the horizon:

We've torn down integrity.
We've torn down purity.
We've torn down honesty.
We've torn down respect.
We've torn down national pride.
We've torn down ideals.
We've torn down dreams.
We've torn down our sense of shame.
We've torn down political aspiration.
We've torn down everything we began building at the birth of our nation.

We began the new millennium with terrorism on our own soil, with high school shootings, and with dramatic rollbacks of traditional moral boundaries. The Cleavers, the Brady Bunch, and the Huxtables no longer mirror our complex families. Diversity is the new state religion, with tolerance demanded in all things except for traditional Judeo-Christian values.

Paul tells us not to be surprised:

Don't be naive. There are difficult times ahead. As the end approaches, people are going to be self-absorbed, money-hungry, self-promoting, stuck-up, profane, contemptuous of parents, crude, coarse, dog-eat-dog, unbending, slanderers, impulsively wild, savage, cynical, treacherous, ruthless, bloated windbags, addicted to lust, and allergic to God. They'll make a show of religion, but behind the scenes they're animals. Stay clear of these people. (2 Timothy 3:1–5 MSG)[3]

Does that sound to you like a picture of today's world? I realize it's easy to be discouraged. We could throw up our hands and simply quit. Such is not a godly attitude, according to the Scriptures. In a time of tearing down, we are to be about His work of building up. In a destructive world, we are to maintain constructive attitudes.

The Final Follow

It will not surprise you to learn that a lot of tearing down and building up have occurred in every generation, including in Bible days. There had been a time for tearing down in the apostle Peter's life. He had watched his Lord arrested and taken for execution—that alone almost tore down the life of Peter. But to make things worse, he himself had failed the most basic test of love and loyalty. Even with a prediction from Jesus that should have served as a warning, Peter had denied his affiliation with his wonderful master—not once but three times.

In spite of our Lord's patient preparation of His impetuous disciple, Peter was constantly demonstrating the frayed fabric of his life. Time and time again Peter proved that without Jesus he was nothing. Now it looked like he would once again be a fisherman—no more teachers, no more dreams.

In the comforting simplicity of the net and sea spray, Peter surely thought back to the last time he had been a serious fisherman. The Master had come along then and said, "Follow me." He had seen a miraculous catch, knelt before the teacher, and said, "Depart from me, for I am a sinful man, O Lord!" That experience, too, had been a tearing down, a humbling, a confrontation with his own unworthiness. Even so, Jesus had wanted him, and he had followed. Jesus had said, "Do not be afraid. From now on you will catch men" (Luke 5:8, 10).

"Follow me." That's what Jesus had said and that's what Peter had done. Now, having failed his Lord, he was just a fisher of fish again. He must have wondered if his following days were finished. The final chapter of John's gospel, however, brings Peter full circle. Again, Jesus will say to him, "Follow me." This will be the final "follow." And again Peter will drop his nets and go—this time to the Ascension; to Pentecost; to the building of the Jerusalem church; and all the way to Rome, where he will die (according to tradition) as a martyr, a coward no more, but the courageous man Jesus had said he would be.

We all love Peter. And why not? There is so much reality, so much familiar humanity that comes through the ancient pages of Scripture to make him real for us. There is Peter who was the first to recognize Jesus as the Christ; Peter who denied he was even a friend. There was

Peter who stepped out of the boat, and Peter who almost drowned when his faith short-circuited. Jesus called him "the Rock" one time, "Satan" another. Peter was so much like us—one step forward, two steps back, animated by wild faith and paralyzing doubt. He was a man of highs and lows, mountains and valleys, and that's why he makes a perfect study for times like these. As a preacher I tend to operate on the "what comes next" principle. I keep things simple and chronological, starting at the first verse and moving along. This chapter is an exception. The novelist Kurt Vonnegut Jr. once advised writers to start as close to the end as possible.[4] That's what I'm going to do here. I find it intriguing to start at the end of the story in John 21, then go back to pick up the details.

John 21 is the final chapter of the final gospel. It's considered a kind of epilogue and contains the last recorded words of the Savior before He ascended to heaven. There are more recorded conversations between Jesus and Peter than with any other disciple, so it's fitting that this last one is also with Peter. It's also fitting that it's a tale of restoration because that's what Jesus does. He is always reconciling, always reconstructing, always bringing people home.

Jesus is completing a conversation with Peter, once again foretelling what lies ahead for the fisherman. "When you were younger you dressed yourself and went where you wanted," He says. "But when you are old you will stretch out your hands, and someone else will dress you and lead you where you do not want to go" (John 21:18 NIV).

On the night of His arrest, Jesus had correctly predicted an act of denial. Now He predicts an act of devotion. According to tradition, Jesus is saying that Peter will reach his latter years, but that he will die with his hands outstretched—a euphemism for what He Himself has been through. Tertullian and Eusebius, early historians of the

Christian movement, each report that Peter followed his Lord to the cross.

Jesus saw it through the mist of the future and foretold Peter's three denials—just as He sees our future with its failures and successes. Now that Peter is a fallen disciple, Jesus repeats once more the words that defined His disciple's life mission: "Follow Me." It is as if none of the heartbreak in between has ever happened. Jesus looks beyond it and says, "Follow Me."

"What About Him?"

As this exchange occurs, Peter notices that someone else is already following. According to John 21:20, Peter turns and sees "the disciple whom Jesus loved" keeping pace with them. This, of course, is John, the only disciple who rivaled the closeness that Peter enjoyed with Jesus. So much is happening right now between Jesus and Peter, but the impetuous disciple momentarily loses sight of all that. He wags a thumb at the trailing John and says, "But Lord, what about this man?" (v. 21).

The preceding conversation has been gentle and compassionate, soothing the bruising of Peter's soul. Now Jesus is blunt. He says to Peter concerning John, "If I want him to remain alive until I return, what is that to you?" And one more time, He says these words with an added urgency: *"You must follow me"* (v. 22 NIV; emphasis added). In His answer to Peter, Jesus mentions His own "return," reminding us again that instructions for practical living are often found in the context of future predictions.

Jesus' final words to Peter were—*You must follow Me!* His last command to Peter should be the first concern of each of us today. Whatever things distract you—what is that to you? You must follow Him!

I wanted to begin right there, framing the story for this chapter with that crucial command. Now let's go back and examine the fascinating conversation that led up to it—the story of the recommissioning of a fallen disciple, a failure who became a follower again.

Moving back to John 18 we find the disciples in crisis. Jesus has been arrested, and two disciples have followed at a distance. One, loving and loyal John, will follow all the way to the cross; the other, Peter, will experience another relapse of doubt. Just as he has sunk into the waves after a glorious moment of water-walking, now he sinks back into an alley. Hours previously, he has promised to follow Jesus to death itself—to occupy the next cross (Matthew 26:35). Peter is always so near, and yet so far. He has followed Jesus to the point at which his courage fails. And beside a fire, where peasants warm their hands, a stranger voices the very question which Peter is silently asking of himself: "You are one of His disciples, are you not?" (John 18:25).

Peter hears himself say, "I am not!" Worst of all is the growing suspicion that he is telling the truth. Peter is given two more chances to redeem himself, but each time the answer is the same. Three is a number of completion, and Peter understands himself to be a complete failure in following Jesus.

We've all been there, doing or saying something wrong, feeling the sting of conviction, and hearing the voice inside us asking, "You are one of His disciples—are you not?" We also know that our first act of disobedience can be a slippery slope that becomes an avalanche.

Love or Like?

Now there is another fire, this one on an early-morning beach at the Sea of Tiberias. A few of the disciples had gone with Peter when he said, "I am going fishing" (John 21:3). Their fishing trip ends just as on that memorable occasion when they fished all night and caught nothing. One of the disciples notices a man watching them by the shore. It's Jesus, though He is initially unrecognized. And soon He's duplicating the wonderful miracle of the net-bursting catch—one hundred fifty-three fish are suddenly spilling over the nets. John counted them. And soon, there is a campfire, a breakfast, a reunion, laughter, and probably many, many questions. Ignoring all the chatter around the fire, however, John wants us to know only what Jesus said to Peter.

Three times Jesus asks him, "Do you love Me?" and Peter answers in the affirmative—but there are certain significant variations on the theme. We see the word *love* in our Bibles all three times. But in the Greek it's not so. For the first two questions, Jesus uses the word most associated with godly love—*agape*. This is supreme, sacrificial love. "Peter, do you love Me with the love of God, committed and costly?" Each time Peter answers with a different word—the one that means "brotherly affection." *Do you love Me? Yes, I'm fond of You.*

The first time Jesus asks, "Do you [*agape*] Me more than these?" Peter replies that he is fond of Him.

The second time it is, "Do you [*agape*] Me?" He has dropped the phrase of comparison. Peter offers the same reply.

The third time, Jesus makes another change. He abandons the elevated *agape* and asks if Peter is fond of Him. It may be one of Jesus' saddest remarks, and it has the effect of, "Well, Peter, are you even *fond* of Me? Really?"

Peter, wounded from his great failure, no longer wants to boast of his unmatched love or how he will follow Jesus to the cross. Humbled, he is saying, "I can give you only this much from my heart," and Jesus is asking, "Are you sure you even have that much to give?"

As we read this passage, understanding the Greek language and all its implications to their subtle discourse, we can almost make out the sound of Peter's heart breaking. It is a time for tearing down. Jesus had called him the Rock. What kind of rock can be shattered into so many pieces?

Feed and Follow

What we've just discussed is the content of a sermon countless pastors have preached. The intricacies of the conversation between Jesus and Peter make for such a terrific lesson that we often miss elements in the story that are equally important. We focus on the love, but we miss out on the lambs. Let me tell you what I mean.

Jesus is asking Peter about the depth of his love and commitment. But He is also giving Peter a commission with every response. The first time, when Peter says, "Lord, You know that I'm fond of You," Jesus immediately says, "Feed My lambs." The second time, Jesus says, "Tend My sheep." And the third time Jesus combines the two and says, "Feed My sheep."

What Jesus is saying to Peter is this: "Peter, it's not about some abstract love that you have, and how that love might be measured on some emotional scale. It is about your willingness to do what I do—to care for My children." Jesus instructs Peter to feed the lambs; tend them; feed the sheep. These words *feed* and *tend* refer to providing spiritual nurture to the soul, or building someone up by promoting their spiritual welfare, in the way a shepherd would care for his flock. "This is what I do," Jesus is saying. "You do it too."

And Jesus adds the final commandment, which sums up everything: "Follow Me." In that conversation, Peter may be feeling smaller than he ever has, having the very measure of his love for Jesus sized up. And yet Jesus is saying, *"Follow Me!"*

I read that chapter one more time, in the light of all that is going on in our nation and world, and I'm struck by the way Jesus takes something broken and rebuilds it into something strong and fruitful. He does that with twelve confused, slow-learning disciples. In our broken world we are witnessing just the opposite. I'm a Christian and a patriot, someone who loves his country and believes God has blessed it. But as I write these words our nation is being deconstructed, torn down piece by piece.

I could write another chapter, or perhaps another book, about the things that are being destroyed before our very eyes. And the temptation for each of us is to either throw up our hands in surrender, or climb onto a soapbox and start condemning the ones doing the damage. But I believe that if Jesus were to counsel us on how to respond, He would say just what He has said to Peter. He would say, "Tend My lambs. Feed My sheep. And keep following Me."

The Art of Body Building

One of the beautiful words in our language, in both sound and sense, is *edification*. The Greek version has a nice ring to it too: *oikodomeo*. It is two words combined, *oikos* ("house") and *domeo* ("to build"). So when we speak of edifying—building up—one another, the Greek understanding is building one anothers' house. The word *edifice*, or building, comes from this root.

Here's an example of how it's used in the literal sense, in the New Testament: "Therefore whoever hears these sayings of Mine, and does them, I will liken him to a wise man who builds his house [*oikodomeo*] on the rock" (Matthew 7:24). In Matthew 24:1, we find the word used in reference to building the temple—the *oikodomeo*, or the edifice. That's a house, but it's God's house.

Through the years, the meaning of this word has shifted. We use this expression to talk about building people rather than buildings. In other words, we've taken the word exactly where I believe God would want us to take it. If you'll remember, Jesus had a history of making things. His early occupation was carpentry, making things with His hands. But even before that, He is the One who made the universe by the power of His Word (John 1:1–3, 10; Colossians 1:16, 17; Hebrews 1:1, 2, 10). His earthly ministry involved shaping people into living stones.

When He ascended to heaven, we, the living church, became His body, and one of the great themes of the New Testament is the building up of the body of Christ. Peter writes, "You also, as living stones, are being built up a spiritual house, a holy priesthood, to offer up spiritual sacrifices acceptable to God through Jesus Christ" (1 Peter 2:5). This is a divine metaphor telling us that we are one great building under construction, so that God can come to take residence in that building. At the same time, we are *individual* buildings—Paul said that your personal body is God's temple as well (1 Corinthians 3:16). We build each other up individually and corporately.

This should be the most beautiful process visible on this earth: people constantly edifying one another, building each other up to be holy dwelling places for God. Yet sometimes it goes awry. I've read books about the "toxic church," describing church leaders who have broken people down instead of building them up. And nothing could be more tragic. The Bible exhorts us to edify one another, to build up one another. As a pastor, my passion is to be in the building business, raising up men and women to be beautiful structures of God.

When Jesus said, "I will build My church, and the gates of Hades shall not prevail against it" (Matthew 16:18), He was referring to the eternal body of believers that was christened on the day of Pentecost. Many empires have raged against that church and failed. It continues to rise taller and taller with each generation. The exterior is built through evangelism, and the interior through edification.

Today, the world is doing everything in its power to tear down the church, and often within the church, we are tearing each other apart. We seem to have forgotten that *we are God's building*. We are eternal; we are the living body of Christ. When we feel beaten down by this world, we should be strengthened by our knowledge of God's plan for His church. And then we should love one another as the eternal living stones of that church, and continue to build each other up instead of tearing down. Here are some things to keep in mind as we strive to become better builders.

Edification Is Not About You: It's About Others

I only know of one passage that speaks of self-edification. The New Testament is a collection of "we" writings. It's always speaking in the second person plural. The major emphasis is upon the building up of one another.

Sadly, we have more than our share of demolition experts. I'll never forget being a young preacher and traveling to various churches to preach. One day I was the guest preacher at a church in northern Ohio. As I often did back then, I sang a solo and then delivered my sermon.

A woman walked up to me afterward and said, "Son, I've heard you preach a lot. You need to sing more."

The interesting thing is that she was trying to do exactly what we're talking about—she wanted to build me up as a vocalist. But I was devastated because my passionate calling was to preach. We need to be thinking, lovingly and sensitively, about the best way to uplift others. Paul gives us a solid tip: "All things are lawful for me, but not all things are helpful; all things are lawful for me, but not all things edify. Let no one seek his own, but each one the other's well-being" (1 Corinthians 10:23–24).

These are challenging words for the "Me Generation." In Erwin McManus's book, *An Unstoppable Force*, he bemoans the fact that we seem to have lost sight of this core value of the church. He writes: "Unfortunately, for too many people, when the conversation is no longer about them, there's not much left to be said."[5] To that assessment he adds that since we are each the center of the universe (is that even possible?), everything is evaluated on whether or not it meets our own specific and "special" needs.

The logical phenomenon derived from that mind-set is what I would call "church shopping myopia." This malaise has become as common in Christians as seasonal allergies. Physical myopia is a condition that causes vision to become defective—it sees things only within a very narrow range. The myopic church shopper's spiritual vision is distorted by a focus on convenience—"What does the church have to offer me?"—instead of focusing on relevance—"How will this church help me to 'serve the lost and broken world?'"

Rather than obediently following Jesus' command to feed His sheep, church shopping is too much about being fed and too little about exercising our faith.

While there is only one visible body of Christ on earth today, no one person is that body. All of us together as followers of Jesus, each doing the part ordained for us by God, make up His body.

For the church of Jesus Christ, it's always "*We* over *Me*." As the athletes say it, "There's no 'I' in *team*." Paul uses this principle when he writes, "He who speaks in a tongue edifies himself, but he who prophesies [that is, *preaches*] edifies the church" (1 Corinthians 14:4). The implication is that what serves the body takes precedence over what serves the individual.

In the New Testament there are many references to "one another" and "each other." Here's one of them: "Therefore comfort each other and edify one another, just as you also are doing" (1 Thessalonians 5:11). I've met many self-educated men and women, but no self-edified ones.

I read about a group of women who were having dinner together shortly after one of them returned from Europe. One of the women, a stay-at-home mom, was particularly low in spirit that day. She hadn't been to Europe or anywhere else exciting. Her life felt so drab she felt like she was invisible. She was surprised when her returning friend presented her with a gift. It was a book about the great cathedrals of Europe. Inside the cover, her friend had inscribed, "With admiration for the greatness of what you are building when only God sees."

Inside the book she read the account of how one of the cathedrals was built. A visitor saw a workman carving a tiny bird on the inside of a beam. He watched the craftsman's concentrated movements for a few minutes then looked up at the entire massive edifice, under constant construction for a century. He asked the carver, "Why are you spending so much time chiseling a tiny bird into a beam that will be covered by the stone roof? It will be hidden from everyone's view?"

Without looking away from his work, the craftsman replied, "Because God sees."

As the woman read this story, she thought of the things in her life that were hidden from view: baking for church receptions, sewing patches on children's jeans, bandaging scrapes, cleaning the house, then cleaning it again when it was left messy—she remembered now that God saw, and she felt better. Most of all, she realized that her friend had done a little carving on the weary beams of her soul. It was uplifting, edifying encouragement from a friend just at the right time—which is the way God uses us within the body, even when we don't realize it.[6]

We must try to be ready for those moments, watching closely for the moods of our friends, ready to apply the salve of a good word in season. That's the work of edification. On the other hand, there is a corresponding warning to heed: "Let no corrupt word proceed out of your mouth, but what is good for necessary edification, that it may impart grace to the hearers" (Ephesians 4:29). Even our most casual words are to be spoken with regard to the ripple effect that ensues. It's not about us, but about others.

Edification Is Not What You Profess: It's What You Pursue

Building is long and deliberate work, but destruction is the work of a thoughtless moment.

Some of us build up while others tear down. It seems as if cynicism and sarcasm are a kind of cultural lingo these days. It takes a conscious effort to be a positive, uplifting person when we have so few role models doing it. I catch myself slipping into a sarcastic mode as I talk to staffers at our church. Someone kids me, I zing him back, and pretty soon it escalates into sarcasm that leaves a bruise somewhere behind the smile.

Have you ever realized that aggressive humor can be hurtful? Humor has a double edge. It can be used to strengthen a bond or to strike a blow.

"Therefore," Paul tells us, "let us pursue the things which make for peace and the things by which one may edify another" (Romans 14:19). Pursuit is intentional—it's not something that happens on its own. As far as humor goes, the joke that comes naturally will often be at someone's expense. The joke you'll need to be intentional about is the one that sets others at ease, perhaps by making it at your own expense. I do this, for example, when I tell you I'm directionally challenged. We laugh together, no one is hurt, and the laughter bonds us.

Pursuing edification means staying on task. Paul writes to Timothy to avoid those time-wasters "which cause disputes rather than godly edification which is in faith" (I Timothy 1:4). So many silly distractions keep us from building each other up. By the way, what do we call those time-wasters? That's one of those ideas that needs a word of its own. I've invented one: *posteriorities*. I'm hoping that all the new dictionaries will pick up on my brilliant new word!

Here's what it means. If priorities are all those things you intend to do, in the order you intend to do them, then posteriorities are all the things you're *not* going to do, in the order you don't intend to do them. If our priorities are to edify one another, then what are our posteriorities? Silly arguments about inconsequential religious questions; squabbles over church politics, carpet colors, and who gets to be on what committee; and all that kind of thing. Let's establish our posteriorities and start avoiding them immediately.

If it is true that Christ is coming back soon, shouldn't we feel a sense of urgency over the things at the top of His list for us to accomplish? Building up one another is a priority, not a posteriority. Wouldn't you love for churches to chart all their activities and all their budget expenses, and find out which ones edify people and which don't?

On a personal level, how are you measuring up with your priorities? Use this little poem to chart your own profile:

> I saw them tearing a building down,
> A group of men in a busy town,
> With hefty blow and lusty yell,
> They swung with zest,
> And a side wall fell.
> Asked of the foreman,
> "Are these men skilled?
> The kind you would hire if you had to build?"
> He looked at me, and laughed, "No, indeed!
> Unskilled labor is all I need.
> Why, they can wreck in a day or two,
> What it has taken builders years to do."
> I asked myself, as I went my way,
> Which of these roles have I tried to play?
> Am I a builder with rule and square,
> Measuring and constructing with skill and care?
> Or am I the wrecker who walks the town,
> Content with the business of tearing down?
> —Author Unknown

Edification Is Not About How Much You Know: It's About How Much You Care

"Knowledge puffs up, but love builds up" (1 Corinthians 8:1 NIV). Another translation reads: "While knowledge may make us feel important, it is love that really builds up the church" (NLT).

Have you ever been hurting over something when someone wanted to give you a detailed advice list—when all you wanted was a listening ear and a soft shoulder? It's amazing how few of us learn that those in pain need comforting more than they need information. We men in particular can live our whole lives without figuring that out. We want to tell our wives how to fix things; what they want is to know that we care, we empathize, and we hurt with them.

We need to realize that with everything we do at church. Doctrine and instruction will never cease to matter, but people wander into church because they are lonely, hurt, and disconnected. Why did people seek Jesus out? He loved them and cared for their needs. Then, through tears of gratitude, they heard His teachings. Jonathan Edwards, America's great preacher and theologian, said, "Our people do not so much need to have their heads turned as to have their hearts touched, and they stand in the greatest need of that sort of preaching which has the greatest tendency to do this."[7]

It's Not About Your Gifts: It's About Your Goals

What about the question of spiritual gifts? Paul says, "Now concerning spiritual gifts, brethren, I do not want you to be ignorant" (1 Corinthians 12:1). The Barna research organization has identified the fact that Paul is not getting his wish; many people are ignorant on this subject.

As you may know, we all have at least one spiritual gift that we use within the body of Christ. These aren't the same as natural abilities, but are specially adapted to strengthen and unify the church. More than 20 percent of those surveyed by Barna claimed "gifts," such as: sense of humor, creativity, and clairvoyance.

The problem is that these are not spiritual gifts by any New Testament definition. As for the genuine gifts, 28 percent of American Christians failed to claim a single one of them. If they are indeed followers of Jesus Christ, they can be certain that they possess at least one of the gifts specified in Romans 12:6–8, 1 Corinthians 12, Ephesians 4:7–13, or 1 Peter 4:10–11.[8]

Spiritual gifts aren't like Christmas or birthday gifts, intended for private enjoyment. They are for the express purpose of building up fellow believers. Whether your gift is teaching, service, faith, helps, or any of the others, it is "for the edification of the church that you seek to excel" (1 Corinthians 14:12). Therefore the question is not which gift did you receive, but how you intend to use it.

When we bring these gifts to church, Paul says, "let everything be done for edification" (1 Corinthians 14:26). Paul saw people boasting about tongues or prophecy, and he pointed out that the only thing we should boast about is how strong and unified the fellowship is becoming. Self-centeredness slips into the church, reflecting the world we live in, while the work of building one another must be humble and unselfish. Our gifts are nothing to brag about—they are on loan from God for the wonderful work of body building.

It's Not About Your Wisdom: It's About His Word

There is a final principle that will help us be the encouragers and edifiers that God wants us to be. When Paul visited Ephesus, he delivered a beautiful address to the elders there, including these words: "So now, brethren, I commend you to God and to the word of his grace, which is able to build you up and give you an inheritance among all those who are sanctified" (Acts 20:32).

The Word of God is a Book that builds. When you feel torn down by all that is happening in this world, you'll find so much strength and encouragement in the Bible. When you think you're in no condition to help others when you need so much encouragement yourself, it is all here for you in the ageless Scriptures. God speaks through this Book. He takes its inspired words and applies them to your life so that you feel a ray of hope in the darkening gloom.

It's a difference maker. But don't make the mistake of believing a weekly sermon, a book like this one, or even a fellowship group will make this happen for you. It's important that you delve deeply into the Word yourself. You need to be studying it and reflecting on it every day of your life. The word of His grace, according to Paul, is able to build you up. And do you remember earlier in the chapter when I mentioned finding only one passage that speaks of building ourselves up? Jude 20–21 is that very passage: "But you, beloved, building yourselves up on your most holy faith, praying in the Holy Spirit, keep yourselves in the love of God, looking for the mercy of our Lord Jesus Christ unto eternal life."

So yes, the real work is done in fellowship. But we must never neglect the deep, private work of building that only the Holy Spirit can do within us, through the Scriptures, through prayer in the Holy Spirit, and through privately entering into his presence.

My question to you is, who said you need to choose between the two? You can excel at both, keeping the discipline of a daily appointment with God, to build the inner person, and also ministering among the body at your church. What a wonderful balance it makes when we do both well. What a great joy to be found doing them both when Christ appears in the sky.

Many people stop during the autumn to take in the spectacle of geese migrating in flocks, high in the sky. They fly in a distinctive V formation. We enjoy the natural beauty of that, but have you ever wondered about its functionality? The V is more efficient than flying in a line or randomly. The flapping of the wings creates an uplift of air, an effect that is increased at the rear of the formation. There is one goose at the point of the V, and after a certain time, he'll drop off and fly to the end of the formation. The weaker birds also remain close to the rear and on the inside where their work is decreased. In this way, the geese take care of one another. The stronger birds lead until others rotate to the front and take their places. By cooperating and uplifting one another, the geese achieve long migrations that would be otherwise impossible. In numbers, they're better protected. I think those geese have something to teach us.[9] We are so much stronger together than we are on our own.

I cannot predict what the condition of the world will be as you read these words. Nor do I know anything of the circumstances of your life. But of certain truths I can be extremely sure. One is that Christ's return is closer than it was when we began this book together. Another is that His church will endure because it is eternal. And finally, I know that you have a place in that church—a place where you can heal and be healed; a place where you can take the lead and fall back for rest; a place where you can build up others, and be built up yourself.

The world outside can grow only to a finite level of darkness, but inside the church, we've yet to see the ultimate brightness of pure light. We've yet to see the perfection of genuine love. We've yet to become those people that we're destined to become, through the strengthening of the body of believers, and through the work of Christ Himself.

When He returns, we'll see the brightest, most intense, most beautiful light in all creation. Jesus said, "I am the light of the world" (John 8:12; 9:5). I hope you are drawn to that light like a moth to flame. What on earth should we do now? Gather together. Serve Him. Await His return.

There Is a God. Christ Is Returning. The Best Is Yet to Come.

You can put that on your bus, and drive it!

FOUR

Stay Challenged

FOR ALL OF HIS SEVENTY-SIX YEARS, ROMANIAN-BORN LIVIU Librescu met life's challenges head-on. As a child in Romania during World War II, he was confined to a Jewish ghetto while his father was sentenced to a forced labor camp. But he survived the Holocaust, determined to fulfill his dream of becoming an engineer. And he did, in spite of the Communist Party ruling Romania during his young adult years. He completed an undergraduate engineering degree at the Polytechnic University of Bucharest and then a PhD at the Institute of Fluid Mechanics at Romania's Academy of Science. As a brilliant professor he was widely esteemed—within Romania. Communist rule prohibited him from publishing his research outside of Romania. So, at great risk, he smuggled his papers out of Romania to publishers in other countries.

After three years of overcoming obstacles, Dr. Librescu and his wife were granted permission to emigrate to Israel in 1978. After teaching at Tel-Aviv University for seven years, he accepted a one-year position as a visiting professor in the Virginia Tech (Virginia) Department of

Engineering Science and Mechanics. In 1985 his family joined him in Blacksburg, Virginia, and they became part of the university family. He became one of Virginia Tech's most popular and respected professors and researchers in the field of aeronautical engineering. Throughout his career, Dr. Librescu compiled a list of awards and recognitions too long to detail here, but they were evidence of how the man lived his life—with strenuous and lavish commitment and generosity to his opportunities, his vocation, his family, and his university.

Dr. Librescu was Jewish. For all of his seventy-six years, he exemplified in his life the kind of diligence that reflects the image of God in human beings. Dr. Ishwar Puri, head of Dr. Librescu's department at Virginia Tech, said of his colleague, "He loved his position as a professor. A prolific researcher and wonderful teacher, he devoted himself to the profession, solely for the love of it."

When the professor himself was asked, in 2005, why he continued to work so hard, he said, "It is not a question of organizations or calculations. If I had the pleasure to do this, then I will put time aside to do this. It is personal freedom. If you are limited, then you miss the freedom. And I—I would like to be fluid. I would like to be free as a bird and fly everywhere."

The way Dr. Librescu lived his life—overcoming obstacles for more than seven decades to give his all to what he loved—would be a lesson by itself in diligence. He continued to teach at Virginia Tech well past retirement age because life itself was a challenge for him. He never gave himself permission to stop as long as his students needed him. In fact, it was his diligence that cost Dr. Librescu his life, and served as the ultimate illustration of what it means to live with no reservations.

On April 16, 2007, when a heavily armed, deranged student entered the classroom buildings on the Virginia Tech campus and began randomly killing and wounding students and staff, Dr. Librescu was teaching a class of around twenty students. As soon as it became obvious that the shooter might target his classroom, the seventy-six-year-old professor immediately threw himself against the inside of the classroom door while instructing the students to flee out the windows to safety. One of the last students to exit the classroom remembers seeing the professor leaning against the door and then falling, fatally wounded by bullets that came through the door. All twenty students, some with broken legs from the two-story fall, survived.

What would make someone sacrifice himself for the sake of others? For Liviu Librescu, it was the culmination of a life of overcoming challenges and remaining diligent to the end. After the attack, a student summarized the professor's actions: "It's one of those things where every little thing you do can save somebody's life."

I tell Liviu Librescu's story for a reason expressed by Dr. Puri, his department head: "[Professor Librescu] was an extremely tolerant man who mentored scholars from all over our troubled world." The professor was no stranger to trouble, but he wasn't intimidated by it. From childhood his commitment to living for others created peace in "our troubled world." Christians live in the same world. And we are called by God to take up our cross and march into the trouble for the sake of Christ—not knowing but that one little thing we do might save someone's life in time or for eternity.

Learning to live an exceptional life—a life of sacrifice, diligence, and generous commitment—is a process that never ends.[1]

The apostle Peter clues us in on the importance of living this kind of life: "Therefore, beloved, looking forward to these things, be diligent to be found by him in peace, without spot and blameless" (2 Peter 3:14). As always, the theme is that Christ is returning, so how shall we then live in this chaotic world? As you can see, the idea this time is to be diligent.

It isn't the first time Peter has used this word. Note what he has already written in an earlier chapter: "But also for this very reason, giving all diligence, add to your faith virtue, to virtue knowledge" (1:5). His message to us is to be motivated because our Lord is coming back. Don't stop the good things you're doing, but work even harder. If you do that, the world will never trip you up.

The Purpose of Diligence

At the beginning of this epistle, we catch a glimpse of how the idea of diligence fits into Peter's overall theme: "As his divine power has given to us all things that pertain to life and godliness, through the knowledge of him who called us by glory and virtue, by which have been given to us exceedingly great and precious promises, that through these you may be partakers of the divine nature, having escaped the corruption that is in the world through lust" (2 Peter 1:3–4).

You may need to read that rich paragraph more than once. As you do so, note that Peter offers two focal points. First there is the astonishing idea that every follower of Christ has been given everything pertaining to life and godliness—not some things, not most things, but *everything*. Have you ever realized that? All that you need is already yours.

But wait! Where can we find these things? Peter says they have been given to us through the "exceedingly great and precious promises" of God's Word. That means your Bible is a full utility kit for everything you need to live with confidence in this chaotic world.

There's nothing else tangible in life that is as wonderful and complete as the written Word of God.

My wife, Donna, was recovering from surgery recently, and it fell to me to buy groceries. That is one of those things in life that just wasn't meant to be. She gave me a nice, neat list, and I wandered in confusion from aisle to aisle, occasionally finding some product but clueless as to why it was in the place where I found it. Yet I can find my way through the Bible like an old scout.

The Word is so beautifully organized and presented for us. We have history, poetry, and prophecy neatly grouped and giving us the story of God's people. Then we have the Gospels and our narrative of the early church, then the letters of those apostles that offer so much clear guidance for life. Everything we need for life and godliness is found in a neat package you can hold in a hand and bury in a heart. You can carry a New Testament in your shirt pocket or even, in software form, inside a cell phone these days.

Those who know me know how I feel about God's Word. But there's a disclaimer. It's possible to become so enamored of the Bible that we forget we need to interact with it. It's not enough to say, "What a beautiful leather Bible," and promptly stick it away on the shelf or under the car seat. Some Christians hear that "it is God who works in [us] both to will and to do for His good pleasure" (Philippians 2:13), and they think they can sit back and relax. They tend to miss the verse that came right before it, telling them to work out their own salvation "with fear and trembling" (2:12). That doesn't sound relaxing to me.

We do need to be careful how we speak of "working out" our salvation. This doesn't mean we can earn salvation—only the blood of Jesus Christ can give us that. In terms of the true reconciling work of forgiveness, we have no part. But we are to work *out* what God has worked *in*. I call that the "divine cooperative." The gift is delivered to us through the work of God, and we take it and practice due diligence in working to perfect ourselves as followers of Christ.

Isn't this how we look upon all gifts? If someone gives you a nice shirt for your birthday, it's up to you to wear it. If you receive a book, you're the one to read it. We are the recipients, but we must act on what we have been given or the gift is wasted upon us. Donna and I have two athletically gifted sons. I often told them while growing up that their ability was God's gift to them, and what they did with it was their gift to God. We receive gifts from the Holy Spirit too. I hope you have a firm grasp on what your spiritual gift is and that you are intentionally using it rather than tucking it away to admire.

We have the gift in hand. We've been provided with everything we need for life and godliness, and the Bible is the set of instructions that will get us up and running. More than that, it can make the very difference in our survival during the toughest of times. Consider the example of Geoffrey Bull, a British missionary who was taken prisoner when the communists took over China in 1949.

Geoffrey was kept in solitary confinement, but that wasn't the worst of it. His cell wasn't much larger than a phone booth. For twelve years his captors made him the subject of constant brainwashing attempts. "Not only did they want my confession," he said, "they wanted my soul." Convinced he was a British spy, the Chinese were after him every day, using diabolical mental tortures. But one thing made a difference for Geoffrey Bull. As a boy, his parents had encouraged him to memorize impressive portions of the Scriptures. Those verses lived in his heart, in the one stronghold the wardens could not penetrate, and they gave Geoffrey strength and power.

One night, with the cell doors bolted and padlocked, Bull knelt to pray. The guard began shouting through the keyhole, "You are not to pray!" He entered the cell and forced him from his knees. Even so, Geoffrey clung to every word of Scripture he possessed, turning it over in his mind, feeling its warmth. God gave him a patience and peace that few of us can imagine. When he would finish with the verses, he would name the names of his captors, praying for every one of them. The seeds of bitterness found no place in his heart.

After he was finally released, Geoffrey Bull faced many months of recuperation. After that, you might have expected him to retire. Not him. He married and resumed his missionary career, this time in Borneo. There was still much work to be done—to be done *diligently*.[2]

The Prerequisite for Diligence

Faith is the prerequisite for diligence. Peter begins right there, telling us in verse 5 what to add to our faith. A list of "add-ons" follows, but the steam engine that pulls the train is faith. Without it, we're going nowhere.

Faith is the lowest common denominator in the mathematics of this passage. Have you noticed? Grace and peace are "multiplied" in verse 2, then a number of sums are "added" in verses 5–7. If you pay close attention, you will notice that God does the multiplying, and we do the adding. That's the divine cooperative at work.

So faith is the beginning of the process. We accept Christ by faith and are saved completely by God's grace. We want to move forward as believers by adding on to this faith. How do we do it? By taking responsibility for our growth. And this is what Peter wants to help us understand.

The Principles of Diligence

Now it's time to understand the meaning of the word that I believe is the key to the Christian life. What is the word *diligence* all about?

- *To strenuously give of yourself.* *Strenuous* is an athletic word. It is demanding and sweat-producing. It means "to give all strenuous activity toward." Indeed it comes from the athletic world of intense concentration on the goal of becoming a champion. Diligence is the picture of the sprinter coming around the bend toward the finish tape, exerting every muscle in his body, even when it seems like he has nothing left to give. He has practiced for months or years, working on every tiny characteristic of his motion. He has run countless miles, pushing his body toward faster finish times. And now, as he runs the big race, he is even more focused. Just saying *strenuous* seems to make us huff and puff.
- *To lavishly give of yourself.* Understanding what it means to strive strenuously can include the idea of *lavish* extravagance. In New Testament times, wealthy patrons loved sponsoring Greek plays. Fierce competition ensued, as each patron tried to top his rivals in financing the latest and the greatest props, scenery, and performers. When his friends viewed his lavish production, they'd have a new benchmark, and they'd be determined to set yet another. These wealthy donors were "out-lavishing" one another. Peter uses the Greek word *choregeo,* which means to supply things extravagantly, without limit or cost considerations. It is the word from which we get

our word *choreography*, and it is what we mean when we say, "Money is no object."

The great age of the Greeks has passed, but the idea lives on. The college bowl games, televised around New Year's, strenuously try to out-lavish one another in their glitzy halftime shows. But they all pale in comparison to the Super Bowl, when tens of millions of dollars are spent on world-class performers, fireworks, light shows, and whatever else will make the viewers say, "Wow!" The official sponsors of the game spend budget-busting sums to produce the TV commercial that will be most discussed around tomorrow's water cooler. As for those who actually play the game, they hold nothing back, either. They are strenuous in their ferocity. No one gives half of his effort during the biggest game of the season.

We see the same phenomenon every four years in the Olympic Games. Each host city wants to be proclaimed the best ever at putting on a show for the entire world. More than one hundred million dollars was spent in Beijing, more than doubling what was spent four years earlier in Athens.[3]

Many of the athletes compete with one another all through the year at other venues, and they know each other well. But they save something extra for the world stage of the Olympics, and we love seeing strenuous competition at its very best.

With all of that modern imagery in mind, think about what the Word of God, through Peter, asks us to do. We are to be characterized by a strenuous diligence, lavishing all that we are, and all that we have, upon growing in Christ. He tells us that we have all the tools when it comes to life and godliness. Now it's up to us to pour it on as we make our lives the most exciting, adrenaline-pumped, God-glorifying testimonies of service that we can produce through the power of the Holy Spirit.

In his book *Knowing Scripture,* R. C. Sproul writes about the "Sensuous Christian." Sproul doesn't mean that in the usual physical use of that word. He defines that term as the domination of the Christian life by the intangibles of feelings. "Many of us" he writes, "have become sensuous Christians, living by our feelings, rather than through our understanding of the Word of God. Sensuous Christians cannot be moved to service, prayer, or study unless they 'feel like it.'"[4] This hapless believer does good things when he is feeling close to God. But when he is depressed, he does nothing of service to Christ. He therefore looks for stimuli to ignite his emotions because he wants to *experience* God rather than genuinely know Him. The sensuous Christian evaluates the Word by his feelings rather than the other way around, and he stays immature because he believes this is childlike faith, when it's actually childish. The Word constantly admonishes us to grow in our faith, but the sensuous Christian simply wants an experience of some kind. What eventually happens? He encounters tough times but he lacks the wisdom to meet the challenge.

Sproul makes me realize I need to ask this question of myself, just as I ask you to ask yourself: *Is my walk with God all about emotions and feelings? Or is it driven by faith and the Word?* When I have one of those days when I don't feel the victory of my faith, do I continue to serve Him in obedience? Or do I let my feelings hurt my faith? Strong faith is based upon the facts of God's Word—the truth of our salvation, the historic fact of Christ's resurrection, the understanding that He will come again. Those things are true even if I'm not as excited about them as I should be on a gloomy day. Peter is talking about laying a foundation of faith based on the solid and substantial Word, so that no bad day, no bad event, no national recession can shake it. These are the times when God smiles upon our response—when the world is treating us poorly, when our spirits are low, yet we pray anyway; we serve anyway; we open the Word anyway and say, "God, I'm not my best today, but all that I have is still yours." Any child that tells Him that is going to be taken up in His embrace and comforted.

His promises don't fluctuate with our whims. We can cling to those promises and find a powerful emotional equilibrium. Living based on feelings is like riding a roller coaster without a seat belt. Living rooted to His Word is more like building a house with a foundation of pure, tempered steel. You're going to be ready for anything that comes along. What Peter is saying to us is, "Start digging! You have your shovel, you have your earth-moving equipment, now lay down that sure foundation." You do so by applying all that is in the Word.

I'm the first to admit that I process through a series of emotions as I prepare to preach. Like most communicators, I'm always putting myself into the shoes of my listeners. How will this sound to them? What if they hear this sermon and it drives them away from striving for Christian maturity? There's always the temptation to give the people what they want, which may not be the same as what they need.

Every preacher of the Word struggles with this urge, but in the end, he knows that God has called him to be true to the Word. He knows the terrible implications of conforming his message to the world, rather than letting his message be transforming through the true Word of Christ. I get a sense of Peter having these same thoughts as he wrote the first chapter of his letter:

> For this reason I will not be negligent to remind you always of these
> things, though you know and are established in the present truth. Yes,

I think it is right, as long as I am in this tent, to stir you up by reminding you, knowing that shortly I must put off my tent, just as our Lord
Jesus Christ showed me. Moreover I will be careful to ensure that you
always have a reminder of these things after my decease (2 Peter
1:12–15).

His "tent" is the old, tattered human body that he knows will soon
perish. He can't make small talk. He can't spend time telling people
the feel-good messages that massage the ear. The situation is urgent,
and he is already making arrangements to see that his words outlive
him—as they have certainly done, in that we're discussing them right
now. Peter is nothing if not strenuous and lavish in training his
brothers and sisters in the faith.

The Priorities of Diligence

Peter offers us seven priorities of diligence, all built upon that foundation called faith. Like many biblical lists, this one isn't exhaustive—
other positive traits could be listed. But I believe these seven are special.
They form the basic girders that make up the architecture of the
Christian life that we build. These are the seven elements you should
look for periodically when checking up on the vital signs of your walk
with Christ.

- *Faith + Virtue.* "Add to your faith virtue" (2 Peter 1:5). Do you
  know what virtue is? *Courage.* This is the New Testament word
  for moral goodness: having the courage to do the right thing
  no matter what the circumstances might dictate. People with
  strong integrity are consistent from one situation to another.

They act from their moral base rather than from consensus or popular opinion. This kind of virtue develops as we become steeped in God's Word and begin to show the mind of Christ in our actions. The Spirit of God, rather than the spirit of the age, guides our decisions.

- *Virtue + Knowledge.* "To virtue knowledge" (1:5). This one means exactly what it says. We are to continue growing in the knowledge of God's Word. In fact, the word *knowledge* is found five times in the first chapter of 2 Peter. What we need is knowledge anchored in truth, and we have it in the Scriptures. It only remains for us to extract that knowledge and make it part of us. You'll never find a devout believer who doesn't have a deep familiarity with the Word of God. This is simply essential.

- *Knowledge + Self-control.* "To knowledge self-control" (v. 6). Most of us are very comfortable hearing that we're going to be gaining knowledge, but our smiles fade a bit when we hear about self-control. This concept implies that we have choices. We can choose what we do, what we say, and what we think. This is about (here comes another unpleasant word) *discipline.* Anything worth achieving in life is going to come because of personal discipline and self-control. You might have shown a little of it by picking up this book rather than turning on the television. You exercise it by rising from bed to attend church when you're a little sleepy. We could all use more self-control.

I spoke to a San Diego Charger about his routine for personally motivated discipline. Every morning his alarm clock would sound at a very early hour, and he would take off running toward the hills. He did this day after day, and how could he keep it up? He told me that with every footfall he would say to himself, "My competitors are still in bed. My competitors are still in bed." He wanted to attain that slight edge that would set him apart, win him a starting job, earn him a place on the All-Pro team, and help him contribute to team goals. In the end, he realized every one of his goals.

- *Self-Control + Perseverance.* "To self-control perseverance" (v. 6). Perseverance is a glorified synonym for patience. It is to "voluntarily and continually endure difficulties and hardships for the sake of honor."[5] Self-control gets the football player out of bed in the morning, but perseverance finishes the routine today, tomorrow, and the next day. Many of us have the self-control to start diets or exercise programs, but lack perseverance, and therefore never cross the finish line.

  Perseverance is silencing your body when it begins to complain. It's forcing yourself awake to study the Bible in the morning when you know you could use another fifteen minutes of sleep. Perseverance is the trademark of champions.

- *Perseverance + Godliness.* "To perseverance godliness" (v. 6). What exactly is godliness, and how does it grow from perseverance? The word means reverence and deep respect toward God, and it begins to take form in us only when we continue with Him—serving Him as Lord, growing through His Word, accepting the Spirit's correction and guidance, all across time. It's not about being a Sunday Christian or a mountain-top experience believer, but an everyday, long-haul follower of Jesus Christ.

  We need real godliness all the time, but it is especially

necessary in chaotic days like the ones we are currently experiencing—and I don't mean the everyday run-of-the-mill pattern that passes for "godliness." Today we seem to be presenting our concept of God in a more casual, user-friendly way, and I see certain dangers there. We want unbelievers to see a positive faith, and that is good. We want them to see a God of love instead of one who is relentlessly angry, and that, too, is good. But I worry that bit by bit, we're losing the concept of His holiness, His majestic and infinite magnitude, and yes, His judgment of sin. Our God is an awesome God, a glorious King, and so much more than a kindly grandfather in heaven.

I bring this up because the godly Christian is the one who is truly humble before Almighty God. It is impossible to pursue our Lord over the years and still maintain a childish, superficial, lame and tame conception of him. To be godly is to reflect, more and more clearly, His image in us. Our minds can't take in His greatness, but we need to at least be humbled by the thought of it.

- *Godliness + Brotherly Kindness + Love.* I have combined the last two priorities of diligence because they are so closely related. To godliness we are to add brotherly kindness, and to brotherly kindness, we add that supreme mark of the Christian called love (v. 7).

Does it seem strange that we first add self-control, which is tough, then perseverance, which is a little harder, then we begin to become godly, which is an ultimate goal of life—and then we add, of all things, brotherly kindness? It almost seems a step backward, something rather mundane compared to godliness. But brotherly kindness and love are what truly set us apart as believers, when we practice them consistently. You can have knowledge without love and kindness. You can have faith without it, perseverance, and all the rest. But godliness makes love overflow from within us!

It's a tribute to the goodness of God that if we are truly like Him, the first thing people will see in us is the warmth of brotherly kindness. All of the Ten Commandments are summarized in the word *love.* Jesus spoke constantly of love, and showed this trait more than any other in His life. And it's the one and only virtue that God is described as *being*: "God is love" (1 John 4:8, 16). That's how significant love is in our faith.

This list is a kind of godliness obstacle course for the believer. Make a checklist of the seven traits, put it where you'll see it every day, and evaluate how you're running the course. It's a slow process, but trust me—be a diligent disciple and one day you're going to look at the list, notice you're beginning to match up with it, and you'll realize that you have become a different creature.

The Possibilities of Diligence

Peter now offers us two three-part pictures—one for the diligent life, one for the nondiligent.

Three things that will happen if you are diligent:

- *You will have stability in your Christian life.* Peter wants us to know that if we pursue God and focus on these qualities, we'll see them begin to come together for us. Character is the result of persistent action, and a pattern of diligence will lead to stability. One by one, old and unhelpful habits will fall by the wayside in your life. You'll simply find that you don't want to do those things anymore because walking in the Spirit is so much more satisfying.

You'll be more resistant to the ups and downs of the world that trouble most people, and therefore you'll have stability. What about sin? You'll never be totally free of its everyday challenge—not in this life. We're not talking about a plan for perfection, but a life of constant growth. None of it comes easily. If it did, we would see stable and fruitful lives all around us. The church would be filled with supersaints! No, it's not easy, but those who are diligent, those who continue to pursue the consistent Christian life, will enjoy a maturity that causes them to live with confidence in chaotic times.

- *You will have vitality in your Christian life.* Vitality is defined as abundant mental and physical energy. It's what people tend to lose when they leave their youth behind—that ability to spring out of bed and greet the new day; the propensity to embrace change rather than fear it; and so many other signs of a lively heart. Make a close study of the mature saints you know, and you'll see that vitality, even deep into their golden years. There's some quality about them that remains forever young. Wouldn't you love to grow with grace like that? These qualities, lived out diligently, make it happen.

Christ came into this world to give us life and to give it *abundantly*, as Jesus tells us in John 10:10. He's not interested in helping us survive. He wants us to thrive. Peter is telling us in verse 8 that we'll come to the place where all these qualities of diligence will create a joy and vitality that overflows from us, as if we were fountains of God's goodness. The godlier qualities of our lives will become infectious, so that other people begin to seek Him because they want what they see in us.

- *You will have reality in your Christian life.* Third, Peter tells us that we'll have true reality in our lives. Peter says we will be neither barren nor unfruitful in the knowledge of Jesus Christ. That means we'll know His truth deeply, and it will bear real fruit all around us. We will be involved in the real world, connecting the truth of the gospel to the needs that we see. Some people believe faith is some kind of fantasy world in which we escape the problems of the day and become "so heavenly minded that we're no earthly good." That's not the profile of the truly devout follower. Real Christians keep it real.

Now, what about the other side of the coin? What does life look like for the believer who chooses not to pursue this course?

Three things that will happen if you are not diligent:

- *You will lack spiritual power.* Peter speaks of life "for he who lacks these things" (2 Peter 1:9), referring to the list he has just given. There are millions of people who profess to be Christians, yet manage to avoid going after virtue, knowledge, self-control, patience, godliness, brotherly kindness, and love. You can have a reunion with them after thirty years and find they're at the same level of spiritual maturity now as then—a real tragedy. Once, a little boy fell out of his bed during the night and told his mother, "I went to sleep too close to where I got in." That's what happens to too many of the children of God. They remain children by dozing off at the very entry point of their faith. They don't learn to pray through a trial. They can't minister to a friend who needs loving care. They have no idea how to grow in grace, and the voice of the Holy Spirit is so still, so small, that they can't hear it above the culture's clamor. They lack spiritual power.

- *You will lack spiritual perception.* "Shortsighted, even to blindness," is the way Peter speaks of the immature Christian (1:9). We live in an era in which keen eyes are essential spiritual equipment—and you realize what kind of sight I'm talking about. We need to see truth, as if looking through the eyes of God. Growing believers enjoy increasing communication with the Holy Spirit, their counselor and advisor in all things. Nongrowing ones are like armies without reconnaissance reports, fighting away in the fog. They are shortsighted to the point of blindness.

  As we read the headlines, consider our own business and housing decisions, and wonder what's just around the corner in our culture, we need to pray daily that we be granted the ability to see with the eyes of God, think with the mind of Christ, and walk in the power of the Holy Spirit. Do those things, and you have an outrageous advantage on those who don't! We have a direct line to the One who knows what happens on the next page because He has written the whole story.

- *You will lose spiritual privilege.* Thirdly, the nondiligent believer will eventually come to the place where he "has forgotten that he was cleansed from his old sins" (1:9). These sins, of course, were those committed before salvation. Can you imagine experiencing the miracle of salvation, the cleansing of Christ's blood, the arrival of the Holy Spirit, and the joy of Christian fellowship, only to forget that miracle that started it all in motion? It seems impossible, but when we look at the world, we see how often it happens. Christians live in such a way that there is no discernible difference between their lives and those outside the kingdom. In other words, they have lost all the spiritual privileges and graces that make life worth living. These are the people who ask, "Am I really saved? How can I be certain?" If the question even needs to be asked, there is something terribly wrong.

This is why we want to live with passion, focus, and diligence, growing in the traits that Peter mentions. Everything we could possibly need to be difference-makers in this world has already been given to us. There's really no limit to what we can achieve in this life for the glory of God, and our own abundant life.

The goal of my life is to reach that place where diligence to God's will is my total passion.

The Promise of Diligence

Now God offers us this promise: "If you do these things you will never stumble" (2 Peter 1:10). What is a stumbling block to anyone else becomes a stepping-stone for us. This doesn't mean we'll have no problems. To the extent that we diligently pursue the Christian life, however, we will walk victoriously and upright, and we'll avoid the classic mistakes.

There is another intriguing promise. "For so an entrance will be supplied to you abundantly into the everlasting kingdom of our Lord and Savior Jesus Christ" (1:11). What kind of entrance? This is actually a nautical image. Heaven, in Peter's imagery, has a harbor. We sail Godward toward that harbor, moving through the storms and rocks that lurk in the waves. Some ships barely make it into port—the crew is exhausted and near mutiny, the rigging is torn, supplies are low, and the ship has sprung many leaks. It's not exactly a hail-the-conquering-hero kind of arrival. But we don't have to float into the harbor with our sails down and our spirits defeated. Peter is telling us that diligent believers are like diligent captains and sailors: they sail with discipline, manning the watchtower, maintaining the ship, keeping morale high among the crew. That's a picture of the well-lived Christian life. The storms will come, but God has given us what we need to come through them all the stronger.

In other words, this isn't about going to heaven. If you have trusted Jesus Christ, your name is on that crew list by order of the Captain. What's at issue here is the quality of your voyage. Think about the sailors of old—the life they led on the sea, the confinement of a small ship, the dangers of storm, snare, and shipwreck. The hard life of the open sea required absolute discipline, unquestioned diligence, and particularly an unquestioning obedience to the admiral—no matter how desperate the voyage became.

How strong is your faith? Are you disciplined and diligent enough to weather the storm? Think about that as you hear the story of Sabina

Wurmbrand. She was a Jewish convert to Christianity in the Romania of the 1930s and '40s. She and her husband, Richard, accepted Christ and together founded an underground church. Sabina was arrested for covert Christian activities, including smuggling Jewish children out of the ghettos.

The Romanian Communist Party sponsored a "religious conference." Ministers were required not only to attend but to profess loyalty to Communism. Sabina insisted that her husband stand up for Christ, even if that would make her a widow because, she told him, "I don't wish to have a coward for a husband." Four thousand were on hand to watch, and the whole nation listened on radio, as Richard Wurmbrand professed allegiance only to Christ. He was imprisoned and placed in solitary confinement, much like Geoffrey Bull in China. His book, *Tortured for Christ*, describes fourteen excruciating years of suffering for his Lord.

Sabina's story is less famous, though she spent much time in prison and under house arrest as well. When the family was finally ransomed and allowed to leave Romania in 1966, Sabina begin a speaking ministry, telling the world what it meant to live behind the Iron Curtain as a disciple of Jesus Christ, particularly from a woman's point of view. The women worked for hour upon hour at slave labor, scooping out a canal by hand. Empty stomachs kept them awake at night, though they were bone-tired. Sabina wondered about her nine-year-old son, Mihai, now a homeless orphan. Her captors would gather children and beat them, just to torment the parents in the camp.

The wardens kept them alive and working with promises that they might see their children if only they would keep laboring. This hope energized them when all heart and strength should have been gone. Finally the day came for Sabina to meet with Mihai. There were only a few moments, and her heart was too full for speech. Little Mihai was pale and thin. As they led him away, she managed the words, "Mihai, love Jesus with all your heart!"

Those words and the intensity of her love were more powerful than all the cruelty of the Eastern Communist Bloc. Her husband and son both came through those dark days as strong Christians, pushing on boldly for the kingdom of God.[6]

Don't you hear the voice of the Spirit saying the same words to you? "Christian! Love Jesus with all your heart!" I don't know what dangers, toils, or snares life has thrown in your path in these recent months. I can't say exactly what the coming months will hold. But I know that on this wondrous gospel ship, daily diligence to the chores of kingdom life will bring us through—no matter what we face.

FIVE

Stay Connected

"I HAVE YOUR CHILD!" IS THERE ANY MORE TERRIFYING NEWS? Add to that the words, "You will never see this child again," and you have a serious situation. Authorities on the East Coast had one of these on their hands early this year. A nine-year-old Athol, Massachusetts, girl had been taken by her grandmother. The little city of Athol has some big-league, technically savvy police officers. The police first connected with the grandmother through the girl's cell phone number. She promised to return the girl. When she failed to do so, Officer Todd Neale went into action.

He was aware of a fact that many people do not know. He knew that since 2005 there has been a US law that requires mobile phone providers to be able to locate 67 percent of callers within 100 meters (0.18 miles).[1] The technology can only be used in cases of lost or missing people or when a life is clearly in danger.

Officer Neale contacted the girl's cell phone service provider to request that they provide him with GPS coordinates every time the phone was used. While he knew enough to take those steps, he needed the services of a more experienced cell phone tracker. He called on Athol's Deputy Fire Chief, Thomas Lozier, who had that experience. The two successfully tracked the kidnapped girl through GPS and Google maps to a hotel six states away from her home. The local state police took over from there, arrested the grandmother, and reconnected the girl with her frantic family. The cell phone posse rejoiced.

Cell phones are wonderful tools for making connections. Besides their obvious use for making voice contact with friends or loved ones, they can also be used to text silent messages when a verbal conversation would be rude—like in a restaurant. Newer phones even have full keyboards for doubled-handed input.

But simple texting has become "so last year." Today there is Twitter. With one action you can send a 140-character message with all of the minutiae of your life to two hundred of your closest friends simultaneously and in real time. "The social warmth of all those stray details shouldn't be taken lightly," says *Time* in a recent cover story.[2] In this increasingly impersonal world, people really want to connect with one another. Twitter became the primary real-time connection within Iran and to the rest of the world during the demonstrations following the disputed presidential election of June 12.

So many people seek to make connections with someone who will care about them that it is apparently very common for a Twitterer (if that is a word) to receive an error message: "Twitter is over capacity. Too many Tweets! Please wait a moment and try again."[3]

May I suggest a better place to make meaningful connections—without busy signals? The church.

Oh, I know. There are those like *Newsweek* who are proclaiming the "Decline and Fall of Christian America." Others like the *Boston Globe* have also carried stories about how that state's mainline churches are dying slow deaths; in the Roman Catholic Church, the Archdiocese of Boston has closed nearly one quarter of its churches during the last decade.[4] A report from March 2009 shows significant declines in both of the two largest faith communities, Roman Catholic and Southern Baptist. Until recently, both of them had steady growth.[5]

The American Religion Survey, also released in March 2009, indicates a sharp uptick in the number of people who profess no religion at all. In fact, "no religion" is the only area of growth—and that's across the board, in every state in the union. True, a few faith groups are reporting growth: evangelicals, Mormons, and Muslims. According to the report, Muslims in America have doubled since 1990.

In his book, *Bowling Alone: The Collapse and Revival of American Community*, Robert D. Putnam observes that since the 1960s, Americans have become 10 percent less likely to be church members and 25 to 50 percent less likely to be involved in religious activities. In other words, there are now fewer church members, and a great many are less active ones. During the 1950s, there was a boom in church attendance. Putnam believes those strides have been reversed—and perhaps even overcompensated for in the other direction.[6]

People are not only staying away from churches, they are staying away from community groups such as clubs, service organizations, and adult sports leagues. Charles Colson notes that the age of personal computers has pushed individualism to a new level. Rather than connecting with people face to face, they do it electronically through Internet social networking, e-mail, and instant messaging—much of the time with "handles" rather than names, and faceless anonymity replacing deep, knowing friendship.[7]

Cyber-community seems nice until something bad happens, and then we want face time rather than Facebook. In the aftermath of

September 11, 2001, people came looking for genuine community. The same thing happened with the subsequent series of crises that followed. On the Sunday after 9/11, our large sanctuary couldn't contain all the members and guests who wanted to be part of a worship service. When we feel insecure, a computer screen seems cold and irrelevant. Television is impersonal. We need to be with fellow members of the human race, created, like ourselves, in the image of God.

When the economic bottom fell out late in 2008, the *New York Times* had this headline: "Bad Times Draw Bigger Crowds to Churches." The article studied the spikes in attendance of evangelical churches during every recession cycle of the last forty years. Each time, growth jumped 50 percent in the wake of the bad news—before settling back into its routine as people became more comfortable.[8]

How does this affect society? How does it influence individuals? Theologian Leonard Sweet writes that "each of us lives on many levels, and we need multileveled relationships with different kinds of people to be healthy and whole. With the decline of extended families in Western cultures, this becomes all the more important."[9]

We could be seeing the results of that already. Two studies found that over the last nineteen years, the number of people reporting that they had no one with whom they could really share important issues had tripled. Nearly half of all Americans, claimed the studies, had either one intimate friend or none at all. Meanwhile, virtual social networks have become all the rage. We suspect that people long for authentic community, and perhaps they're looking for love in all the wrong places. Online friendship isn't ultimately satisfying. It's possible to have three hundred "connections" on Facebook, two hundred "following" you on Twitter, and still feel as if no one really knows you at all.

During tough times, we're seeing a widespread craving for genuine soul-to-soul connection.[10] How many online friends will come to visit us if we check into the hospital? How many will hold us accountable for living with godly integrity?

A Church that Looks Like God

It was our Creator who said, "It is not good that man should be alone." He brought Eve into the world to provide rewarding human interaction for Adam (Genesis 2:18).

Relationships are part of our basic design. We require a relationship with God's only Son, Jesus Christ, in order to be saved. After that, a great deal of our growth as believers comes through the accountability that fellow Christians provide within spiritual community. Together, we become something much larger than the sum of our parts. According to the New Testament, we are the one body of Christ—an assembly of parts that only function in unison. This we call the church.

Have you ever noticed the great "3:16" verses in the Bible? The greatest, of course, is John 3:16, which tells us God loved the world so much that He sent His only Son. "The world" is all of us together. 1 John 3:16 tells us "we know love because He laid down his life for us. And we also ought to lay down our lives for the brethren." In other words, God set the pattern that we follow with each other. Philippians 3:16 encourages us to "walk by the same rule [and] be of the same mind"—a definition of community. And in Malachi 3:16, in the last book of the Old Testament, we read: "Then those who feared the LORD spoke to one another, And the LORD listened and heard them; So a book of remembrance was written before Him for those who fear the LORD and who meditate on His name."

That last verse tells us that when God-fearing people begin to speak to one another, He listens to them and their conversation becomes part of eternity through His "book of remembrance." Remember, Jesus said, "For where two or three are gathered together in My name, I am there in the midst of them" (Matthew 18:20). We can always experience the presence of God alone, and we should do so every day. But special things happen when believers gather together to share in Him.

Dr. Russell Moore of Southern Seminary believes there is a reason for that. He says that our need for connection, communion, and community is rooted in the triune nature of God himself. Genesis 1:26 and 11:7 quote the Lord as saying, "Let *Us* . . ." He is multipersonal, and as individuals created in His image, we need the multiple personalities available to us through community. Moore also points out that the members of the Trinity glorify one another. God is glorified on the divine level by the Father glorifying the Son, the Son glorifying the Father, and the Spirit glorifying the Son.[11]

A close study of the gospel of John shows these triune relationships as a clear theme. For example, Jesus answers our prayers to bring glory to the Father. He said, "And I will do whatever you ask in My name, so that the Son may bring glory to the Father" (John 14:13 NIV). John 17:1 in particular shows the power of this mutual glorification: "Father, the hour has come. Glorify Your Son, that Your Son also may glorify You."

As We See the Day Approaching

There is a powerful and positive relationship among the three Persons of the Godhead as each glorifies the other. Any strong church or fellowship reflects this principle. When we love and perfect each other, we are reflecting the work of the Holy Trinity and participating in His ancient and everlasting love. As we mentioned earlier, the New Testament has a pattern of "one another" and "each other" tasks (encourage one another, love one another, bear with one another, to name three). As we carry these out, we experience a unique form of godliness that can't be attained as separate human entities. We reflect the roles and relationships of the Triune God, and we really do become the people of God, the body of Christ, and the fellowship of the Holy Spirit.

If we are going to be able to live courageous lives in these chaotic days, we will need to be calm in our hearts, compassionate toward others, constructive in our relationships, challenged to grow, and connected to the church. We were created to live in community, not in isolation.

Mary Saunders, a Southern Baptist missionary in Africa, described a regular meeting she had with a new Christian in Somalia. The regular appointment was secret because the area was predominantly Islamic and often intolerant. On this particular evening, Mary reviewed the memory verse the young Somali had been learning: "This is the day which the LORD hath made; we will rejoice and be glad in it" (Psalm 118:24 KJV). After discussing the verse, Mary sang the familiar chorus based on that verse. The young man was delighted. The idea of singing raised a question for him: "When there is more than one Christian, what other things do you do?"

Mary realized that the ideas of corporate worship, music, praying together, Bible study—all these things she took for granted—were unimaginable to someone whose experience was limited to private Bible study and prayer.[12]

This book is about what on earth we should be doing in times like these, based on passages about the return of Christ. The Bible teaches that we should be living every day with an attitude of expectancy, and the New Testament writers had to preach that same message: "And let us consider one another in order to stir up love and good works, not forsaking the assembling of ourselves together, as is the manner of some, but exhorting one another, and so much the more as you see the Day approaching" (Hebrews 10:24–25).

We follow daily events and realize that this present age could end very soon, and that Christ's return could be approaching. The realization of that motivates us, more than ever, to be busy with our Father's business. And it's very clear that part of that business is to stay connected to one another through the fellowship of the church. We are to devote ourselves to one another and to begin preparing the body of Christ, as we prepare ourselves, for that day when He arrives to reclaim us. As we "see the Day approaching," in the words of Hebrews, we should be gathering together more frequently instead of less.

Hebrews 10:24–25 constitute the New Testament's central statement on the connectivity of God's people. By the way, in the course of this chapter, you're likely to notice that this is one of my favorite words: *connectivity*. In the current climate, people hear that term and think of networks, the Internet, and the world of business. Our world of spiritual business is the ultimate connectivity, the kind Jesus described to His disciples when He said, "I am the vine, you are the branches. He who abides in Me, and I in him, bears much fruit; for without Me you can do nothing" (John 15:5). In that marvelous analogy, we are all interconnected through our attachment to the true vine, Jesus Christ. We cannot afford to be cut off from each other or from the vine that sustains us, that feeds us, and that helps us to grow.

As we have that connectivity with Him and with one another, we begin to bear much fruit (15:8).

The Imperative of Connectivity

Let's take a closer look at this passage to discover the imperative of connectivity. Notice the wording: "Not forsaking the assembling of ourselves together, as is the manner of some."

There are three exhortations given to us by the Lord through the writer of this passage in Hebrews which are set apart by the key words, "let us."

- "*Let us draw near* with a true heart in full assurance of faith" (v. 22). This is our responsibility to God—coming to him wholeheartedly.
- "*Let us hold fast* the confession of our hope" (v. 23). This is our responsibility to ourselves—to live hopefully.
- "And *let us consider one another* in order to stir up love and good works" (v. 24). That's our responsibility to one another, and we fulfill it by "not forsaking the assembling of ourselves together" (v. 25).

For the writer of Hebrews, worship attendance isn't an option for Christians. Take a close look at the first generation of believers, and you'll see how strongly they felt about it. According to Acts, the narrative of that era, those first Christians assembled in two ways: publicly and privately. One was the more formal expression of the church in the temple and in synagogues; the other more informal and intimate, in homes.

Connectivity in Public Meetings

Those first Christians were "continuing daily and with one accord in the temple" (Acts 2:46). Did you notice that I said "in the temple and in synagogues"? Isn't that the last place you would expect Christians to gather, in the wake of the hostility against Jesus? You'd think that the followers of Christ were looking for trouble by gathering there.

The truth is that most of the first Christians were also Jewish. The temple was the greatest symbol of worship and spiritual community that they could imagine. And a closer examination of the language in Acts 2:46 shows that it was actually the temple *courts* where the believers met. The crowds were tremendous in the wake of the Resurrection, which was followed, a few weeks later, by the coming of the Holy Spirit.

As impressive a city as Jerusalem was, there weren't any modern civic or convention centers available for the huge crowds coming together to worship Christ. So the temple, with its expansive courts, made sense.

This matter of gathering together is highly significant. The phrase is actually a single word in the language of the New Testament. It occurs only a couple of times—once here in Hebrews 10 and again in 2 Thessalonians. In his second letter to the Thessalonian church, Paul writes these words: "Now, brethren, concerning the coming of our Lord Jesus Christ and our *gathering together* to Him, we ask you . . ." (2 Thessalonians 2:1).

From these uses of this word, we learn that there are two "gathering together" seasons in the church: a present day gathering together on earth, and a future reunion with Christ in the air. That ultimate event is thrilling to the soul, but the current fellowship is just as exciting, just as supernatural, and Christ is just as present. As we come together, we are slowly causing each other to conform to His image. We also experience His presence on an entirely different level as He comes to be enthroned upon our praises. As a matter of fact, gathering together in His power in the midst of a world in turmoil is very much like those first believers who boldly ventured every day to the temple, where they could not help being seen by the Pharisees and the priests. That Judean world was in turmoil, too, and it's no wonder that people were flocking to the joy and hope they witnessed among the believers.

The devil would love for us to hang on to our mundane ideas and images of fellowship: doughnuts and coffee, a handshake, a little football talk—little more than what happens at the water cooler from Monday to Friday; the fellowship of the saints reduced to a friendly chat at the country club. Yet New Testament fellowship—*koinonia*—includes the idea of a holy partnership, of genuine communion of souls, best illustrated when we share the bread and the cup together in the Lord's Supper. It connects us as children of the same Father, blessed by salvation from the same Savior, and filled with the same Spirit. We experience a supernatural oneness with each other when we meet in the name of Christ. And if you've ever been a part of that, you know that Monday morning at the water cooler can't ever compare to Sunday morning at the throne of grace. Country clubs and lodges all pass away, but Christ's church is eternal.

Regardless of the stern warning in Hebrews, many believers don't take church attendance seriously. As a pastor, I hear words such as, "Oh, I'm spiritual, but I don't particularly need the church or 'institutional religion.'" When someone tells me, "I've learned to worship God on the golf course," I'm tempted to reply, "That's a good trick, and just about as easy as playing golf in the sanctuary." Indeed, I would love to see ordinary people approach sporting events with the same attitudes they bring to Christian fellowship. An anonymous wit posted a tongue-in-cheek sampling of what that would be like. Here is his list of reasons for no longer attending professional sports games:

1. Every time I go, they ask me for money.
2. The people I sit by aren't very friendly.
3. The seats are too hard and uncomfortable.
4. The coach never comes to call on me.
5. The referees make decisions I don't agree with.
6. Some games go into overtime, and I'm late getting home.
7. My parents took me to too many games when I was growing up.
8. My kids need to make their own decisions about which sports to follow.

It's true that some have legitimate reasons for not attending church, and those people are one of the reasons we have a radio and television ministry. But our faithful listeners are familiar with the point I regularly make on Friday broadcasts: our programs can never take the place of participation in the local church. The church is an up-close-and-personal thing; accept no substitutes. We must not forsake our assembling together. We need public connectivity.

Connectivity in Private Meetings

There is also a need to connect with other believers in smaller gatherings. This requirement may be less well known, but it's just as important. We crave the sense of belonging that comes through a more intimate group of like-minded believers who can hold one another truly accountable. The last part of Acts 2:46 captures this necessity: "Breaking bread from house to house, they ate their food with gladness and simplicity of heart." Isn't that a wonderful description of what goes on in many home Bible study and fellowship groups today?

The early church had a wonderful balance between corporate worship in the temple court and dinner meetings in individual homes. Every day there were brand-new believers in Jerusalem, coming to the large gathering and funneling into the small one for growth and socialization in God's kingdom. At my own church, we first called our home groups 20:20 groups because of Acts 20:20: "I kept back nothing that was helpful, but proclaimed it to you, and taught you publicly and from house to house." Spiritually speaking, it's a good way to gain 20/20 vision.

Small group ministry is commonplace in churches today, but the very first network was in Jerusalem, and the groups were led by apostles and the growing leadership of the new church. What a wonderful, balanced way for us to mature in Christ together—through "big" church and small group. Wherever this pattern is imitated, we see the same thing happen as what transpired in the birthplace of our faith. Rapid growth occurs.

When we think about all the good things that come out of church fellowship and small group ministry working together, we can't help wondering why or how anyone could ever live without it. Yes, we come together out of obedience to God. But we also do it because nothing else gives us such joy and sustenance.

The Importance of Connectivity

What are some of the good things that happen because we are connected? A single chapter in a book would never be sufficient for naming them all, but we can touch on a few.

One is simply that it's a priceless privilege. Can you imagine how you would feel about freedom of worship if it were ever denied you? Joel Rosenberg tells about a rapidly growing church in Iran. It's made up of converts from Islam, and the pastor broadcasts his weekly worship service and teaching via satellite. People are eager to hear these sermons and lessons because they worry about what would happen if the secret police were to catch them attending a Christian church. They don't dare play Christian music in their homes or sing praise songs aloud because neighbors could turn them in. So they depend completely upon the pastor's broadcasts for their worship and fellowship in the Word.[13]

Consider what happens when we become a part of each other's lives.

We promote love. "And let us consider one another in order to stir up love" (Hebrews 10:24). Here's the phrase again. "One another" is one of Paul's favorite phrases: he uses it thirty-eight times in his epistles, and we find it occurring sixty-eight times from Acts through Revelation. The New Testament is a "one another" book, not something written for the hermit in the wilderness. The writer of Hebrews wants to remind us that coming together keeps us connected by *agape* love.

Simple togetherness is one of the main ingredients of love—so simple we almost miss it. If we neglect to gather together, we drift apart from one another and become disconnected. Being together reminds us of the needs we each have. We share the concerns of our hearts, we laugh and eat together, we worship at the throne of grace side by side, and God knits our hearts in love. Then human love increases our love for that same God who binds us.

Faith, hope, and love grow within us as we come to church and interact together: faith in Christ, hope in the future, and love for each other as our hearts intertwine into a true spiritual family. That's something we all long for in this crisis-driven world. Deep in our souls, we don't want to sit anonymously in the pews. We are unsatisfied by coming, hearing a sermon, and going home. We want to know and be known, not only by God but by His children. We have to put ourselves forward, and we have to risk the bumpy stretches that come with any kind of relationship. But this is a deep need, to stir up the love that God has given us to share.

The phrase *stir up* is translated, "to provoke, to incite." In the Greek, it suggests an "exasperated fit." The choice of words would seem strange in association with love and good works, but it's very intentional. Fellowship should have an energy that provokes everyone toward God's work. We should get stirred up!

The baseball player Reggie Jackson referred to himself as "the straw that stirs the drink."[14] Cocky and outspoken, he had a knack for keeping the adrenaline flowing among his teammates. Hebrews is telling each of us to be the straw that stirs the drink in fellowship together as we stir up love among God's people. I envision a church that is, if you'll pardon the expression, "stir crazy"—a place in which people rise from their beds each week with a relentless purpose and think, *By the grace of God, I will find a way to show love to a new friend today. Lord, please give me a word of encouragement and guide me to just the soul who needs to hear it! My life is filled with blessings, and I'm going to be a blessing to at least one person today.*

A friend told me about an example of that recently. At church, Barbara sat next to Sherry, a younger woman she vaguely knew. Then, at a certain time in the service, Barbara touched Sherry's arm and whispered, "I bought this little angel ornament yesterday. It's just a tiny thing that I thought was pretty—and I felt God leading me to give it to you, Sherry. I've also sensed He has been guiding me to get to know you better." That afternoon, Barbara called the young woman on the phone. She was just a little nervous, being unaccustomed to such assertiveness. But she said, "Please don't think I'm a crazy woman! I really did feel my heart moved to make friends, and I thought I would call you and break the ice."

From there, the two had a wonderful conversation. Barbara's friendly gesture had moved the younger woman to tears. Sherry had been desperately seeking the personal and genuine touch of God. She had wanted to know if He really acted in this world, or if it was all just talk. This unexpected encounter, just as she was wondering, eventually led her to Christ. That's the kind of event that Hebrews is telling us about when it says, "Please! Don't drift out of fellowship. Stir each other up!"

We provoke good works. We are better together. Together we can do more for Christ that we could do by ourselves. Together we can attempt great things for God and expect great things from God. Together we can reach out to the whole world in providing financial and intercessory support for multitudes of missionaries. Together we can link up with radio, television, Internet, and print media . . . literally touching every person on planet Earth.

Being among the people of God should be provocative—not a retreat from the world but an order to advance! The sermon should bring on an "exasperated fit" to go tell people about the Lord. The music should inspire the soul and provoke us to bring our friends to hear it. Hearing what God is doing overseas—or on the other side of town—should stir us up to go and help. The question for believers is this: Is your church fanning your gifts into flame? The question for pastors is this: Are your church's ministries stirring up people for service?

Let's be certain we're clear. We are not saved *by* good works, but we are saved *for* them (Ephesians 2:10). Throughout its history, the church, at its best, has blessed the surrounding world. In the first centuries there was persecution. But as soon as churches became free to gather throughout the empire, Christians began helping the sick. St. Basil built the first hospital in Caesarea of Cappadocia, and soon institutions like that began appearing in many cities.

In his book, *How Christianity Changed the World,* Alvin J. Schmidt tells how Christians had been erecting hospitals for nearly four centuries before Arabs took their example and began building them in their own countries. So the Christian influence led to the healing of the sick not only in Western but in many Middle Eastern countries. Then through the missions movement, believers were helping the sick and needy across the globe. Schmidt concludes, "Christ's parable of the Good Samaritan had become more than merely an interesting story."[15] Our faith was designed by God to be a productive one.

Philip Yancey is one writer whose books I read from cover to cover. In his book *Reaching for The Invisible God,* he tells about a time when a man came up to him after a speaking engagement and said blusteringly, "You wrote a book titled *Where Is God When It Hurts,* didn't you?" When he nodded yes, the man continued, "Well, I don't have time to read your book. Can you tell me what it says in just a sentence or two?"

After some thought, Yancey replied, "Well, I suppose I'd have to answer with another question, "Where is the church when it hurts?"

You see, he explained, the church is God's presence on earth, his body. And if the church does its job—if the church shows up at the scene of disasters, visits the sick, staffs the AIDS clinics, counsels the rape victims, feeds the hungry, houses the homeless—I don't think the world will ask that question you asked with the same urgency. They will know where God is when it hurts: in the bodies of His people, ministering to a fallen world. Indeed, our consciousness of God's presence often comes as a byproduct of other people's presence."[16]

We provide encouragement. "Not forsaking the assembling of ourselves together, as is the manner of some, but exhorting one another" (Hebrews 10:25). Another translation of the word *exhorting* is the word *encouraging.* In other words, we should be constantly encouraging each other as we gather in fellowship. If you're discouraged with life—out of a job, worried about health concerns, or simply stressed out by the modern pace—church activity should encourage you rather than give you even more stress.

Ted Engstrom tells about a literary group that once gathered at the University of Wisconsin. The members wanted to be poets, novelists, essayists, and authors—and they had the talent to be successful. These young men met regularly to read and critique each other's work. After a while, they began calling themselves the Stranglers because they were very tough in their evaluations. Members competed with each other to see who could parse each word and phrase most critically. After a while, it was like having one's precious creativity dissected with a sharp scalpel.

That group was all male, which may explain the competitive spirit. But a group of women formed a sister group and called themselves not the Stranglers but the Wranglers. When they read their works aloud, something much different occurred. They offered constructive suggestions tinged with positive encouragement. They erred on the side of motivation rather than mutilation.

Twenty years later, an alumnus studied the careers of his classmates and made a surprising discovery. Not one of the gifted male Stranglers had made a significant literary accomplishment. But at least six successful authors were former Wranglers. One of them was Marjorie Kinnan Rawlings, author of the classic *The Yearling*.[17]

To encourage is to "pour courage" into someone who needs it. Christians are blessing dispensers and hope ambassadors. Wherever they go, accomplishment and fruitfulness should bloom all around them because of the relationships left in their wake.

When the church goes about its business and becomes a greenhouse for inspiration and evangelism, you cannot stop it from growing or from turning the world upside down. Who wouldn't want to be a part of a place that makes everyone stronger and more confident? In our time, the world has all the Stranglers it needs. It specializes in finding fault, knocking people down a peg. The workplace is making people angry. Marriage and parenting seem harder than ever. We are brewing a culture of despair, and that's fertile soil for the church to step in and provide real encouragement, real relationships, and real love through the authentic power of Jesus Christ. Nothing else can come close to competing with the hope and the peace we can offer.

Living outside the fellowship of the church carries its own penalty. It's like a world with no sky, or one with no music but plenty of noise. Why would anyone want to deprive himself of the good gifts of God? Fellowship in a local church is the most beautiful of all.

Yes, the church—as we experience it—has its faults, but remember: the church as God sees it is perfect and spotless because of the cleansing blood of Christ.

The Power in Your Hands

I've always been fascinated by the life and ministry of Charles Spurgeon, the "Prince of Preachers," whose preaching took England by storm during the 1800s. I recently read a new biography of him and learned a brand new tidbit about his conversion—a subject I thought I knew well.

As a teenager, Spurgeon was a nonbeliever. He was planning to become a farmer when he decided to study Latin and Greek instead. He really didn't know where his career was heading. At the school in Newmarket, his life was impacted by one particular individual. No, it wasn't a professor or instructor; neither was it a classmate or friend. Charles Spurgeon had his life changed by the school's cook, an elderly woman named Mary King. She invited him to attend her church one day, and that led to many conversations with her about her faith, eventually setting him on the path to salvation. Years later, he learned of Mary King's retirement, and supplemented her income from his own pocket.[18]

Here's what that story says to me. If a cook from the kitchen can prepare the path for the greatest preacher of the century, what does that imply God might do through you? We rarely recognize the full extent to which God has used ordinary, available human beings for His greatest purposes. Many millions of people owe Mary King a debt of gratitude because of Spurgeon's contribution to their faith.

If such power was in Mary King's hands, it's in yours as well. It's not difficult to encourage, inspire, and edify another human being. You could do it today, using the telephone, a written card, an e-mail, an automobile, your spoken voice—or a strategic pew. What if you made a covenant with every other believer you know concerning this goal? You and your coconspirators would be determined to give a powerful word of encouragement to at least one soul every time you came to church. And someone just might walk up and encourage you. If you were to do this, God would make a determination of His own. He would begin sending people across your path from every direction—hearts in need of hope, ears in need of edifying words. You can't imagine the joy you would experience simply by being a willing vessel for holy encouragement.

I realize there are times when you need a lift too. Don't forget the very best source of all: God's Word. "For whatever things were written before were written for our learning, that we through the patience and comfort of the Scriptures might have hope" (Romans 15:4). Open the Bible and God will begin speaking to you through it. I have my own set of Scriptures that always lift my spirits. I hope you have yours as well.

The Incentive of Connectivity

The writer of Hebrews tells us that our faithfulness in church attendance should increase as we see our Lord's return on the horizon. We don't know when the day of His return will be, though many signs seem to be coming into alignment. It is a sure thing that each day that passes draws us closer to its eventuality. Each day it doesn't happen, it's that much more likely that tomorrow it will.

If there were no promised Second Coming, the condition of the world itself would be all the incentive we needed to cling to the wonderful fellowship of God's people. But we know that Jesus will return. I want to be found faithful to everything that matters to Him, and nothing matters more than His church.

Even in the midst of national crisis, when worship attendance temporarily surges, the habit of most is to find other things to do; Sunday is the new Saturday. In what is being called a "post-Christian America," church attenders are now in the minority compared to the Sunday golfers, joggers, and late-sleepers who see no particular reason to worship their Creator.

As we see the day approaching, we should be motivated to build the body of Christ into something that justly glorifies God. We should take fewer Sundays off and be more faithful to our church classes and small groups. And when we are in attendance, not only should we be there, but we should be there body, mind, and spirit, devoting all of ourselves to the work of Christ through the church, giving generously of our resources as the first Christians did. When your pastor announces a need, whether it's workers for the nursery, people to cut the church lawn, or funding for missions, he should be overwhelmed by volunteers. And when the new members are introduced, he should have to read so many names that he becomes hoarse.

The church is not a building. No, it is not even the people. It is actually the living presence of a holy God in a fallen world. It is the tangible evidence of an invisible hope, dressed in the skin of all the people who have found that hope. And when society comes unglued, as we've seen it do lately, the church becomes God's lighthouse, shining the way for our ships to avoid the rocks, survive the tempest, and come into safe harbor. If there was ever a day when we needed the church, this is it. If there was ever a greater opportunity to invite our faithless friends, we have it now.

There's a legend about a church in southern Europe called the "House of Many Lamps." It was built in the sixteenth century and had no provision for artificial light except for a receptacle at every seat for the placement of a lamp. In the evenings, as the people came to church, they would carry their own light with them. When they entered the church building, they would place their lamp in the receptacle as they began to worship. If someone stayed away, his place remained dark. If more than a few stayed away, the darkness seemed to spread. It took the regular presence of every member to illuminate that sanctuary.[19]

When you forsake assembling—when that little light of yours is not allowed to shine—you leave a spot of darkness. If enough people heed your example and take Sundays off, a great darkness begins to fall across the house of many lamps. It's discouraging to walk into a half-empty house of God, and there are a great many today that have more empty seats than full ones. In Europe, the darkness has nearly engulfed a continent that once dominated Christendom—a continent that gave us Luther, Calvin, Wycliffe, Wesley, Spurgeon, and so many others. The absence of your light also produces a sense of cold emptiness.

On a cold and blustery winter evening, a husband and wife made themselves as comfortable as they could before the crackling fireplace as they awaited the arrival of their pastor. He had made the appointment earlier in the day. The husband steeled himself against the anticipated rebuke. They had previously been in the habit of attending every service, every week. But over the past year, they rarely made it once a month. "We're just as good as some people who go to church twice every Sunday, and I am going to make it clear to our pastor too!" the husband blustered.

The doorbell rang, and the pastor entered. Remaining in his overcoat, he silently walked directly to the fireplace, took up the tongs, lifted a brightly glowing coal from out of the fire, placed it on the hearth, and, still silent, stepped back to watch.

The husband eventually joined him in an oddly silent observation. After a very long time, the once red-hot glow turned into a cold, dark mass. Finally, the pastor wordlessly turned to the man and gave him a look that spoke volumes. The man got the message. Like that coal, we burn brightly when we are together, but we burn out when we stand alone.[20]

As for me, here I stand—squarely on the side of God's church. As a young man, I gave my heart to Christ and my hands to the church. I have had wonderful days there, as well as a few painful ones. If Christ comes tomorrow (a wonderful thought), I want Him to find me faithfully serving in the fellowship of the saints, the gathering of the holy priesthood.

SIX

Stay Centered

LAURA LING AND EUNA LEE KNEW THEY WERE TAKING A GREAT risk when they went to the border region between China and North Korea earlier this year to film an investigative report on human trafficking. Ling had previously produced a television documentary on the underground church in China and was working in conjunction with a Christian agency from South Korea. The women were captured, tried, and convicted of a "grave crime" against the regime of Kim Jong Il.[1]

On the same day that the journalists were sentenced to twelve years at hard labor, the government threatened the world with a "merciless offensive means to deal a just retaliatory strike to those who touch the country's dignity and sovereignty even a bit."[2] This rhetoric is couched in the context of UN Security Council discussions about stronger new sanctions against North Korea for their recent nuclear test and barrage of rocket tests.

Two days before the women were sentenced, the Voice of the Martyrs organization received a threat via fax from North Korea.

"Something very bad will happen to you," the communiqué read, if the ministry continued its weekly outreach into the Communist nation with faxed messages of Christ's love.[3]

To be a follower of Christ in North Korea is considered equal to being a traitor to the government, where only worship of the ailing President Kim Jong Il and his late father is permitted. North Korea has the dubious distinction of holding the number one spot on Open Doors World Watch List not just for 2009 but for the seventh straight year. The list contains the names of the fifty countries of the world where Christians are most severely persecuted for their faith in Christ.[4]

Despite the extreme poverty and intense persecution of Christians in North Korea, it has been estimated that there are as many as four hundred thousand Christians who risk their lives to gather in secret worship services![5] As many as 10 percent of those believers are currently incarcerated in North Korea's notoriously atrocious political prison camps.[6]

North Korea is a hostile environment in which to be a follower of Jesus Christ, but so are forty-nine other countries. Even right here in America Christians are reporting greater persecution. When we hear such things, many of us are caught off guard. But if we believe the Word of God, we know that persecution has always been part of the believers calling (2 Timothy 3:12).

Most of us will never experience the persecution that Laura Ling and Euna Lee are facing. But neither can we escape the new hostility and intolerance that is being directed toward followers of Christ in our post-Christian nation. As never before, we must build our lives around the core values of our faith. We must stay centered on Christ, or we will become discouraged and defeated warriors.

When the apostle Paul wrote to a group of Christians who were living in a time similar to ours, he helped them to find their spiritual center: "If then you were raised with Christ, seek those things which are above, where Christ is, sitting at the right hand of God. Set your mind on things above, not on things on the earth. For you died, and your life is hidden with Christ in God. When Christ who is our life appears, then you also will appear with Him in glory" (Colossians 3:1–4).

In Paul's last statement, in verse four, there is a reference to the return of Christ, so we know that we're on the right track. Practical instructions follow prophetic insights. What Paul wrote to the Colossian believers, he wrote for us.

Set Your Hearts on Christ

Think back to a time when you set your heart on something. Can you remember how that idea loomed before you, galvanizing your spirit every single day?

I need only talk to people for a few minutes before their "heart-set" comes tumbling out. They want to find their life's partner and marry. They long to start families, or they have compelling visions to build their own businesses. They dream of becoming famous musicians or faithful missionaries.

When we set our heart on something, it motivates us, changes us, and energizes us: it makes our eyes shine, puts a spring in our step, and focuses all our divided attentions into a single, laser-intense direction.

Kevin Everett lay facedown on the Buffalo Bills' home turf, trying desperately to get up. The crowd silenced as the Bills and Broncos gathered in prayer. Kevin realized that he was paralyzed from his fierce tackle in the season opener. He tried to give a thumbs-up as he was finally lifted off the field. "I tried my hardest, you know, put all my heart into it. Just to let them know that I was all right. But it wasn't all right."

Early reports indicated it was a potentially life-threatening injury, and should he live, the chances of his walking were almost nonexistent. Through a series of miracles, some of which were medical, and a lot of intense work on his part, Everett not only lived but also walked unaided onto that same playing field one year later. His heart had become set on doing whatever it took to make a recovery. One reporter asked Everett if he had ever thought about giving up. "That's not me," he responded. "I don't give up. I don't settle for less. I kept plugging away, working hard."

Although he will never play the game again, he has a new heart-set. Gratitude to the Lord has become his transforming strength and has given him a new focus in life. "You put your faith in God and let him show you the way."[7]

I'm sure you've been through trying times, perhaps the loss of a job or a loved one. While surrounded by sorrow, you might have found that it helped to fix your mind on one thing, something positive and productive. For instance, work can be a true blessing. We call it "staying busy." But Paul counsels us to set our hearts on Christ in such a way that every facet of this life is transformed by its relationship to Him.

We know we are destined for heaven. We realize we are citizens of another world. Therefore we are to set our hearts on the things of God, which are perfect and beautiful, rather than the things of this world, which are in disarray even at the best of times. When Paul wrote this statement, he used a verb tense that means "keep on doing this," as opposed to a one-time action. In other words, it's not "think about heaven at this moment." It's "*Keep on* keeping your mind immersed in God and His Word, all the time." This is a discipline too few of us have mastered: the art of heaven-based thinking. Some call it the practice of the presence of God.

We need to understand what it means to "set our hearts." According to Paul it means that our "desires and thoughts, wishing and thinking, the whole of our emotional and intellectual energy is to be directed toward [heaven], where Christ reigns at God's right side."[8] I imagine every one of us has centered our desires and thoughts, all our emotional and intellectual energy, on various earthly goals in the seasons of life. Can we think and feel with the same intensity about Christ?

In times such as these we have to look somewhere for answers. The psychologist tells us we should look within. The opportunist tells us we should look around. The optimist says we should look ahead, and the pessimist says we should look out. But God says we should look up—even when we feel down.[9]

Think for a moment about a compass that you might carry on a hike. You can turn your feet in any direction, but the arrow of the compass will faithfully point to magnetic north. That way, should you ever become lost, the compass will align your position for you. In life, our true north is Christ. Whatever direction our world's path may twist, however off-path it may wander, our lives should point faithfully to the one and only Lord of every place, every time, every situation. When He is our determining point, everything will find its proper orientation.

"Our citizenship is in heaven, from which we also eagerly wait for the Savior, the Lord Jesus Christ" (Philippians 3:20). The wise old preacher Vance Havner put it this way:

"Christians are not citizens of earth trying to get to heaven, but citizens of heaven making their way through this world."[10]

If we reach deep into Christian history, back to about AD 149, we find a letter called "The Epistle of Mathetes of Diognetus." The unknown writer described Christians this way:

> They dwell in their own countries, but simply as sojourners. As citizens, they share in all things with others, and yet endure all things as if foreigners . . . They pass their days on earth, but they are citizens of heaven. They obey the prescribed laws, and at the same time surpass the laws by their lives. They love all men and are persecuted by all. They are unknown and condemned; they are put to death, and restored to life. They are poor, yet make many rich; they are in lack in all things, and yet abound in all; they are dishonored, and yet in their very dishonor are glorified.[11]

Or consider the oath of allegiance that is required of newly nationalized US citizens, in which they "declare on oath" that they "freely and without any mental reservation" relinquish ties of loyalty to their former homelands and that they will defend the United States against all enemies.[12]

As Americans, we expect new citizens to be loyal and trustworthy, never betraying their new home. How much more important is our role as citizens of heaven. This is the most basic statement of our true identity, and it's more critical than any other fact about us.

Set Your Minds on Christ

We've discussed matters of the heart; now let's talk about the mind. Having our hearts set on Christ means that our wills, our emotions, our hopes and dreams are centered on Him.

The phrase *set your mind* means "to have understanding; to be wise; to feel, to think, to have an opinion, to judge; to direct one's mind to a thing; to seek or to strive for, to seek one's interests or advantage." In other words, it is the mental discipline of directed thinking.

That's the positive command, but it is accompanied by a warning against the negative: "Seek those things which are above . . . not those things which are on the earth" (Colossians 3:1–2). Immediately we find ourselves questioning that way of life. Paul isn't telling us to forego the physical challenges and chores of everyday life, while sitting and ruminating on heaven and angels. He *is* saying that our ultimate concern should be with heavenly realities and values, governed by the presence and power of Christ, who sits at the right hand of the Father.[13] Therefore the physical impulse may be to roll over in bed on that Saturday morning and catch an extra hour of sleep, but the Holy Spirit may be whispering in your ear that He wants you to go and minister to someone's needs. The Christian trains his mind to see those two alternatives, and to give precedence to the things of God.

Sometimes, God wants you to take care of earthly business. We do live in this physical world, and we should do everything, including everyday responsibilities, as unto the Lord. In the ancient world, it was the Gnostics who wanted to twist Christianity into bearing contempt for this physical realm. But that's not the teaching of Scripture. Christ is Lord of body, mind, and spirit.

In his letter to his friends in Corinth, Paul gives us a heavenly perspective on earthly things: "Because of the present crisis . . . the time is short. From now on, those who . . . buy something [should live] as if it were not theirs to keep; those who use the things of this world, as if not engrossed in them. For the world in its present form is passing away" (1 Corinthians 7:26 31 NIV).

So is it okay to buy a car, to invest in a home? Of course. But we don't set our hearts and minds on perishable things because they will pass away. The eternal things have our allegiance. Allow me to share with you an analogy that helps me think of what it means to have an earthly life with a heavenly mind.

Travel is a necessary portion of my ministry, and that means I must often move between time zones. If I fly across the United States, that three-hour time change can really make a difference in such matters as eating and sleeping. In the airports I'll see people stepping from the jetway as they reset their watches to the local time. Me, I'm too stubborn. My watch shows Pacific Time, all the time. I glance at my wrist and do the math, based on how many times zones I'm separated from the home I love. I also think about what's happening back home according to the time. If it's Sunday, I'll visualize people getting ready for worship in our sanctuary, and a little pang of regret will pass through me because I'm absent. It may be nighttime where I am, but in San Diego, "God's Country" to me, the skies are sunny and the aisles are filled with people chatting, finding their seats, and preparing to worship God.

For some reason, the consistency of the watch connects me to home. I don't mind adding or subtracting the necessary hours, and calculating my local time in relation to Pacific Time. I believe Paul is making a similar point here in this passage. Keep your mental clock set on heavenly time. Look to Christ first, and then do the math to know how to function in this world. You have to live in this world for a time, just as I have to leave California from time to time. Learn to say with the psalmist, "Whom have I in heaven but You? And there is none upon the earth that I desire besides You" (Psalm 73:25).

The discipline of centering our hearts and minds on Christ will require us to focus. Here, from Paul's written words to the Colossians, are four truths that will help us to stay centered on Christ:

Focus on His Connection to You

Colossians 3:1–4 reads, "If then you were raised *with* Christ . . . your life is hidden *with* Christ . . . you also will appear *with* Him in glory" (emphasis added).

I've highlighted the word *with* to show just how critical it is in this frame of thinking. *With* is a word of connection, our lifeline to Christ. When He died, we died with him. When He was buried, so were we. And we shared in His glorious resurrection, so that now we can be seated in the heavenlies with Him.

When the Bible says that Jesus died for us, it doesn't mean simply that He died in our behalf; it means He died in our place. He died where we should have died. Just as Adam was the personal embodiment of our fall into sin, Christ is the personal embodiment of our salvation and glory. "For as in Adam all die, even so in Christ all shall be made alive" (1 Corinthians 15:22). We fell with Adam, but we were resurrected with Christ.

Do you see the importance of that little word *with* in our spiritual destiny? The great Chinese Christian preacher and writer, Watchman Nee, grasped it. In 1927, he had been struggling with issues of temptation and his sinful nature. One morning he was sitting upstairs reading the book of Romans, and he came to the words, "Knowing this, that our old man was crucified with Him . . ." (6:6). For Nee, it was as if the words had come to life on the page. He leapt from his chair, ran downstairs, and grabbed a kitchen worker by the hands. "Brother," he shouted. "Do you know that I have died?"

The worker only stared in puzzlement. Nee blurted out, "Do you not know that Christ has died? Do you not know that I died with Him? Do you not know that my death is no less truly a fact than His?"

It was all Watchman Nee could do to keep himself from running through the streets of Shanghai, shouting about his death and new life. From that day on, his faith was confident and strong. His biographer wrote that it was impossible to say anything that might offend Nee. Why should he be offended? That Watchman Nee was long since dead![14]

Charles Spurgeon had his own way of explaining this amazing phenomenon of dying with Christ:

> I suppose that, if you were to meet your old self, he would hardly know you, for you are so greatly altered. I dare say he would say to you, "Come, old fellow, let us go to the theater, or turn into this beer-shop, or let us go home, and find out some way of amusing ourselves."
>
> You would reply, "No, sir; I cut your acquaintance a long time ago, and I do not mean to have anything further to do with you, so you may go about your business as soon as you like. I am not what I was, for I have been crucified with Christ, and I am dead, and my life is hid with Christ in God."[15]

One day Martin Luther was answering a knock at his door. "Does Dr. Martin Luther live here?" asked the visitor. "No," Luther answered, "he died. Christ lives here now."[16] Can we understand that this truth is just that radical? The old you is dead and in the grave; the new you is raised to walk in newness of life, and to live victoriously for Christ. Why not take a few moments today and mull this truth over in your mind!

Focus on His Control over Everything that Concerns You

What image comes to your mind when you think of Jesus? Do you think of the uninspiring media stereotype of "gentle Jesus," a rather weak teacher? Or do you imagine the risen and ascended Lord, the glorious one in whose name "every knee should bow, of those in heaven, and of those on earth, and of those under the earth, and that every tongue should confess that Jesus Christ is Lord, to the glory of God the Father" (Philippians 2:10–11)?

Mental images make a difference. The reality is that Jesus is risen, that He sits at the right hand of the Father, and that when we see Him again, He will be revealed in all His magnificence. When we focus our attentions on *that* Lord, on His power and authority, our faith surges. I love the way Eugene Peterson captures it in his creative paraphrase of Ephesians 1:20–23:

> All this energy issues from Christ: God raised him from death and set him on a throne in deep heaven, in charge of running the universe, everything from galaxies to governments, no name and no power exempt from his rule. And not just for the time being, but forever. He is in charge of it all, has the final word on everything. At the center of all this, Christ rules the church. The church, you see, is not peripheral to the world; the world is peripheral to the church. The church is Christ's body, in which he speaks and acts, by which he fills everything with his presence (MSG).

Let those words soak through your mind for a few minutes. Afterward, I challenge you—no, I *dare* you—to feel the same anxiety over the state of current affairs. Our Lord sits enthroned at the center of this universe, ruling all things. Do you think He can handle a stock market in turmoil? He defeated death itself. Do you feel confident He could defeat a tough housing market? All nations, all creatures will bow before Him. Under His protection, do we have anything to fear?

Even when the world seems to spin out of control, be calm: this is only how it seems. In reality, Almighty God is still on His throne, and in the words of that old spiritual, "He's got the whole world in His hands."

Focus on His Care for You

Colossians 3:3 reads, "For you died, and your life is hidden with Christ in God."

Hidden. Just as your hand might gently enfold a rose petal, God's hand gently enfolds you—again, *with* Christ. The phrase is "*with* Christ, *in* God." I certainly can't think of a more secure place to be.

I don't feel secure about my own abilities. I have no ultimate faith in our economy, our military prowess, or anything else in this poor, fallen world. But in Christ, I do feel utterly safe and secure. He is my rock, my shelter in a time of storm.

Note that we are not commanded to hide ourselves in God. Your life "is hidden." In other words—done! This is an accomplished fact, a here-and-now thing, not something for which to anxiously hope. If you are a Christ-follower, then you are with Christ, in God, and you are ultimately free and safe. Next time you feel worried, go somewhere alone and simply reflect on that.

The Bible is actually filled with imagery and language about this security. We imagine ourselves with Shadrach, Meshach, and Abednego, thrown into a roaring furnace yet receiving not even a deep tan. A fourth man is beside them—that would be Christ (Daniel 3:25). We ride the whirlwind with Elijah, and ordinarily it might be frightening. But Elijah finds peace there, and so do we. With the mighty arms of the tempests buffeting him, whirling and thundering all about him, he smiles, as comfortable as if he were home in bed (1 Kings 19:10–12). Instead of sitting around worrying about the stock market, housing, or unemployment, is there any reason, after all these thousands of years, for God to no longer protect us? Our security is not found in the things of the earth, but in our position with Christ, in God—where we are *hidden*.

Focus on His Commitment to You

Colossians 3:4 reads, "When Christ who is our life appears, then you also will appear with Him in glory."

Part of being with Christ is becoming more like Him. Today, we are being transformed to something just a bit closer to His image every day, but when He returns in glory, the change will be sudden and dramatic. He will come in His glorious resurrection body, and we will then have perfect resurrection bodies too.

Paul reiterates this point that Christ will "transform our lowly body that it may be conformed to His glorious body" (Philippians 3:21). Does that sound good to you?

As we grow older, we have a deepening appreciation for bodily wellness. I don't know about you, but my "tent" is growing a bit more tattered all the time. One day I get to trade it in on a new and deluxe model. This is Christ's commitment to me, and to you as well. Place your faith in Him, and you will be fully and wonderfully renewed—spirit, mind, and even body—upon His return.

In John Ortberg's book, *Faith and Doubt*, he reminds us that to stay centered in Christ, we will need to learn the difference between hoping *for* something and hoping *in* Someone. Hoping for something, he writes, means wanting a particular outcome—a job, a house, a cure. But all these earthly hopes ultimately disappoint us. They wear out, fall apart, melt away, or perhaps they never materialize. All of us learn to live with the inevitability of dashed hopes.

At those sobering moments, the question becomes, "Is there some deeper hope?" Is there anything, anyone in this life that will never once disappoint us? The Bible, Ortberg writes, points to one Man, one hope, one God who is worth trusting, not because of any particular thing He can give us. We trust Him because of who He is. He is the one *in whom* and *by whom* we can hope. "Hope," he concludes, "is faith waiting for tomorrow."[17]

Three Ways to Stay Centered in Christ

Hopefully, I have convinced you of the importance of staying centered in Christ. If so, then your question may be, *Just how do I go from being earth-centered to being heaven-centered?* Here are three suggestions to help you in your quest for Christ-centeredness.

Seek God's Will. "But seek first the kingdom of God and His righteousness, and all these things shall be added to you" (Matthew 6:33).

What is it about this verse? People insist on reading it backwards, as though from some spiritual strain of dyslexia: "Add all these things unto you, then seek the kingdom of God and His righteousness in whatever time is left." Blessed are those who read it as written, as intended, as the truth happens to be. One missionary rephrased it well: "Take care of the things that are important to God, and He will take care of the things that are important to you."

As a college student Richard Greene learned this lesson. He was fretting over bills and he grew agitated and afraid. "Where will the extra money come from?" he asked aloud. "Please, Lord, help me pay these bills."

A short while later he received an unexpected scholarship. Then a friend handed him a check for the month's rent. All these things were added unto him. God cared for Greene's educational needs, and he went on to serve the Lord at Trans World Radio, beaming the message of Scripture around the world.[18]

Search God's Word. Jesus was a guest in the home of Mary and Martha one day, as Luke's gospel tells us. He found Himself caught in the crossfire of warring priorities. Martha was playing hostess and housekeeper, while Mary sat at Jesus feet and listened intently to His teaching. It didn't seem fair to Martha, and she told Jesus so—Mary, she said, should do her part. As always, Jesus gave the least expected response: "Martha, Martha, you are worried and troubled about many things, but one thing is needed, and Mary has chosen that good part, which will not be taken away from her" (Luke 10:38–42).

We face this choice every single day. Staying centered on Christ requires us to stay focused on God's Word. Geoffrey Thomas has written, "The love of Christ is the strongest constraint to knowing the Scriptures, and if we have little desire for the Bible, we should ask if we indeed know the Savior." In other words, our relationship with the Bible mirrors our relationship with Christ.[19]

At the age of fourteen Jerry Bridges was the lone witness to his mother's very sudden and frightening death. His dad became lost in his own sorrow and neglected to minister to his son. Years later, Bridges was an ROTC engineering student at the University of Oklahoma. One night while studying, he happened to reach toward the shelf for a textbook. His eye caught a Bible his parents had given him when he was a boy. A thought flashed through his mind that now that he was really a Christian, he ought to read the Bible. And he followed up on that impulse over many years.

As it turned out, hearing deficiencies kept Bridges from the naval career he had wanted. He settled in California and worked as a writer of technical manuals for an airplane manufacturer. Though his career wasn't following the intended script, Bridges turned even more attention to what his Bible said about life in this world. He found a passion for the Scripture that led him to fifty years not with the Navy but the Navigators, the international ministry dedicated to Bible study and memorization.[20]

Along the way, Bridges found himself writing booklets, which led to major Christian books that have fed millions of hungry souls. All his literary endeavors sprang from his own intimate walk with God and his daily navigation of the Word—his lifeline when he was seeking to cope with his deflated career dreams. His book for troubled times, *Trusting God,* has this to say: "The moral will of God given to us in the Bible is rational and reasonable. The circumstances in which we must trust God often appear irrational and inexplicable . . . It is only from the Scriptures, applied to our hearts by the Holy Spirit, that we receive grace to trust God in adversity . . . The faith to trust God in adversity comes through the Word of God alone."[21]

This is what it means to set our minds on God through His Word. As Bridges affirms, the Scriptures often turn worldly logic on its head. People may think we are unreasonable. The truth is that only those with their minds set on God know what reason really is; only God's course is the course that will ultimately prevail.

Support God's Work. Our final secret to staying centered in Christ is so simple, so powerful, and so often forgotten. Simply go where His action is—and if you can't go there, find other ways to get involved.

In the Sermon on the Mount, again through the rewording of Eugene Peterson, Jesus tells us, "Don't hoard treasure down here where it gets eaten by moths and corroded by rust or—worse!—stolen by burglars. Stockpile treasure in heaven, where it's safe from moth and rust and burglars. It's obvious, isn't it? The place where your treasure is, is the place you will most want to be, and end up being" (Matthew 6:19–21 MSG). We might call that an investment manifesto for children of the kingdom. Pour yourself into eternal things, things that affect the invisible world; things that change the population of heaven.

Jesus says that our hearts naturally follow our treasures. What we value most is a magnet for our thoughts and emotions. Therefore we must learn to value God's things the most. The more we give ourselves to His purposes, the more centered on Christ we will become. Here's a quick way to test that: Talk to someone who has just returned from short-term mission work. Maybe you've had that experience yourself. How did you feel upon returning? What was your experience of giving a few days or weeks completely to the advancement of the gospel? Most of us feel like entirely different people. As the old song reminds us, "the things of earth will grow strangely dim, in the light of His glory and grace"[22]—and in the sanctified sweat of His service.

Our earthly treasures begin to look shabby indeed when we place them next to the treasures of God's kingdom. And all we need to do to prove that is to support the work of God. In his book *The Treasure Principle,* Randy Alcorn writes, "By telling us that our hearts follow our treasure, Jesus is saying, 'Show me your checkbook, your VISA statement, and your receipts, and I'll show you where your heart is.'"[23]

Alcorn offers the illustration of buying a stock for investment purposes. (His principle is especially valid given the current market volatility.) When we buy a particular stock, we have a vested interest in that firm. Its forecasts, its dividends, and its earning statements can directly affect our personal financial fortunes. They can rise or fall, depending on how that company performs in the marketplace. So we watch the financial pages and read our Google alerts for any hint of change. When we see articles about "our company" or even any industry related development, we read every word. A month earlier we would not have given that same news a passing glance.

This is simply the logical behavior of the wise investor, and when we invest ourselves in God's kingdom, our minds and hearts follow in that same way. If we begin sending money to help African children with AIDS, Alcorn continues, we begin to read more on that subject than we used to. If we're supporting a new church in India and we hear of an earthquake, we are glued to the news, praying all the while. The compass point always goes north, and our hearts go where our money leads.[24]

It may be simple, but it's also a matter of obedience. Are you willing to reallocate your resources to help center your heart and mind on Christ? It will work every time. The more you give to His purposes, the more centered on Him you become.

There are many other means of staying centered on Christ in chaotic times. But if we start with seeking Him first and searching for Him in the Scriptures, if we remember that our heart follows our treasure and we invest that treasure in things above, we will be well on our way toward staying centered in Christ.

When tough times come, as they've done lately, it serves us well to look to the examples of those who have suffered much more deeply. We often have a great deal to learn from them. A perfect example is Viktor Frankl, who survived a Nazi concentration camp. Cruelty, torture, hard labor, starvation, and an environment of death were his daily life for several years. He was married for only nine months when he and his young wife were separated. She was deported to Bergen-Belsen, and he was sent to Auschwitz.

In his book *Man's Search for Meaning*, Frankl describes an early morning prison march with a regiment of hungry, listless men, stumbling through the darkness, tripping on stones, and splashing through the mud as the guards shouted viciously and clubbed them with rifle butts. No one added a word to the icy wind. But finally the man next to Frankl muttered through the cover of his coat collar, "If our wives could only see us now! I hope they are better off in their camps and don't know what is happening to us."

When he said that, Frankl's thoughts immediately turned to his own young wife. He thought about her face, examining every feature in the sanctuary of his memories where even the Nazis could not invade. He thought of her encouraging smile and serious mind. The sun was beginning to rise, but the thought inside him was brighter, and it somehow strengthened his legs and insulated his body.

Over the coming months, stronger men gave up hope and died all around him. Why did Frankl trudge onward through the miserable landscape of his days? He credited this to the power of the human concentration. He simply kept his mind fixed on the powerful image of his wife, and he derived strength and comfort there, purpose and meaning for a life starving for it. "I understood how a man who has nothing left in this world may still know bliss," he wrote. "Be it only for a brief moment in the contemplation of his beloved."

Love, he discovered, is the most profound of all motivators. He could finally comprehend the words of an old proverb: "The angels are lost in perpetual contemplation of an infinite glory."[25] Those angels know, better than we, where the real joy is to be found. That abundant source is a well with no bottom, and when we are weak and thirsting from the trials of this life, we would be well advised to find that well and drink deeply.

Several years ago, my wife and I were invited to Oxford, England, to attend the expository preaching conference sponsored by *Preaching Magazine*. The meeting was held at St. Andrew's Church, and I was invited to give one of the sermons from the historic pulpit where Dr. G. Campbell Morgan had once taught the Word of God. When I returned to the United States after the conference, I was the surprised recipient of several books about G. Campbell Morgan, including the book *In The Shadow Of Grace: The Life and Meditations of G. Campbell Morgan*.

I discovered in the reading of this book that G. Campbell Morgan had ministered the Word of God during a period that included the sinking of the *Titanic*, the First World War, and the Second World War. All these events personally impacted the lives of members of his congregation.

In The Shadow of Grace presents portions of the sermons that Morgan preached during times of tragedy and war. According to his own words, Morgan was a pacifist. Yet with the advance of the German armies toward England, he found it necessary to speak in favor of the war and the protection of his nation.

On March 3, 1916, G. Campbell Morgan preached a sermon he

called "The Fixed Heart in the Day of Frightfulness." In his own words, he simply encouraged his listeners to stay centered on Christ.

Men who are strong are always men who are fixed somewhere, who have a conviction from which they cannot be separated by argument, which cannot be changed, whatever the circumstances in which they live. Sometimes these men are very narrow, but they are wonderfully strong; they are singularly obstinate, but they are splendidly dependable. Consequently, we always know where to find these men. The fixed heart is the secret of courage. Courage is an affair of the heart; courage is the consciousness of the heart that is fixed . . . What, then, shall we do in the day of frightfulness? We shall do our duty; the thing that is nearest; the thing we have to do tomorrow morning. We will do that, and do it well; and do it cheerfully . . . What this nation needs, now just as much, and perhaps more, than anything else, is the multiplication of strong, quiet souls who are not afraid of evil tidings, even though the zeppelins may be coming, and will not add to the panic that demoralizes, but will do their work.[26]

That's called being centered. No level of persecution, no newspaper headline, no stock collapse, no housing bubble can taint the tiniest drop of that peace, joy, and love. Give Christ your mind and your heart. Invest yourself in the things that matter to Him. You'll find there a whole new world, one ruled perfectly and lovingly by our Lord—and pretty soon, you'll understand that the events of this earthly life are just as firmly in His wonderful hands.

SEVEN

Stay Confident

BILL MAHER IS BEST KNOWN AS THE HOST OF TWO NIGHTTIME television talk shows. The name of the second show—*Politically Incorrect*—pretty well sums up Maher's tone, personality, and subject matter. As a stand-up comedian, he is known for his acid-tongued commentaries on everything traditional—especially faith.

But in 2008 Maher added to his comedic résumé by writing and starring in a documentary film called *Religulous* that opened in theaters on October 3. His goal was to attack organized religion, especially Christianity and its belief in the Bible. Being an equal-opportunity agnostic, Maher also tried to split open the foundations of Judaism and Islam as well.

And because each of the three major religions is based on the teachings of a holy book—Islam, the Koran; Judaism, the Old Testament; Christianity, the Old and New Testaments—these books became the targets of Maher's focused scorn. In an interview on *The CBS Early Show* with host Harry Smith, Maher said, "My motivation [with *Religulous*] is to make people laugh. I mean, religion, to me, is a giant elephant in the room of comic gold because, you know, we're talking about a garden with a talking snake. If you can't find humor there—people are just used to [these stories]. That's why they don't laugh at [them]."[1]

Some people are surprised when they hear Maher say he's not an atheist—but less surprised when they read his answer to the question, "Is there a God?" Since he rejects the divine origin of the Bible, he rejects what it says:

> I believe there's some force. If you want to call it God—I don't believe God is a single parent who writes books. I think that the people who think God wrote a book called The Bible are just childish. Religion is so childish. What they're fighting about in the Middle East, it's so childish. These myths, these silly little stories that they believe in fundamentally, that they take over this little space in Jerusalem where one guy flew up to heaven—no, no, this guy performed a sacrifice here a thousand million years ago. It's like, Who cares? What does that have to do with spirituality, where you're really trying to get, as a human being and as a soul moving in the universe? But I do believe in a God, yes.[2]

Bill Maher is not the first skeptic in history to doubt the veracity of the Bible, and he won't be the last. But he is certainly emblematic of something the apostle Peter wrote nearly two thousand years ago: "Scoffers will come in the last days, walking according to their own lusts" (2 Peter 3:3). Having been raised in the church as a young person, Maher also fits the description of some the apostle Paul predicted would come: "Now the Spirit expressly says that in latter times some will depart from the faith, giving heed to deceiving spirits and doctrines of demons" (1 Timothy 4:1).

My prediction, though not divinely inspired, is that we haven't seen anything yet. There will be more arrogant skeptics to join Maher's critical and comedic chorus against the Bible and the faith. The warning for true Christians is not, "The skeptics are coming!" but that they have such a well-publicized, public platform. Their voices enter the ears of believers through the media. Christians, therefore, must be prepared to "always be ready to give a defense to everyone who asks you a reason for the hope that is in you, with meekness and fear" (1 Peter 3:15).

One man who has learned to do just that—defend his faith with meekness and fear—started down a road not unlike Bill Maher: the road of scathing skepticism of the Bible's authority. Piyush Jindal, better known as Bobby Jindal, is the governor of Louisiana. He's the first Indian-American elected to statewide office in US history. Governor Jindal's story has captured national imagination over recent months for a variety of reasons. Helping to rebuild a state devastated by storm and flood, he understands the idea of public crisis.

Jindal, born and raised a Hindu, converted to Christianity after a careful reading of the Bible. It began a spiritual journey to Christ he describes as "gradual and painful." Young Jindal first picked up the Word with ulterior motives: He wanted to disprove a faith—one he both "admired and despised." This is a familiar old story in Christianity: the skeptic who is converted by following an investigative trail, undermining his own skepticism in the end. Our Bible does a powerful job of defending itself when confronted.

Jindal was expecting to find a pack of myths inside those covers. But something happened as he opened his New Testament. Its pages worked like a mirror. "I saw myself in many of the parables," he says. Jesus seemed to be speaking across the centuries, telling stories written just for him.

His curiosity now in overdrive, Bobby Jindal began to seek out works about the historical accuracy of the Bible. To his own surprise, he found himself convinced that here were sacred words that had traveled with integrity through two thousand years—firsthand accounts of the ultimate miracle, God in human form. It was intellectually impossible to deny that Jesus Christ had risen from the dead, then ascended to heaven.

"However," he says, "my perspective remained intellectual and not spiritual." Jindal was shaken by what he found, but he was unwilling to give in to what his mind told him was the real thing. After many hours of counseling with a patient pastor, he finally embraced his new Lord and Savior.[3]

Bobby Jindal is an emblem of his era. Last year the *New York Times* reported on a change in the interests of college students. After decades of obsession with the more "practical" curriculum, many young scholars are gravitating toward courses in philosophy. They're feeling a deep need to make sense of the world, and they're finding that contemporary thinkers and leaders give them no ultimate answers. Therefore, they are digging into the wisdom of writers from distant centuries.[4]

We Christians believe there is only one of those ancient texts that is eternally relevant. The pressing questions of our past, present, and future are all answered by this Book because the Scriptures, like Christ, are eternal—authoritative yesterday, today, and forever. They explain life, but they also give us strength and comfort for the rigors of life's journey. Perhaps greater than anything we have discussed so far, the Bible is the key to living with confidence in a chaotic world.

If the history of human experience teaches us anything, it is this, the Bible is no ordinary book. Composed of sixty-six shorter books, written by some forty different authors over many centuries, it is a kind of multicentury anthology with no earthly reason to be so perfectly unified. It is incredible that it should speak with one authoritative voice, or that all its various sections, chapters, and verses should hold such power over human lives after several millennia. There is no explanation for any of this unless it is the eternal Word of God. I am convinced that this miraculous Book provides an accurate account of history and the *only* account of the future. We need the life-changing message of the Bible right now.

Beth Moore writes that we should desire a steady diet of Scripture because of what it says about itself: it is "living and active" (Hebrews 4:12 NIV). This is no dusty, ancient document with a lingering passage or two of vague interest. The Greek word for *living* suggests that the Word is teeming with life. Moore concludes that if we believe this, and if we accept that it is "God-breathed" (2 Timothy 3:16 NIV), "we might say that every breath comes to us still warm from the mouth of God. As if He just said it."[5] I wish I had written that!

When you open this Book, you are not just opening a book. When you read the Word, you are doing more than reading words. You are not simply taking in information; you are taking in *life*, warm from the breath of God. Nor are you studying the works of dead writers—rather you are hearing the voice of the living Lord. And when this world is in crisis, and up seems down, and right has gone wrong, this Book holds the answers you need. You and I should inhabit its pages more fully than we reside in our physical houses. We should consume its truth as surely as we eat the food upon our tables. When there's no other visible source of confidence, we can stay confident in the Word of God.

A Cure for Itching Ears

Timothy was a young man with an uphill struggle before him. His mentor, the apostle Paul, had left him in Ephesus to guide its church. That was going to be no easy task.

Paul understood the encouragement his young protégée needed. Sitting in prison shortly before his execution by the Romans, Paul could have used a little encouragement himself. But the tentmaker from Tarsus was wise and godly by this late season of his life, and he wasn't given to self-pity. Always abounding in the joy of God's work, he wrote a letter counseling Timothy to stay focused on a task with eternal implications. The letter carries an urgency that stands out among his New Testament epistles. Perhaps he felt what Jesus felt in the Upper Room: time was short, and the stakes were high for the kingdom of Christ.

Ephesus was a cultural melting pot in which people, even believers, were becoming more worldly every day. God's inspired Word was being trivialized, so Paul wrote to Timothy, "I charge you therefore before God and the Lord Jesus Christ, who will judge the living and the dead at His appearing and His kingdom: Preach the word! Be ready in season and out of season. Convince, rebuke, exhort, with all long-suffering and teaching" (2 Timothy 4:1–2).

Notice the phrase "I charge you." It's used on six other occasions in Scripture. It always precedes a clear and urgent command. Even without the charge, these words would have carried the same weight as any other scriptural command. But the extra notice is a way of underlining the words that follow. It tells us, "Listen very carefully—this next part is life-and-death stuff." Then comes the phrase, "before God and the Lord Jesus Christ, who will judge the living and the dead at

His appearing and His kingdom." Can you feel the solemnity with which Paul fashions this word of counsel? Once again, here is an end-time reference in a present time call-to-action context.

The twenty-first century is not dissimilar from the first. Our culture, like the city of Ephesus, subjects the Word of God to scorn and ridicule. Paul wrote of a time when people will "not endure sound doctrine, but according to their own desires, because they have itching ears, they will heap up for themselves teachers; and they will turn their ears away from the truth, and be turned aside to fables" (2 Timothy 4:3–4).

We live in an age of ten thousand competing voices, all of them tantalizing, all designed to scratch the itching ears of a directionless society. People are inventing new religions by the day. If Paul were writing in our era, he might call them "ear candy." They sound sweet but have no nutritional value whatsoever. Consider the books that ride the best-seller list at the moment of this writing, each of them offering a "new," suspiciously convenient way to find truth, meaning, and purpose without breaking a sweat. Listen to the gurus who populate the talk shows. You'll notice that the trendy new "religions" play to the ego while making almost no demand on obedience or sacrifice.

Pluralism and tolerance are the watchwords of the day, but they result in more turmoil, not more peace. All the answers people seek are in the Word of God, where they've awaited us for two thousand years. But the masses would rather have their ears tickled than their souls renewed.

A Famine of Hearing

Long before Paul, the prophet Amos warned: "Behold, the days are coming . . . that I will send a famine on the land, not a famine of bread, nor a thirst for water, but of the hearing of the words of the LORD" (Amos 8:11). It's a strange kind of famine, isn't it? The problem is not with the corn but the ears.

We may well be in the early stages of the hearing famine. For generations, God's Word has been at the center of church preaching. Today, even in the major faith communities, questioning scriptural authority is in vogue. Popular speakers advocate processing God's Word through the cultural filters of the day, rather than the other way around. We once understood that we don't stand in judgment of the Bible; it stands in judgment of us. But many today are air-brushing the Word of God to make it palatable to those who go in for spirituality that costs nothing but the cover price of a best seller. Instead of our being conformed to the image of Christ, we want to conform His image, and everything else in Scripture, to our sad conditions. Thirty years ago, people were saying, "If it feels good, do it." Today, it's more subtle. We say, "If it sounds good, believe it."

When we are trying to figure out how on earth we can live with confidence in this crazy, chaotic world, we ought to be running to the Bible and not away from it, as so many are doing. We are like survivors of the *Titanic*, the great luxury ship, floating helplessly on the tides. At that boat's launch an employee of the White Star Line boasted, "Not even God himself could sink this ship."[6] No matter how modern and luxurious the ship was, however, it went down— and its passengers were left scrambling for scraps of wood to keep them afloat.

That's a picture of you and me right now. Our culture of prosperity seemed to be an unsinkable vessel, but it's in pieces right now. Though everything else may fail us, God's Word never will. Jesus, who calmed the storm and walked across the waves, is still in control. Double-digit unemployment, trillion-dollar debts and bailouts—what are these to One who created every star in the sky? He still reigns, He still speaks, and His Word still offers the provision for every need we have in such a time.

So what exactly are these needs? Paul is going to give us a clue. In so many ways, the great apostle is telling Timothy what the church in Ephesus, and the church in our own cities, need to hear when the preacher stands up to speak.

We Need a Sure Word from God

Paul gives Timothy five commands in this text. The mentor's directives nearly jump off the page in their urgency and forcefulness:

> Preach!
> Be ready!
> Convince!
> Rebuke!
> Exhort!

Remember, Paul has been working in a state of urgency for three decades, planting churches across as much of the globe as he can possibly reach. He knows that his ministry is almost complete, even though the fire still burns within him for new lands and new souls. Now he must place the future of all his labor in the hands of the next generation of evangelists, preachers, and teachers—including Timothy, his prize pupil. Paul yearns to see the Holy Spirit take hold of Timothy's young life.

He writes, "For I am already being poured out as a drink offering, and the time of my departure is at hand. I have fought the good fight, I have finished the race, I have kept the faith" (2 Timothy 4:6–7). Can't you hear the passion in his words?

In the previous chapter of this letter, Paul has spoken to Timothy about truth and the importance of upholding it. He has foreseen a time when religious leaders will be addicted to pleasure rather than fellowship with the Father, and will clothe themselves in the appearance of godliness—without the power of it. "From such people stay away!" he has concluded (2 Timothy 3:4–5). Now, in the fourth chapter, Paul tells Timothy that it's not enough to just *acknowledge* what is right, he must *announce* what is right. He must preach this truth!

The word he uses for *preach* means "to proclaim with formality, gravity, and an authority that must be listened to and obeyed." We know that from the beginning, preaching has been God's vehicle for inviting people into His kingdom. Paul speaks of "the foolishness of preaching" (1 Corinthians 1:21) because the very words that are divine revelation to the believer seem like nonsense to the rest of the world. The Holy Spirit, of course, makes the difference. Puritan Thomas Watson explained, "Ministers knock at the door of men's hearts; the Spirit comes with a key and opens the door."[7]

Turning Point is our international ministry for doing exactly what we're discussing: preaching the Word to the world. We use television, we use radio, we use the Internet, we use prerecorded media, print media, and sometimes we do it the good old-fashioned way: we go to the various corners of the world and preach the gospel in person.

On one such trip to Wake Forest, North Carolina, I was preparing to speak at a dinner meeting. Someone told me that a US Army chaplain wanted to share a word. This is not something that occurs at our meetings with much frequency, but God had big things in mind that evening. Let me share his incredible story with you.

His name is Brad Borders. He was a young man whose life had been characterized by poor decisions. From his mid-teens he had been confused and aimless, and the future seemed to hold no promise for him. But one day in 1994, while driving through the Smoky Mountains of North Carolina, he concentrated on keeping his car on the road through the precipitous turns as he turned up the radio. Of all things, it was some Bible preacher—and of all subjects, he was preaching from the book of Revelation, one of the most difficult books in the Bible.

Brad described for our audience the strangeness of listening to biblical teaching as an atheist. As Paul said, it can seem like nothing more than sheer folly to an unbeliever. Brad had always rejected this kind of thing quite easily. But on this day, the message finally came in loud and clear. It must have been like listening to someone speaking a foreign language, then, in one moment, receiving the ability to understand every word being spoken. It just *clicked.*

There is a God, he thought abruptly.

The next thought was, *And Jesus Christ is His Son. And I don't know Him. And if that doesn't change, my life will remain in shambles.*

Strange how you can be driving along a road, he said, and suddenly you believe your entire destiny hinges on the words from a two thousand-year-old book! What would make someone believe that? What mysterious power could bring an adult mind to that conclusion in the space of one instant?

Suddenly the pastor (that was me) was speaking directly to Brad. He was calling on every listener to stop for a moment and consider one question. *What's going to happen on the day you die?*

Brad had absolutely no answer for that question. He had no defense, no diversion. He needed Jesus. He needed forgiveness. He was certain that God, the maker of everything, was alive, and suddenly Brad wanted more than anything in the world to know him. Sitting behind the wheel of a '92 Saturn, Brad prayed his heart out. He asked for forgiveness, for salvation, and for the privilege to know Christ personally. God granted his every request.

Fourteen years passed, bringing this same man to a microphone at our dinner, where he held the audience spellbound. During the intervening years, he had been mentored and discipled, just as Paul had done with Timothy. He had gone through seminary, been ordained as a pastor, enlisted as a chaplain, and commissioned as a servant of the gospel, traveling to places he never dreamed he would see. I was amazed as I listened to his story. I had never met Brad or heard a word of his story. I only learned it because I happened to visit North Carolina. I had to wonder what else God was doing out there through our ministry that he hadn't let me know about. Praise God, this is the tip of the iceberg; His Word never returns void. He has promised us:

> For as the rain comes down, and the snow from heaven,
> And do not return there,
> But water the earth,
> And make it bring forth and bud,
> That it may give seed to the sower
> And bread to the eater,
> So shall My word be that goes forth from My mouth;
> It shall not return to Me void,
> But it shall accomplish what I please,

And it shall prosper in the thing for which I sent it.
(Isaiah 55:10–11)

In case there's any doubt about the return on God's Word, consider this. Since Brad Borders became a chaplain, he has led more than seven hundred soldiers to Jesus Christ.

That's the ultimate power of the Word of God through preaching. It has nothing to do with me. Believe me, I couldn't convince you or anyone else to believe in the reality of Christ and to commit your life totally to Him—not unless the Holy Spirit empowered the words of my mouth. In ordinary circumstances, Brad, an atheist without direction, could never have suddenly turned his life on a dime, becoming someone capable of leading more than seven hundred soldiers to Christ. Even then, it would be even less likely to happen based upon a sermon from the book of Revelation. Although Brad didn't believe a word of it, the preacher obviously did. In other words, it was a sure word from God.

You'd be amazed how many times something as unlikely as that has happened, always beginning with the Word being preached. There is an account of a woman on her deathbed. She described how she was saved by reading a crumpled, ragged piece of wrapping paper in a package shipped from Australia. Someone had used the printed text of a sermon by Charles H. Spurgeon to wrap a package for shipment. The sermon was preached in England, printed in America, shipped to Australia, then sent back to England as wrapping paper, where the woman read it and encountered Jesus Christ. The Word traveled thousands of miles on the cheapest, most crumpled and smeared newsprint. But the truth shone brilliantly through the simplest of media, and God's Word did not return void.[8]

We Need a Serious Word from God

We need a sure word but also a serious one. Paul writes, "Be ready in season and out of season."

The words *be ready* mean "to stand by; to be on hand." This phrase conveys more than the idea of just being alert. There is urgency and vigilance in being ready the way Paul describes. It's the idea of a soldier standing on the wall at midnight, knowing the enemy is within firing distance. "In season and out of season" basically means this: the right time *and* the rest of the time. We proclaim the Word of God when it is readily accepted, and we proclaim it when it is not. People always need a serious word from God.

Those of us who are charged with the responsibility of teaching God's Word must understand that it is serious business! Nothing could be sadder than the feast of God's Word served up at lukewarm heat, with little flavor. We're approaching issues that concern our hearts, our souls, and our heavenly destiny. The element of solid reasoning is important, as we'll see, but the heart of preaching is . . . the heart. We preach the Word to change lives.

It is possible to be intellectually stimulated without being changed from within. This is why we are to proclaim the Word, to the hearts of our people, with authority and certainty.

A cartoon by my friend Rob Suggs in *Leadership Journal* showed a sad pastor studying a chart that showed his plunging church attendance. Apparently most of his congregation had drifted away. A friend was gently suggesting to the pastor, "I'm no expert, Bob, but maybe it would help if you didn't close each sermon with, 'But then again, what do I know?'"[9]

Paul commands Timothy to boldly proclaim the message of the

Gospel. People need a serious word from God, so we need to deliver our message as if tomorrow depends upon it; the truth is, it does.

We Need a Systematic Word from God

We also need a systematic word from God. We must be bold with our message. We share it with most certainty and urgency. But we must also share it intelligently.

Paul uses three important words here: *convince, rebuke,* and *exhort.* Those are known to writers as "strong verbs"—action words in which the action is aggressive. What can we learn from these words that will help us during times of national and world crisis?

Our Minds Need to Be Convinced by the Word. To convince is "to present an argument or a strong appeal"—something like an attorney presenting a brief. We're trying to change the mind of the hearer.

J. Sidlow Baxter wrote: "To my own mind, the most satisfying proofs that the Bible is divinely inspired are not those which one 'reads up' in volumes of religious evidences or Christian apologetics, but those which we discover for ourselves in our own study of the Book. To the prayerful explorer the Bible has its own way of revealing its internal credentials."[10]

The nineteenth-century scholar, A. T. Pierson, agreed: "Every study of the Bible is a study of the evidences of Christianity. The Bible is itself the greatest miracle of all."[11]

That miracle once did its work upon a young G. Campbell Morgan. He had grown up in a Christian home, never questioning that the Bible was the Word of God. But in college, his faith was severely challenged and he began to entertain doubts. "The whole intellectual world was under the mastery of the physical scientists, and of a materialistic and rationalistic philosophy," he later said. "There came a moment when I was sure of nothing."

That was an era when it was fashionable to launch attacks on the veracity of Scripture. The new crowd hired out great lecture and concert halls across England for the purpose of attacking the authority of the Bible. Armed with all their intellectual artillery, the army of skeptics troubled the young Morgan. He studied every book he could find—for and against the Bible, for and against Christianity—until his mind was reeling with arguments and counter-arguments.

He finally heaved a sigh, gathered up all the volumes, and locked them in a cupboard. He then walked to a bookshop and purchased a brand-new Bible. He had decided it was time to let the venerable old Book speak for itself. The young Morgan believed that if the Bible truly was divinely inspired, and if he would simply read it with an open mind, then the Book would do its own convincing. So he opened its covers and began to read.

The Bible spoke to him with eloquence and authority. The unity of the sixty-six inspired books, the many literary forms gathered across time, and the depth of the message itself—all these elements of the Bible experience overwhelmed him. The clear power and presence of God could be encountered here! "That Bible found me," he later said. After that year, 1883, he was a devoted student of the Scriptures for the balance of his life.[12]

Our cynical culture would like you to believe that the Christian life is a mindless thing, built around an ordinary book that is a dusty grab bag of mythology. It's all so much emotion, they claim, so much self-deception. According to the stereotype, you check your mind at the door when you take up Christianity, and smart folks should stay away.

Now for the truth of the matter: the Word of God is the most rational, accurate, well-documented body of literature in the history of the world. It requires our God-given intellect to even begin the life-long process of embracing its many dimensions of profound teaching. Great thinkers throughout the ages have discovered just that: Sir Isaac Newton, who gave us our basic laws of physics; Blaise Pascal, world-class mathematician and scientist; Sir Francis Bacon, who introduced the scientific method; Michael Faraday, foundational pioneer of chemistry and electromagnetism. And today, to give one example of many, there is Professor Henry F. Schaefer, one of the most distinguished physical scientists in the world, a five-time nominee for the Nobel Prize, and a devout follower of Jesus Christ.[13] Here is what many of these men would tell you: if it requires faith to be a Christian, how much more faith does it require to dismiss this amazing, timeless book called the Bible? People today say the age of miracles is over, and that they've never seen one. But if you own a Bible, you hold a living miracle in your hand.

Our Wills Need to Be Convicted by the Word. Paul's second word is *rebuke.* It's not my favorite word or yours, but it's a necessary part of life and faith. It means "to reprimand." It is synonymous with the word *convict.* In a spiritual context, it means to speak out against sin where we find it.

In today's church, that can be an adventure. But to some extent, human nature has always been tough on truth-tellers. We understand why pastors often shy away from "telling it like it is," but truthfully, they often find they've underestimated their listeners. People are starving to hear an unvarnished gospel. They need a sure word from God!

Too many modern pastors attempt to be user-friendly and give no offense. I don't set out to preach or not preach about sin. I want to reach seekers too. But my goal is to be faithful to the Word of God. I preach through its pages and disregard the politics of addressing this or that topic. It just so happens that occasionally the Bible has something to say about sin! If the Bible says it, we need to say it too. And more often than not, it's the message people are longing to hear.

John Steinbeck, the author of *The Grapes of Wrath*, was not known for writing from an evangelical perspective. But in another of his books, *Travels with Charlie*, he gives an interesting account of his reaction to a sermon he once heard in a New England church:

It is our practice now, at least in the large cities, to find from our psychiatric priesthood that our sins aren't really sins at all but accidents that are set in motion by forces beyond our control. There was no nonsense in this church. The minister, a man of iron with tool-steel eyes and a delivery like a pneumatic drill, opened up with prayer and reassured us that we were a pretty sorry lot. And he was right. We didn't amount to much to start with, and due to our own tawdry efforts we had been slipping ever since. Then, having softened us up he went into a glorious sermon, a fire-and-brimstone sermon . . . He spoke of hell as an expert, not the mush-mush hell of these soft days, but a well-stoked, white-hot hell served by technicians of the first order. This reverend brought it to a point where we could understand it, a good hard coal fire . . . For some years now God has been a pal to us, practicing togetherness . . . But this Vermont God cared enough about me to go to a lot of trouble kicking the hell out of me. He put my sins in a new perspective. Whereas they had been small and mean and nasty and best forgotten, this minister gave then some size and bloom and dignity . . . I wasn't a naughty child but a first rate sinner . . .[14]

Missionary poet Amy Carmichael wrote: "If you've never been hurt by a word from God, it's probable that you've never heard God speak."[15] The Bible does many things. It will uplift your spirit, it will make you cry tears of sheer joy, and it will drive you to worship. But there are also times when it seizes you by the collar, pulls you up close, and shows you the sin in your life in such a way that there's nowhere to hide. When you listen to the Word—through preaching, through small groups, or through personal study—do you ask God to shine His light on the dark places of your character, convict you of sin, and give you victory over it?

In his letter to Titus, Paul describes what a true teacher must do! "Have a good grip on the Message, knowing how to use the truth to either spur people on in knowledge or stop them in their tracks if they oppose it." (Titus 1:9 MSG).

Paul also touches upon the ultimate goal of preaching: "Warning every man and teaching every man in all wisdom, that we may present every man perfect in Christ Jesus" (Colossians 1: 28). We can't present every man and woman perfect in Christ Jesus without confronting imperfections where we find them. That's just how it works; our wills need to be convicted by the Word.

Our Hearts Need to Be Comforted by the Word. In her book *Edges of His Ways*, Amy Carmichael is right on target when she points out that no matter what our need may be, what dark cloud may hang over us, we will find just the right word in the Bible somewhere; just the remedy we need. It may not be the first passage we see when we open the Book, but if we search the Scriptures diligently, the Bible will answer every issue that arises.[16]

The Bible speaks to every part of who we are. It convinces the mind, convicts the will, and comforts the heart. In Paul's advice to Timothy, the relevant word is *exhort*—*encourage* in some translations—"to encourage with the goal of bringing someone along a path toward a positive end result." There is no comfort, no encouragement, like the kind that can be experienced through God's Word. Paul writes to the Thessalonians, "Therefore comfort one another with these words" (1 Thessalonians 4:18). And in 1 Corinthians 14:3, we learn that prophecy is for the purpose of comfort: "But he who prophesies speaks edification and exhortation and comfort to men."

Yes, God gives us His Word for guidance, but He also gives it for comfort because He loves us. We look around us and wonder what the future holds. We have questions about the direction of our nation and our world. We have worries about our finances. But when we open God's Word, we receive profound comfort. We are reminded on every page that kings, countries, and economies don't hold the fate of the world; only God does, and He is a God of comfort and love. He has a future and a hope for us.

Once our hearts are lifted, we can lift the hearts of others. The Bible tells us in so many passages to encourage and comfort one another, and it's one of the most important things we do as we gather together for fellowship. One stumbles, another lifts him up. One has an anxious heart, her brothers and sisters pray for her and surround her with love and support. The church shines in these moments as we allow the Holy Spirit to minister encouragement through God's Word.

I assure you that the most remarkable and powerful words of comfort and encouragement you'll ever encounter are all in the Bible. But do you know where to find them? The Psalms, in particular, speak to every condition of the human heart, but do you know your way around in that section of your Bible? If you will simply take the time to learn how to find what you need in the Scriptures, you will have an incredible remedy for fear and anxiety. Better yet, if you will memorize key passages, the Holy Spirit will call up those words from your mind again and again. Burying His Word in your heart is the wisest way you can spend your time.

We Need a Sensitive Word from God

We want to notice a final word from Paul in this amazing passage. He has outlined for Timothy both the message and the method for ministry in chaotic times. The leader should convince, rebuke, and exhort. But he must make sure he does so "with all long-suffering and teaching." What exactly does Paul mean here?

As I read the words, I realize that Paul is speaking particularly to me as a pastor. As I teach God's Word, I need to be very patient. We leaders can be discouraged; there are times when we feel that no one is listening. We look out across the sanctuary and ask ourselves, "Is anyone really interested in learning about God's Word today? Is there any chance that someone out there will actually apply this to their lives?" God's instruction for me is to be longsuffering; to wait however long it takes; to do the work of ministry and remember the harvest is His. If I begin to play God, insisting that things work on my schedule, I will drive people away.

And this patience is not just for preachers. For example, there are wives who have grown deeper spiritually than their husbands. They've been able to attend the Bible studies or spend time in personal study while their husbands were devoted to their careers. Wives, too, need to be longsuffering and patient; be gentle and loving while letting God do the work of admonishment and conviction.

All of us, as followers of Christ, need to be sensitive. We forget that the Spirit of God is always on the move, always seeing the big picture that we don't see. We can't know what is in the minds of others or what the future holds. What we can do is be obedient to Christ and to His Word, and that means being loving, patient, gentle, and longsuffering.

Where to Bury the Treasure

It was February of 1944 when the little Dutch clock shop was raided. An agent of the Nazi Gestapo stood in the living room of Corrie ten Boom's family, his eyes studying the books on a shelf. "You! The old man there," he barked. "I see you believe in the Bible."

It was true. Each morning, before he opened his watch shop, Corrie ten Boom's father, Casper, held devotions with his family. The focal point was a large, brass-hinged Bible. Casper would read a chapter, lead a prayer, and begin the business day. Then, as the sun set, the family would gather again and take up where they had left off in the morning's reading.

His youngest child, a daughter, remembered him reading, "Thy word is a lamp unto my feet, and a light unto my path . . . Thou art my hiding place and my shield: I hope in thy word" (Psalm 119:105, 114). The child had wondered what it all meant. A hiding place? What kind? How could a word be a hiding place, and what was there to hide from?

This was the dark day when she would discover her answer. Old Casper, his four adult children, and one grandchild were ordered out of their home and marched to police headquarters. There they awaited an uncertain fate, having been charged with secretly sheltering Jews who were under persecution by the Germans. In the holding cell, the ten Booms ate the meager meal they were given, huddling together in the encroaching darkness. Only one thing gave them a taste of home: time together in the Word. Casper led devotions as if it were any other day, any other place. The great Bible was out of reach, and there was no light for reading anyway. But it didn't matter because he had buried the Word in his heart—the hiding place no enemy could invade. He knew the passages of comfort, chapter and verse.

His daughter Corrie wrote, "His blue eyes seemed to be seeing beyond the locked and crowded room, beyond Haarlem, beyond earth itself, as he quoted from memory, 'Thou art my hiding place and my shield: I hope in thy word . . . Hold thou me up, and I shall be safe'" (Psalm 119:114, 117).[17]

Later, in the concentration camp, she managed to get a Bible and to read it to fellow prisoners. "The blacker the night around us grew," she recalled, "the brighter and truer and more beautiful burned the Word of God."[18] And indeed the nighttime of her life grew black. She endured the deaths of her father and her beloved sister, Betsie. She survived humiliation, cruelty, and neglect. But the Word of God, and the peace of God flowing from it, brought her through the long nightmare so that she might emerge to bless the world with her message of hope.

Hidden in Plain Sight

Does that story or, perhaps, something else in this chapter help you to feel differently about that Book collecting dust on your shelf or on the back seat of your car where you left it on Sunday? It's not my intention to deal in guilt but to motivate and encourage you to experience the great blessing that comes to those who read and love the Bible as people over the ages have done.

Some of the stories in this chapter have shown you how the Word of God has worked miracles in people's lives. It traveled on newsprint across the world to lead a woman to salvation in England. It strengthened a small knot of suffering humanity in a concentration camp. It captured the intellect of a future Indian-American governor of an American state. A rebellious young man had his life changed on a North Carolina road. Do you notice the pattern? These lives reflect many times and cultures; and each dealt with intense crisis in some way or another. Time after time, the Word of God was their lamp, and the light of their way.

That light seems to shine brightest of all when darkness falls upon our surroundings. Our world is now in crisis, and many people I know are living with a sense of loss and a fear of the future. The Word of God is available to convince your mind, to convict your will, and to comfort your heart. If you will read it, cherish it, and let it dwell within you richly, you'll see the darkness retreat as the light of God's truth shines brightly in your life.

If you remember the Bible's warnings—that the Bible and the faith will come under increasing attacks as we get closer to the return of Jesus Christ—you will not cower in fear when skeptics raise their voices. Whether they are comedians who try to soften your defenses with humor, scholars who try to overwhelm your beliefs with intellectual arguments, or religious leaders who try to convince you that the Bible is just a book, you will be ready. You will remember that "the grass withers, the flower fades, but the word of our God stands forever" (Isaiah 40:8).

EIGHT

Stay Consistent

"DO YOU HAVE A REGULAR MEETING IN YOUR HOME?" THE CITY official asked.

"Yes," the pastor's wife replied—she was the one who answered the door.

"Do you say, 'Amen'?" was the next question.

"Yes."

"Do you pray?"

"Yes."

"Do you say, 'Praise the Lord'?"

"Yes."

The city official went on to tell the pastor's wife that the Bible study they held in their home was in violation of local ordinances. A few days later the couple received a written warning that listed "unlawful use of land" and warned them to "stop religious assembly or apply for a major use permit"—a process that could cost tens of thousands of dollars in legal and other fees.

If you think this took place in Albania, you'd be wrong. China?

Nope. Cuba? Not even close. A former Soviet Eastern Bloc nation? Good guess, but no.

Believe it or not, this took place in May 2009 in San Diego, California, in a neighborhood quite near to where I live. The church I pastor has more than two hundred small group Bible studies that meet in our members' homes weekly, throughout our vast county. The saddest part about it is this: when I heard this report in our local news I wasn't really surprised. Not that this is typical of the local governments in our area. Rather, it is indicative of a growing trend in our nation and our world—a trend that requires Christians to be tolerant of everyone and requires no one to be tolerant of Christians.

And this trend—which is going to increase as the world's tolerance for Christianity decreases in the years ahead—is going to present a new dilemma for Christians in America and other nations: do I live a consistent Christian life, or do I compromise when the pressure gets intense?

As it turns out, some neighbors had complained to local authorities about the number of cars that were parked at the pastor's home during the weekly Bible study. And that's all it took for authorities to begin an investigation as to whether a religious meeting was being held without an appropriate permit. As I write these words, the matter is still under deliberation.[1]

I say "Three cheers!" for the pastor's wife, who boldly and truthfully answered the questions the local official asked. She was consistent. Instead of answering yes each time, what if she had said, "Uh, we have met here occasionally"; "No, we don't say 'Praise the Lord' or 'Amen'"; or "Yes, we pray—sometimes we say grace before we eat, but not every time"? Let's face it; she didn't know if she was about to be arrested or something worse. As far as she knew, her fate lay in her answers.

Consistency. It's the act of living true to what you believe regardless of the cost. Christians need to consider how consistent they are going to be before, not after, they hear a knock on their door.

The truth is, the world itself is inconsistent enough. I doubt its condition has grown any less chaotic since you began reading this book. Our stock market is the very study of inconstancy with its roller-coaster gains and losses. Nothing is stable about international politics, and on a social level, we see marriages struggling and careers going bust. The only consistent thing about our world is that it's inconsistent.

What about you? Are you the same person on Mondays that you are on Sundays? Do solid biblical principles guide each section of your life? How about marriage and parenting, if those apply—do you have consistent principles there, and do you live by them? These are hard questions, and issues that aren't always pleasant to consider. But one of the biblical essentials for getting through times like these is to live a life of solid consistency—to be one person through and through, to be an example of tough-minded integrity that does not throw out the game plan just because things have gotten tougher.

Sports fans will understand what I'm talking about. In 2001, rookie head coach Mark Richt led his Georgia Bulldogs up to Knoxville, Tennessee, to play national title contender Tennessee. Georgia was a serious underdog and hadn't won in Tennessee's raucous, one hundred thousand–seat stadium in twenty years. Before leading his team onto the field, Richt told his players, "Men, if they blow the doors off us early, keep your composure. Believe in the plan." As the game began, Tennessee indeed jumped out to a big lead and pushed Georgia's smaller linemen around. The rout-hungry fans were deafening. But

Georgia's players remembered the coach's advice, each man holding to his part in the game plan, and the Bulldogs pulled off an upset still remembered as one of the greatest college games ever broadcast by CBS.[2]

We can all agree that "the doors have been blown off" in our own game lately. Our temptation is to do what undisciplined athletes might do—throw caution to the wind, forget our training, and declare that it's every man for himself. Yet calm assurance and the right plan are the keys to pulling through. We have God's Word in these times. David the psalmist said that those who don't know God are like chaff (dust) that the wind blows away, but the one who loves the Word of God "is like a tree planted by the rivers of water, that brings forth its fruit in its season, whose leaf also shall not wither; and who shall prosper in whatever he does" (Psalm 1:3).

Confidence + Consistency

Not only do we want to lead lives of consistency, but we depend upon it in others. When I climb onto an airplane, I insist upon a consistent pilot—let him be dull and predictable in his routine, as long as he delivers me to my destination in one piece. If a surgeon is operating on me, I don't want him to be the kind of doctor who has good days and bad days; I want to know that his results have been consistent in past operations. Coaches such as Mark Richt want quarterbacks who are reliable, who will make the right reads and throw the ball to players wearing the right color jersey—*consistently*.

As a matter of fact, we want these people to be confident as well as consistent. Their self-assurance becomes our self-assurance. Confident and consistent: Both of these words begin with the prefix of *con*, which means "with." *Confidence* means "with faith" while *consistency* translates to "with a place"—that is, the idea of standing firm like the tree planted by the river. It has a place, its roots are deep, and it's not budging an inch. When we are centered in Christ and confident in His Word, we can be consistent. We can stand firm because our faith is built on nothing less than Jesus and His righteousness. And when the sky is falling and everyone else is running around frantically, we can walk calmly in the Spirit.

Sometimes we read God's Word and think: *What do you want from me, Lord? I'm doing the best I can!* It's a tough world, and we often feel that we have to be many kinds of people to survive—the rough-and-tumble business world requires one kind of performance, parenting another, and so forth. Even Paul wrote, "I have become all things to all men, that I might by all means save some" (1 Corinthians 9:22).

Yes, but Paul was talking about our identifying with all people, as Christ did, in order to bring them the gospel. Paul never wavered from his walk or his true identity in Christ. Therefore we want to follow Paul's model and be strong enough to be faithful, and flexible enough to be useful. God isn't picking on us, far from it. In fact, He calls on us to be faithful because it is for our best good. "And now little children, abide in Him, that when He appears, we may have confidence and not be ashamed before Him at His coming" (1 John 2:28).

We can't escape this biblical message, foreign as it sounds to the vast majority today who never give a thought to His return. The message is that our lives should be shaped by the certainty that we are living between His first appearance and His final one. In the interim, we are visitors to this world but citizens of heaven. He will return here that He may return us there, and the point is that we should not be making ourselves at home in this world, with its ways. The consistency we want is one attuned to the ways of the spiritual world—the reality of Christ.

The Marks of Our Consistency

"And now, little children, abide in Him" (1 John 2:28*a*), John writes as an affectionate father to his family. He refers to his readers as "little children" five times in this one chapter. He is the apostle of love, and he embodies that virtue in all his writing. In his gospel, we know him as "the disciple that Jesus loved" (John 13:23; 19:26; 20:2; 21:7; 21:20). He tells us in this letter that "God is love" (1 John 4:8). He even knows a loving way to describe the idea of consistency: the beautiful word *abiding*.

Abide is found eighty-two times in the King James Version of the Bible and very seldom in our daily language. When we speak of abiding, it is usually in some legalistic sense: a law-*abiding* citizen; one who *abides* by the rules. In John's discourse, the word means so much more than toeing the line. The Greek translates it as "to continue, to stay in a relationship, to remain, to be consistent." When we abide in Christ, we remain consistent in our relationship with Him. We believe His truth, we obey His Spirit, and we stay steadfast in our love for Him and for His children.

J. Hudson Taylor, the pioneer missionary to China, had been working far too hard, pushing himself to the breaking point. His friends feared he was nearing a breakdown. Fellow missionary John McCarthy sent him a letter in which he shared his personal discovery about the joy of abiding in Christ, based on John 15. McCarthy wrote that abiding does not mean striving or struggling but simply trusting

Christ to provide the necessary power. This had been a helpful insight for him, and he shared it in his letter of encouragement. He reminded Taylor that Christ is "the only power for service; the only ground for unchanging joy."

As Hudson Taylor read this letter at his mission station at Chinkiang on Saturday, September 4, 1869, his own eyes were opened. "As I read," he recalled, "I saw it all. I looked to Jesus; and when I saw, oh how the joy flowed!" To his sister in England, he wrote: "As to work, mine was never so plentiful, so responsible, or so difficult; but the weight and strain are all gone. The last month or more has been perhaps the happiest of my life; and I long to tell you a little of what the Lord has done for my soul . . . the Spirit of God revealed the truth of our oneness with Jesus as I had never known it before."

McCarthy had written: "But how to get faith strengthened? Not by striving after faith, but by resting on the Faithful One."[3] That is, *abiding*.

Most of us find ourselves to be sprinters in life rather than marathon runners. We're capable of bursts of speed and productivity, but we can't sustain the effort. Marathon runners have something to teach us about consistency. They find just the right zone of energy exertion, and they abide there physically. It's the same way with abiding in Christ. Many of us go from peak to valley, dedication to dryness, and we struggle with the sustained walk of faith. If we charted our spiritual walk, it would look like the recent stock market—wildly varying. We want that walk to be represented by a line, straight and unwavering as possible, climbing to higher values— what Eugene Peterson has called it in a book titled *A Long Obedience in the Same Direction.*[4] That's the life of godly consistency.

In a *Leadership Journal* cartoon, the pastor is speaking to his congregation: "We have a special gift for a lady that hasn't missed a service in forty-five years. Eleanor Smith! Where is Eleanor sitting? Eleanor? Eleanor . . ."[5] Oops!

I'll admit to hearing a speaker at some event, who informed us that she hadn't missed her morning appointment with God in more than four years. My natural human impulse was one of immediate resentment because I knew I lacked such perfect consistency.

Not long ago, I came across this prayer: "Dear Lord, so far today I am doing all right. I have not gossiped, lost my temper, been greedy, grumpy, nasty, selfish, or self-indulgent. I have not whined, complained, or cursed. I have yet to charge a penny on my credit card. Now, as I prepare to rise from bed this morning, I'll need your help more than ever."

That's someone who feels like many of us: intimidated on the way to the starting line. We've charged into diet plans, certain that nothing could stop us. We've begun fitness campaigns, keep-the-house-clean initiatives, and countless strategies for getting up early for devotions, for the rest of our lives. But the best-laid plans fall apart; sad and dejected, we quietly begin setting our goals much lower, so we won't shame ourselves again. We settle for a life of sporadic progress, fits and starts.

All the while God's Spirit whispers in our ear, "Don't condemn yourself! God's grace covers you. But you need not give up. There is unlimited power in trusting your heavenly Father and moving forward with each new day." He wants us to enjoy a consistent walk. We'll find out how to do that by following this wonderful word *abide* through the New Testament. Each usage gives us another piece of the puzzle in assembling the total picture of consistency.

Consistently Christ-like

Listen to John's words: "He who says he abides in Him ought himself also to walk just as He walked" (1 John 2:6).

If your goal is consistency—defined in this chapter as abiding in Christ—then the key is to follow the Leader. Jesus shows us the way through His own life. We are called *Christians*, "Christ-Ones," and by that definition we want to live as He lived.

Again we feel intimidated—who can live up to the name of Jesus? I've read that Alexander the Great heard that a man in his army shared his name (all but the "Great" portion of it). Whereas the general was wildly courageous and visionary, the other guy might as well have been known as Alexander the Wimp. The leader called the soldier to his quarters, looked him straight in the eyes, and said, "You call yourself Alexander? Then either change your character or change your name."

If we determine to practice the discipline of abiding, we will discover that it isn't accomplished through some rote formula or by adhering to the steps of a self-help book. The only way to become like Christ is to humbly accept Him as both Savior and Lord and allow the Holy Spirit to begin His program of renovation within us.

An old missionary friend told me that his strategy for a consistent walk was to spend time every day meditating on the passion, death, burial, and resurrection of Christ. While he does other things during his devotional time, he always ends up immersing himself in the awesome, love-driven sacrifice of the Savior. He told me that when he began to follow this discipline, it changed his life.

So if you want a consistent walk, begin with consistent focus on Jesus and how He pursued life. A sermon here and a Bible study lesson there will never implant within your heart all that you need to know. You must develop a personal passion to know Jesus Christ as only the Scriptures can help you know Him.

Just as the character in Nathaniel Hawthorne's "The Great Stone Face" stared for years at the semblance of a face on the cleft a rock and in time took on those features himself, so you, if you look continually on the face of Christ, will become consistently like Him.

Consistently Caring

John says, "He who loves his brother abides in the light, and there is no cause for stumbling in him" (1 John 2:10). This is one of John's favorite themes. In his written letters, he is consistently telling us that love is the proof of our being in Christ.

John tells us that we know we've passed from death to life by the way we love one another, and where there is love, there is Christ. As Christians, loving is what we do. Have you ever been among genuine, serious Christians and watched how they treat each other? Nonbelievers don't quite understand; it all seems very strange and unnatural to them. But we understand. We know that when we give our hearts to Christ, He gives us hearts for others. We can then love in a way that would never have been possible without Him.

As far as John is concerned, the full command of Christ is this: believe on the Son; love one another (1 John 3:23). Then he gives us that lovely verse that so many of us have memorized: "Beloved, let us love one another, for love is of God; and everyone who loves is born of God and knows God. He who does not love does not know God, for God is love" (4:7–8). Could anything be clearer? God is all about love, and anyone without love hasn't been in His presence lately, plain and simple.

Finally, John comes at the same message from the opposite direction. Loving God and hating others, he says, is a contradiction in terms. It's impossible to love an invisible God when we can't manage to love a visible brother (v. 20). In other words, if you are Christian, here is the test: love the people you know—really love them. That's what real Christians do. Anything else is simply playing religious games.

For most of us modern Christ-followers, hate is not the issue. The opposite of love is not hate but apathy. Apathy is oblivious to the needs of others. You may know about the thousands of Ukrainian children in orphanages, many of whom have been abandoned by parents who were unable to care for them. Maryna was a Tufts University doctoral student who found out that the care these children were receiving was insufficient. The children got the necessities, but no focused love; as many as fifteen different caregivers would be in and out of their lives in a week. These helpers were trained to avoid bonding with the children because they had to keep moving; there were just too many children for individual relationships.

This sad arrangement guaranteed poor cognitive and emotional development for the orphans. Maryna felt compelled to find a solution. So she started a "Big Sister" orphanage program, designed to provide every child with a university student to talk and play with him or her for five days of the week for one whole year. The difference to the children was profound. Maryna saw a need, felt compassion, and then did something about it.[6]

Mark Richt, the football coach I mentioned earlier, also felt moved by God to do something. He and his Bible group were studying James 1:27, a verse that says "pure and undefiled religion" includes caring for widows and orphans. He realized he couldn't read that verse and just walk away from its implications. Though the Richts had their own children, they traveled to Ukraine and studied pictures of the orphans. "It just seemed like God was prodding us," Katharyn Richt said. They came across the picture of a child born with a terrible facial deformity and learned that no one was likely to adopt such a child. The Richts felt God tugging at their hearts. This would be their new daughter. Finally, they came home with two new adopted children, and the Richts have a large, happy family that has become a wonderful testimony to the power of Christ's love.[7]

Consistently Confident

"I have written to you, young men, because you are strong, and the word of God abides in you" (1 John 2:14).

You've noticed the subtitle of this section, and you're wondering what that verse has to do with becoming confident—and what confidence has to do with consistency. The truth is that as the Word of God permeates our lives, as we reflect daily on the nature of Christ and come to know Him in an intimate way, we begin to feel an inner strength we never knew before. And strength always produces confidence.

I've seen this in my life and in many believers who discipline themselves in God's Word. Its truth and its power begin to radiate from their personalities. The Scriptures are sprinkled through their talk as the Holy Spirit calls up verses from their memories to apply to every conversation, every new situation. You'll notice that Paul is constantly quoting the Old Testament. Do you think he kept a copy nearby, on the ship, in the tent, or inside the prison cell he was occupying, or do you think he kept the Word of God engraved in his heart? Notice how Jesus answered every temptation from the devil with the written

Word of God. These men, and those who have followed their lead, have continued in the Word until it continued in them. As you do the same, strength and confidence will characterize everything you do.

Professors from the Universities of Toronto and York recently announced that they had identified a connection between faith and anxiety. They had investigated whether a belief in God impacted personal stress. What they discovered through their studies was that the brains of spiritually driven people are calmer in the face of uncertainty. The scholars held a firm conclusion that those with a belief in God had 33 percent less brain response to anxiety; those with an outright certainty of God's existence demonstrated 45 percent less anxiety than atheists. Finally it was concluded that religious people are more effective in decision making. Knowing God builds strength, confidence, and a calm approach.[8]

Consistently Compliant

We must be hearers of the Word, but we must also be doers of it. As nice as it is to know we will do better in dealing with anxiety, there is a far richer benefit: "He who does the will of God abides forever" (1 John 2:17). Yes, that's a promise. If you live as God wants you to, then you will enjoy eternal life in His presence.

Who would you say is the most submissive and compliant person you've ever heard about? Jesus may not be the first name that came to your mind, but He is the correct answer. There was nothing passive or hesitant about Him, but every moment of His life was lived in full obedience to God. Even when He faced the unimaginable prospect of arrest, torture, and crucifixion, He affirmed God's will and submitted to it. Here is how obedient He was: "He humbled Himself and became obedient to the point of death, even the death of the cross" (Philippians 2:8).

Jesus said: "My food is to do the will of Him who sent Me, and to finish His work'" (John 4:34). Again: "I do not seek My own will but the will of the Father who sent Me" (5:30). Jesus is the ultimate model of obedience and submission to God's will.

What that will is, of course, is the great question for many people. They seem to believe God has hidden it from them, and it's up to them to go look for it under every leaf. The will of God for your life is spelled out in Scripture. There's no magic formula; you won't discover His will by placing your Bible under your pillow at night. But as you develop a consistent pattern of reading God's Word and meditating on it, you will begin to sense the reality of God's will at work in your life!

The name of the college you should attend or the person you should marry will not be contained in any verse. But you will find many specific directives to get you serving the Lord, and the specific answers will be revealed as you are consumed by the work of God rather than your own self-interests. The Bible will show you what to do; the question is, are you are willing to do it?

Consistently Consistent

I've saved the best for last. How about being "consistently consistent"?

John says, "Therefore let that abide in you which you heard from the beginning. If what you heard from the beginning abides in you, you will also abide in the Son and in the Father" (1 John 2:24). Only as the Word abides in you, will you abide in Christ.

Did you notice that the word *abide* appears three times in that one verse? Substitute it with the word *continue*, and read it again. You'll get the point. If we continue with the basics of the Word, we will continue with God.

So many of us began with a deep devotion to Christ, but we took detours from the narrow path of obedience. We are all prone to wander. Abiding is not about never missing your appointment with God. It is more about finding your way back when you stray. As the old song says, "pick yourself up, dust yourself off, and start all over again."[9]

Amy Carmichael was a product of a wealthy Irish home with every advantage. But Amy's parents had no intention of sheltering their children from the needs of others less fortunate. The whole family got involved in mission and ministry projects, serving the poor and hungry. Amy's father was generous with his resources in a way that made an impression on his offspring.

Sitting in a fashionable teahouse in Belfast one day, Amy looked out the window to see a small girl, barefoot and dressed in rags. As the rain came down, the little girl was pressing her nose against the window, gazing hungrily at the cookies and pastries on display. The image would not leave Amy's mind. That afternoon, she wrote on a scrap of paper:

> When I grow up and money have
> I know what I will do;
> I'll build a great and lovely place
> For little girls like you.

But then hard times came for Amy and her family. When she was seventeen, her father died. Rather than give into the bitterness of her loss, Amy began an outreach in the slums of Belfast. As many as five hundred poor factory girls were helped by this mission. It was just the beginning of what God would do with Amy Carmichael. She went to India as a missionary, and there she fulfilled her old pledge and built a lovely home in honor of the little poor girl in Belfast. She established what we know today as the Dohnavur Fellowship to save children from the human trafficking that was so prevalent in that region.

Amy Carmichael never came home again. She spent her remaining thirty-five years in India, serving Christ with love and boundless energy. She created a lovely home for one thousand children who might have become slaves or prostitutes. And even though Amy herself became an invalid, she kept on keeping on. From the physical pain that was always with her, she had one prayer request: "Ask for me one thing . . . ask for selflessness, power to help, console, lift the edges of the burdens if I can't lift the whole. Ask for love that forgets all but others."[10]

Amy Carmichael is a hard act for us to follow. That's a high level of consistency and submission. But we don't have to match that standard today; we can start right where we are. We do not need to go to India or even Belfast to be obedient to God. He will let us know what He requires, and He will give us the desire and the talent to do whatever that is. What He does expect is for us to begin to be consistently consistent as we follow Him.

The Motive for Our Consistency

Here is our motivation for walking consistently with Christ: "When He appears . . . at His coming" (1 John 2:28). I heard about a woman who had a firm understanding of this point. A preacher friend of mine was in line at a big store. The woman was ahead of him, and she was holding up progress with a request that was out of the ordinary. The previous night, the store had charged her for one pencil sharpener. She had bought two; now she was returning to pay for the other one.

The cashier couldn't figure out how to handle a day-old correction. The manager, equally nonplussed, pleaded with the woman to simply keep both sharpeners with no additional payment. It really wasn't worth the trouble of refiguring. My pastor friend, possibly sensing a great sermon illustration, followed the woman out of the store and asked her why she was so meticulously honest. She replied, "The way things are going in this world, the Rapture is going to happen any day, and I didn't want to be caught with a stolen pencil sharpener."

We chuckle over that one merely because her point of view is so foreign to most of us. At any given moment there are probably fifty subjects closer to the top of our minds than the return of Christ. If it didn't happen yesterday, we believe that means it won't happen today—though in reality, of course, His return is that much more likely. Do you want to be caught with a stolen pencil sharpener? A shoddy job performance? Arguing with your spouse, cheating on your income taxes, inactive at church?

My friend Charles Swindoll worked in a machine shop while he was a college student. Every day when the whistle blew at the end of the shift, the other workers would hustle around to get their lunch pails and their clothes. By 5:15 or so, they'd be walking out the door. There was only one fellow who was way ahead of the pack. It seemed as if he was on his way to the parking lot thirty seconds after the whistle, lunch pail in hand, coat over his shoulder. One day, Swindoll asked him, "How do you get out so fast?"

The man replied, "Listen, boy . . . I stay ready to keep from gettin' ready."[11]

It's not a bad strategy. Christ is going to return, and we need to *stay* ready so we won't have to *get* ready. Keep your house in order and you won't have to put it in order. Keep your marriage from breaking so it won't have to be fixed. And stay on the path of consistent faith so you don't have to find your way back to it. The fact is that when the time comes, "getting ready" will not be an option.

Needless to say, the biggest question of all is whether you have accepted Christ as your Savior. If you have any doubts at all about that, stop right now and turn to the back of this book for a few words about how to surrender your life to him (see pages 233–235). The most important issue of your life, by an infinite margin, is your eternal destination. If you haven't settled it, don't you think it's about time?

The Measure of Our Consistency

So how do we measure consistency? John says we will know we're on the right track because "we may have confidence and not be ashamed before Him and at His coming" (1 John 2:28).

That verse speaks of a bold commitment, and one that may occasionally require courage. When eight hundred buses in England, Scotland, and Wales carried those wide atheistic banners reading, *There's Probably No God. Now Stop Worrying and Enjoy Your Life*, some agreed with the message, some ignored it, but Ron Heather, a sixty-two-year-old bus driver, was horrified as he read the words plastered on his assigned bus. He knew that he just could not drive a bus bearing that message.

Heather took a stand and refused to drive the bus. Since there were no alternate buses he could drive, he simply went home. If it came to quitting his job, he was ready for that, too, even in the economic realities of 2009. He would not support the mocking of his faith.

Heather didn't know what to expect when he returned to work the next day. His supervisors told him he could drive a bus that didn't bear such a banner. And the result was this: Heather's story, told all over the world, is having an influence vastly broader than that of a few buses bearing cynical messages. His courage and consistency are inspiring others to be bold in the workplace.[12] Here is what John would say about that: "You are of God, little children, and have overcome them, because He who is in you is greater than he who is in the world" (1 John 4:4).

When Jesus comes, we will either be assured or ashamed. The Bible teaches that we will give an account of all the things we have done. That fact should cause us to be taking a pre-inventory of those activities right now. Some ask, "What would Jesus do?" Another question to ask is, "Would I be assured or ashamed if He returned right now?"

Our first event after Jesus returns will be an appearance before the judgment seat of Christ. Please understand that we will not be judged for sin. All of that was handled at the cross! But the Bible does say that " . . . we must all appear before the judgment seat of Christ, that each one may receive the things done in the body, according to what he has done, whether good or bad" (2 Corinthians 5:10). Our sins may be forgiven, but our work will not be forgotten!

Will We Be Assured?

How can we be assured and not ashamed? First, our confidence is the result of our productivity. John quotes Jesus as saying to us, "Abide in Me, and I in you. As the branch cannot bear fruit of itself, unless it abides in the vine, neither can you, unless you abide in Me" (John 15:4). If we are abiding in Christ, we are bearing fruit. When we see God at work in our lives, we become confident in His power.

Our confidence also comes from our prayerfulness. Jesus continues, "If you abide in Me, and My words abide in you, you will ask what you desire, and it shall be done for you" (v. 7). Abiding in Christ puts us on the right wavelength with God's will, and we tend to ask for things in tune to what He wants. As we watch Him work in us through prayer, our confidence in Him grows and matures and when we stand before Him on that day, we will be assured.

The Bible says that five different crowns will be presented at the judgment seat of Christ. We won't walk around in heaven wearing these crowns, as if there could be pride or boasting in heaven; instead, we will lay them at the feet of our Savior in an act of worship. I'm convinced that the most coveted prize will be hearing our Lord say, "Well done, good and faithful servant. Enter into the joy of your Lord."

Will We Be Ashamed?

How will it be possible to enter the gates of heaven and be ashamed? Believe it or not, this will occur for many people. Some Christians who have been unfaithful to God will be in heaven. The precious blood of Christ was shed as much for their sins as for the most fruitful and productive of saints. But these will be Christians who have accepted the gift without ever prizing it. Now, standing before the throne, they will see everything clearly. They will know their foolishness and feel shame, even in the midst of salvation. The Lord will say, "My precious child, I bled for you on the cross. I gave all that I had, and what did you do with My gift?" What answer other than remorseful silence can follow?

It is after this, according to the Bible, that God will wipe away every tear, and we will all enter into His joy and perfection. I don't want to begin eternity in a brief instant of self-humiliation. I'm sure you don't either.

So I'm going to stay ready to keep from getting ready. When I rise from my bed each morning, I'm going to ask the Lord to strengthen me, so that my eyes will remain focused on that eternal prize. I'm going to work with all my heart here on earth, but in spirit, my bags will be packed. I'm going to keep short accounts, holding no grudges, having no unfinished business in my personal relationships. And I'm going to understand to the best of my ability exactly what God wants me to do each day and do it with all my heart and soul.

Both of our sons loved football and excelled as quarterbacks. One of them is currently a scout in the NFL. As a guest at his training camp, I've observed the team's preparation for the season. I was especially curious to discover how a quarterback develops consistency. It turns out that the secret is *reps*—short for repetition. A starting quarterback receives all the reps in daily practice. He throws the ball in each drill, working on every route and every play from his team's playbook. Over and over he repeats the precise steps of his footwork, the reading of the defense, and the mechanics of his release. In the end, he has a kind of "body memory" that is close to perfection for executing the attack strategy of a professional team. His movement is smooth, fluid, and confident.

My own sport was basketball. I spent endless hours in the gym, all for the purpose of being an accurate shooter from every angle. A friend would stand under the hoop and toss the ball back after each shot, and I would work on shooting from the left, from the right, from the free throw line, and everywhere else until each shot became part of my DNA. When I got into a game, my body took over and knew exactly what to do, precisely how much "touch" to put on a shot from any position. Reps made the difference.

Here are the reps that will guide you toward perfect execution of the Christian life. The first drill is to study your Bible reflectively each day. The second is to be a person of prayer—regular and disciplined. Do these things over and over, for every situation. There will be days you don't feel like doing these things, just as the quarterback, aching from yesterday's scrimmage, isn't too keen on today's drills. But those hard-nosed decisions to be consistent will separate you from the luke-warm faith crowd. They will cause you to experience Christ in ways you never could have anticipated.

Read, pray, serve, repeat. Do this every day, and on that wondrous day when Christ returns, you will stand before Him without shame. Having walked consistently in this life, you will walk in boundless joy into the perfect consistency that is called heaven.

But before you get there, your consistency in Christ may well be tested in ways you can't imagine today. Indeed, the Bible says that a one-world government, ruled by a man with delusions of deity, will dictate economic, political, and religious policy for the nations. And that everyone on earth will be required to swear loyalty to him upon pain of death for refusing.

If you are a Christian, you won't be on earth during the seven years when the antichrist ruler is fully in charge. But you and I may well be alive when the world begins to experience the birth pangs of his arrival—intense, increasingly frequent, and painful probes into the freedom of our spiritual life. They will start small—like officials saying you can't hold a Bible study in your home—and grow larger. Now, not then, is the time to decide whether you are going to live consistently for Christ, regardless of the cost.

The only way to be strong enough on the day it happens to you is to put in your spiritual reps daily. You can't get in shape for the most important contest of your life on the morning of the big game. You must live consistently today in order to pass the test tomorrow.

NINE

Stay Committed

HE TOLD HIS FAMILY HE WAS GOING BACK TO THE OFFICE. HE drove to the parking lot of the company where he had made his fortune and stepped out into the early darkness of the frigid January evening. Instead of heading to the entrance of the familiar building, he climbed up the embankment, down the other side, and threw himself under the 5:30 train as it sped past his plant. He was seventy-four years old. He reportedly left a note for his family saying, "I'm sorry."[1]

There were many such stories in the newspapers early this year. This one happened to be about the great German drug manufacturer, Adolf Merckle. He was one of the richest men in the world, a billionaire more than nine times over. He lived a quiet life with a wonderful wife and four loving children. Despite their enormous wealth, they reportedly lived quite modestly.[2] As a young man, Merckle inherited his family's chemical business and developed it into one of the world's greatest pharmaceutical companies—Merck & Co.

He seemed to have a Midas-like intuition when it came to business dealings. He grew his family's small chemical/pharmaceutical manufacturing business from eighty employees in 1967 to nearly one hundred thousand in 2008. That year Merckle was the fifth-richest man in Germany, and Forbes ranked him in the top 20 percent of the world's richest.[3]

He was "a symbol of Germany's industrious spirit,"[4] with one notable deviation: a few years ago he began to take greater risks in the stock market. In an interview shortly before his death, he blamed the whole thing on "'a chain reaction' that broke the financial model that had worked 'superbly' before the crisis.'"[5] We will never know what caused the foundation of his confidence to crumble. But he was not alone in his descent into despair.

A day or two after Merckle's death, Wall Street Journal recorded the apparent suicide of the fifty-two-year-old real estate auction tycoon, Steven Good. In his red Jaguar, parked in a wildlife preserve near Chicago, he took his life with a single shot.[6] He left no note.

Then, in the week following that incident, a desperate money manager, who was also an amateur aerial acrobat, faked his own death in an airplane accident. With the controls set on autopilot, Marcus Schrenker, thirty-eight, bailed out over Alabama and left the plane to crash. He then drove his previously stashed motorcycle to a KOA campgrounds in Florida, where he was discovered three days later, unconscious and with a wrist slashed in a failed suicide attempt. In a statement before his trial began recently, he is quoted as saying that he had "snapped" and "it all came crashing down around me."[7] Now it's federal prison bars that are crashing around him.

Frayed nerves will snap. Chain reactions will sidetrack superb financial models, financial and emotional foundations will crumble, and irrational decisions will continue to plague today's society.

I'm not reassured by western political leaders who tell us prosperity is just around the corner. Hopefully, the economy will perk up in the immediate future, but one Wall Street guru warned: "The credit markets are in a shambles, the banking system is hanging by a thread, and the consumer is out of gas. Traders are clinging to the slim hope that the worst is over, but they could be mistaken. There's probably another leg down, and it will be more vicious than the last."[8]

You and I and our spouses and children—each man, woman, and child in America—currently owe thirty-seven thousand dollars per person in national debt, and it's getting worse by the day. A columnist in my home state of California stated the obvious when he wrote, "The severe economic downturn has exposed the state's finances as a delicate house of cards just waiting to collapse."[9] He could have been talking about the entire world economic system. Americans have transferred vast amounts of wealth to Middle Eastern oil producers and, in the process, borrowed over a trillion dollars from the People's Republic of China.

Many people see their jobs hanging by a thread and their own finances teetering like a house of cards. A Charlotte newspaper just reported that paramedics recently responded to eighty-one suicide attempts in eighteen days. It's no accident, said mental health authorities, that the upturn in attempted suicides coincided with the downturn of the economy, which included spikes in the city's unemployment and home foreclosure rates. "I can't believe it's not related to the economy," said one doctor.[10]

Where do people turn when times are tough? One school of thought says they go to church. As we mentioned in a previous chapter, there's evidence to support that. After the 9/11 terrorist attacks and other crises, church parking lots have needed extra spaces. But for every action there is an equal and opposite reaction. "Economic turbulence might give" gamblers, partygoers, drinkers, and smokers "more reason to indulge," says Thomas Anderson in *Kiplinger's Personal Finance* February 20008 issue, making "so-called sin stocks . . . a safe bet."

Isn't it intriguing? A crisis is really a fork in the road. You have two choices, a high road and a low one. Jesus used this kind of language when He said there was a broad way on which most people travel while His own path is a narrow one walked by few (Matthew 7:13–14). During trial and tragedy, some shake their fists at the heavens and say that this proves there is no God. Others come precisely to the opposite conclusion, saying they never found God to be so real or His comfort so encouraging. Testing reveals character—it is true of individuals, it is true of churches, and it is true of nations.

Without question, these are fearful days. Billionaire investment guru Warren Buffett has observed, "I have never seen Americans more fearful. It takes five minutes to become fearful, much more to regain confidence." He adds a profound statement, "The [financial] system does not work without confidence."[11]

Meanwhile, we find that stimulus plans, bailouts, and whatever else that is tried or not tried begins another contentious debate. The stakes are simply so high, and there is so little consensus about the way forward, that we find bickering within and among nations. The current president of the European Parliament called our emergency stimulus program "a way to hell." Furthermore, he said, it will "undermine the stability of the global financial market."[12]

We see all these things and recognize, once again, the signs of a civilization edging toward its final climax. The more chaotic things become, the easier it is for us to gravitate toward some social extreme— a path of least resistance, whether it's despair, anger, or simply closing our eyes and pretending that everything is fine.

An alternate suggestion: what about sitting down, reflecting on the sovereignty of Almighty God, and reminding ourselves that nothing takes Him by surprise? He is in no way confined by the limits of the moment. He rules from outside the realm of time, which is simply one more element of His complex sovereignty. He foresaw this moment at the foundation of the world, and it has its proper place in His great plan. It is woven, along with everything else, into the infinitely fine tapestry of His will and work.

Knowing that fact brings profound peace. If the world believed it, people wouldn't turn to whiskey, gambling, and narcotics. There would be less of a frenzy these days, and that would be good for everybody. People would understand that the true destiny of creation is in good hands, and believers would surge forward with new determination to seize the day for His glory. These are the times in which the hope of our Lord shines most brightly through the world's murky fog. Our destiny is decided: we will be reclaimed by the returning Christ to spend eternity in His presence. For now, we have the exciting task of seeing how many people we can bring along with us on that journey.

Hurry Up and Wait

James, the most practical of New Testament writers, tells us, "Therefore be patient, brethren, until the coming of the Lord. See how the farmer waits for the precious fruit of the earth, waiting patiently for it until it receives the early and latter rain. You also be patient. Establish your hearts, for the coming of the Lord is at hand" (James 5:7–8).

As we await the Lord's return, therefore, we are to be patient. That ability comes from strengthening the foundation of our faith. The stronger our convictions, the better we'll handle challenging times.

There is a direct correspondence between the strength of one's faith and the depth of his patience.

Patience can be one of the most elusive virtues, even for the hopeful. It's certainly not one of our nation's best attributes. During the Reagan administration, Richard Nixon was interviewed about the subject of peace in the world. He was asked whether the nation was better off than it had been one year previously. Nixon replied, "As Americans, we have many great strengths, but one of our weaknesses is impatience. The Russians think in terms of decades, the Chinese in terms of centuries. Americans think in terms of years, and months, and days . . ."[13]

Someone said that patience has a bitter taste, but a sweet aftertaste. I wonder if any of us would labor with the steadfastness of some of the great Christian missionaries of the past—or have the commitment of their boards and overseers who hung in there with them. When the gospel was brought to Western Africa by missionaries, fourteen years passed before a single convert came to faith. It required ten years in Eastern Africa and sixteen years in Tahiti to win the first soul. William Carey is considered the father of the modern missions movement, yet it took him seven years to convert his first Hindu.[14] Adoniram Judson, America's first missionary, labored six years before he baptized the first Burmese believer.[15] More patient than his supporting churches, he once wrote home: "Beg the churches to have patience, success is as certain as the promise of a faithful God can make it."[16]

In all of those places the aftertaste of patience was sweet because workers for Christ—and their sponsors—knew how to wait upon the Lord and trust His timetable. Difficult? Absolutely. But patience is God's classroom for instructing us in faith and obedience. If we didn't have so much to learn, perhaps we wouldn't have so long to wait. We want to do well in this course of instruction. Let's learn what the Word of God has to teach us about waiting, trusting, and hoping.

The Instruction of Patience

I like the way J. I. Packer describes our daily business: "living out the belief that God orders everything for the spiritual good of his children. Patience does not just grin and bear things, stoic-like, but accepts them cheerfully as therapeutic workouts planned by a heavenly trainer who is resolved to get you up to full fitness."[17]

That kind of believer understands that God is in control even when something unpleasant occurs. He accepts it as one more obscure, multisided piece of the jigsaw puzzle of his life—for which he has no box cover pattern. He trusts the One who sees the finished project and seeks to develop trust-based patience. Puritan Thomas Watson wrote, "There are no sins God's people are more subject to than unbelief and impatience; they are ready, either to faint through unbelief, or to fret through impatience."[18]

If you think back over your life, you're bound to realize that while a doctor needs bright light to do his surgery, God likes to work in the dark. We don't learn character when life is cruising along—only when it demands us to reach within ourselves and find new patience, new faith in God, and new resources to overcome the obstacles.

Perhaps your family is coping with difficult times at present. What if you viewed this as a time of revelation from God, an occasion for learning to trust Him, and a stepping-stone to good things in the future? That's how God has always worked, so why would this occasion be any different? If you and your family were to begin the coming week with that attitude firmly entrenched in your collective soul, giving thanks to God all the way, how much better would your week feel?

If you were to thumb through my Bible, you would find all kinds of markings and quick notes. I write these things down as they occur to me because they might be helpful next time I come to the same passage. I've noted that the word *patience* (or a synonym for it) is found seven times in James chapter five. It's remarkable how this idea keeps coming to the top. I've italicized them in this list:

- "Be *patient* . . . until the coming of the Lord" (James 5:7).
- "The farmer *waits* for the precious fruit of the earth, *waiting patiently* for it . . ." (v. 7).
- "You also be *patient* . . ." (v. 8).
- "Take the prophets, who spoke in the name of the Lord, as an example of *suffering* and *patience*" (v. 10).
- "Indeed we count them blessed who *endure*. You have heard of the *perseverance* of Job . . ." (v. 11).

Patience. Waiting. Suffering. Endurance. Perseverance. These are not the ingredients of popular preaching or reading these days. We're addicted to happy thoughts and synthetic optimism—sweet little lies though they may be. Back in the real world, life is filled with waiting and enduring.

Like many of us, the apostle Paul was not the type of man who enjoyed delay. He was visionary and ambitious—a whirlwind of kinetic energy who was evangelizing nonbelievers, mentoring young believers, and shepherding whole congregations all at the same time. Yet he was also a man who knew and trusted his Lord well enough to know how to trust God's schedule. As he wrote letters from political confinement, he might have been expected to rage in frustration against the Roman obstacles that hindered all the things he wanted to do for God. What we find is just the opposite. He wrote his friends at Philippi, "My chains are in Christ" (Philippians 1:13). He recounted how he was able to share the gospel with the palace guard, and how his correspondents had grown bolder in their faith because of his experiences. A letter of anguish for anyone else becomes an epistle of joy for Paul. As long as he knew God was doing something—and when is God not doing something?—he was able to find contentment.

In 1 Corinthians, Paul gives us the greatest paragraphs on love that were ever written, and patience finds its way into the mix. What is the very first attribute of godly love in his list? "Love is patient, love is kind. It does not envy, it does not boast, it is not proud" (1 Corinthians 13:4 NIV). Then, when we check Galatians 5:22 for the fruit of the Spirit—the crucial qualities that develop in us as we grow—we find patience (*longsuffering* in a few translations) in a prominent place, just after the immortal triad of love, joy, and peace. Paul obviously had a high regard for the kind of quality that must not have come easy to a vigorous, eager evangelist.

If patience, longsuffering, and perseverance are so critically important, why then are they so difficult for us? I believe the reason is that this pattern of faithful response can only be learned through tribulation. Paul again: "And not only that, but we also glory in tribulations, knowing that tribulation produces perseverance; and perseverance, character; and character, hope" (Romans 5:3–4).

When I begin a new day, tribulation is generally not on my list of requests to God: "Lord, can you really hit me with something nerve-racking today? My character needs a good test!" I wouldn't expect anyone to include that request in his or her prayer time. Yet in a sense, it would make sense to do so, if Christian maturity is our goal. Tribulation teaches us to hang in there, and hanging in there develops character in us. And that, Paul tells us, produces something incredibly wonderful: *hope*. And when we say *hope*, we're not talking about a mild desire for something to happen, as in, "I hope it doesn't rain today." We're talking about a solid, foundationally positive outlook on life; an absolute persuasion that God has already won any conceivable battle that this day might concoct, and therefore we can smile confidently *no matter what*. Don't you think we need hope like that in times like these?

Again, don't feel compelled to pray for tribulation tomorrow. It's provided free of charge. Trials are coming to a circumstance near you whether you look for them or not. They enter the door without knocking, regardless of any padlock. This is because the world is fallen and also because God wants you to grow. That's why James stands with Paul in telling us to embrace the quality of patience; to look for it in ourselves during tough times, and to depend upon it to inspire us.

But What's the Big Delay?

James was writing to believers who were suffering deeply. It was not easy to be a Christian in the first century. Many believers thought the only positive outcome for them would be for Christ to return as soon as possible; there was certainly nothing in this life to increase their hope. James was telling them, "Just be patient! If Christ delays, it is for good reason—He's not ready to give up on this world just yet, so neither should you or I be."

So true. Our Lord Jesus Christ is "the Alpha and the Omega, the Beginning and the End . . . the First and the Last" (Revelation 1: 8, 11).

He knows the end from the beginning, and sometimes delays occur in life because God still has work to do, circumstances to line up, unfinished business to complete. It's likely to be something wonderful. These are times to learn the discipline of waiting upon the Lord, having patience in His timing, and resting in the fact that His plan is a perfect one. [19]

I'm talking to more and more people who are fervently praying for Christ to return and stop the madness. They repeat the plea that is found in the final words of Scripture, "Even so, come, Lord Jesus!" (Revelation 22:20). According to the Pew Research Center, more than three-quarters of American Christians now believe in the second coming of Christ, and 20 percent feel fairly certain He will return in their lifetime.[20] Those are truly remarkable figures. We have to be pleased that so many understand that Christ will come back, and that this sorry world is not all that we have. Still, we can't get into the business of backseat driving with God. James understands that, and reminds us to be patient and let Him take the wheel.

Have you ever gotten frustrated on the freeway, when traffic came to a standstill? It always seems to happen when we need to be somewhere. We stew. We fume. We think, *What's the big delay here? This is ridiculous!* Then, ever so often, we reach the point of bottleneck and spot the ambulance and the stretchers. We sigh. We hush. We know something tragic has happened here, and we'd have waited more patiently if only we could have seen the big picture from above.

I've been an impatient patient in a few waiting rooms, haven't you? We flip restlessly through magazines and wait for a nurse to open the door and say those words, "The doctor will see you now." We are patients without patience. The word *patience* comes from a Latin word meaning "one who endures" or "one who suffers." At the doctor's office, we're required to wait with a calm attitude, and that's the biblical meaning of the word. Delays don't occur because someone—in heaven or on earth—is trying to irritate us personally. There are very good reasons in most cases; as far as heaven goes, in *all* cases.

A past presidential First Lady—and I mean our literal *first* First Lady—offers us an example of patience. Martha Washington wrote a friend in December of 1789, confessing that she would much rather be at home at Mount Vernon, playing with her four grandchildren, than serving as a symbolic presence in the nation's new capital in New York City. Yet "I am still determined to be cheerful and happy," she wrote, "in whatever situation I may be; for I have . . . learned from experience that the greater part of our happiness or misery depends upon our dispositions, and not upon our circumstances. We carry the seeds of the one or the other about with us, in our minds, wheresoever we go."[21]

That is a fragrant attitude, one pleasing to God. It gives evidence of the kind of maturity God wants to grow in all of us as we set our hearts on eternal things rather than superficial circumstances.

The Illustration of Patience

James, who is always good with word pictures, now gives us a visual reference for patience. He turns to the agricultural world: "See how the farmer waits for the precious fruit of the earth, waiting patiently for it until it receives the early and the latter rain" (James 5:7).

James and his brother Jude both had backgrounds in farming, so that vocation provided a naturally rich field of analogy. In a farming culture, the "precious fruit of the earth" is an apt description of the importance of the soil and what originated from it. If you didn't farm well, you didn't eat. We also need to understand that there were no irrigation systems in first century Hebrew farming. The "early rain" started the growth cycle; the "latter rain" provided moisture to mature the harvest.

As I write these words, we are in the third year of drought in California. Central Valley farmers have learned they will receive no allocation of water this year. When this happens, there is no harvest. The life in the seed remains dormant. Here is what would happen with proper irrigation: Water, lots of water, would be absorbed to activate the process of growth. As the seed grows larger it eventually bursts from its confining walls. The tip of the root emerges, the seed is anchored, and the new plant absorbs water and nutrients directly from the surrounding soil.[22]

In a post-agricultural society such as ours, we don't understand these things intuitively; James did. As a farmer, he knew that nothing transpired without the water. And he could do nothing about that water because it fell from the heavens. His job was merely to cultivate the soil, plant the seed, and, if rain fell by the grace of God, to bring in the harvest. Patience is instinctive for farmers since they can't bring the rain they need from the clouds. As we await the return of Jesus, the analogy is crystal clear. Our job is simply to till the soil, to nurture each other, to make good use of the "early rain" (when Christ came to earth the first time), and to prepare for the "latter rain" when He will come to bring the harvest.

We smile when we think of first century impatience for the return of Christ. They'd been waiting for three decades, whereas we've been waiting for two hundred decades—two millennia. If we were farmers, we would say that the clouds had closed up forever, and that the rain would never fall again. It's been a while. So what is the evidence of His return? I'd like to suggest that we view the issue from this angle. How long did people wait for the first coming of Christ? We believe Genesis

3:15 offers the first mention of the coming Redeemer. In the second chapter of Luke, the prophecy comes to fruition. How long in between? No matter how you date the first pages of Genesis, it was a very long time. Two thousand years have passed since Christ promised His return, but that's less than half the number of years between Genesis and Luke. According to Jewish tradition we are in the year 5769; subtract 2009 and the result would be nearly four thousand years between Adam and the birth of Christ.

Alfred Edersheim, the Jewish historian and Hebrew scholar, describes the ancient rabbinic conversations on the delay of the Messiah's appearance. Some rabbis believed the Messiah was waiting for Israel to repent. Others felt that He was the One who would come and call for that repentance. According to the Talmud, there were rabbis who believed the Messiah would appear exactly four thousand years after the creation of the earth. Isn't that intriguing? Jesus Christ fit that estimate—He came during that very time frame. Rabbis were limited in what they could do. They could crunch the numbers on their calendars, they could peruse the words of the old prophets, they could hope and dream, but in the end, all they could do was wait. Edersheim writes, "One by one, all the terms had passed, and as despair settled on the heart of Israel, it came to be generally thought that the time of Messiah's Advent could not be known beforehand."[23]

So much for getting ahead of God.

Heaven Standard Time

From the rabbinical perspective, the Messiah was delaying His appearance. God saw things differently. We find His own perspective in the book of Galatians: "But when the fullness of the time had come, God sent forth his Son, born of a woman, born under the law" (Galatians 4:4). That phrase "the fullness of the time" means God's chronology. Only He knows when time is "full" of all the elements He wants to have in place. Jesus came to earth the first time, for example, when the Romans had built roads and connected a vast empire; when an ideal language, perfect for explaining the gospel, united that empire; when the Jews had established synagogues all over the Mediterranean region to become "seed walls" for that gospel to burst forth; and when all the Hebrew prophecies concerning His coming had been uttered, so that the prophets had fallen silent. We can now see just how precisely God selected His timetable for sending His Son the first time. Is there any reason to believe that the time of His second coming will be any less precise?

For most people, the problem is not intellectual but spiritual. Even in the apostle Peter's time, people simply did not want to accept any possibility of Christ's coming; many were comfortably ensconced in their sin. Peter wrote: "Scoffers will come in the last days, walking according to their own lusts, and saying, 'Where is the promise of His coming? For since the fathers fell asleep, all things are just like they were from the beginning of creation'" (2 Peter 3:3–4).

Kevin Miller says that he knows an executive coach who asks the following question to CEOs: "What are you pretending not to know?" Miller writes:

This is the same question Peter is asking of the people who think there's never going to be a Second Coming—who think that there's never going to be a final judgment or an end to the world. Peter says: You can tell yourself whatever you want, but the thought that there's never going to be an "end of the world" is not coming from an objective, impartial evaluation of ideas. It's coming from your deep, unacknowledged desire to do whatever you want to and get away with it.[24]

Peter suggests that we never forget one fact: "That with the Lord one day is as a thousand years, and a thousand years is as one day. The Lord is not slack concerning His promise, as some count slackness, but is longsuffering toward us, not willing that any should perish but that all should come to repentance" (2 Peter 3:8–9).

Translation: God sets His watch to a time zone not accessible to us. Once again we need to remember that He is the one who created time, like everything else, and He uses it for his own purposes. He is not within it, wondering what's around the next bend, as we are; He is outside of it, in the eternal "now." He *made* the next bend.

The Puritan Stephen Charnock wrote: "He is not a temporary, but an eternal God . . . He is the dwelling place of His people in all generations . . . If he had a beginning, he might have an end, and so all our happiness, hope, and being would expire with Him . . . When we say God is eternal, we exclude from Him all possibility of beginning and ending, all flux and change."[25]

I like the little story about the foolishness of quantifying God's timing. A little boy asked God, "How long is a second in heaven?" God said, "One million years." The boy asked, "How much is a penny in heaven?" God answered, "One million dollars." The boy said, "Could I have a penny?" To which God answered, "In just a second."

The Why of the Wait

God has His timetable. From our perspective, He waits. And what is He waiting for? In particular, for us to share the news about Him.

There is someone who needs to hear about Christ at this very moment, someone within your sphere of acquaintances. There are countries and peoples who are on the verge of hearing the good news or on the edge of a true revival. As Peter said, He is not willing that any should perish, and like the captain who won't push the lifeboat away until it is absolutely filled with people to save, God waits for the biggest throng that can be ushered into His heaven.

Jesus spelled it out for us: "And this gospel of the kingdom will be preached in all the world as a witness to all the nations, and then the end will come" (Matthew 24:14). The Great Commission and the return of Christ are intertwined in that way. If you want to see His return, go and tell others about Him.

Robert Ingersoll may well have been one of the most famous atheists of all time. Not only did he have no faith, but he had no hesitancy in telling others that they shouldn't either. He was a bit like those of our own era who blame Christians and their belief in God for nearly every crime or tragedy that has ever happened. In his traveling lectures, Ingersoll ridiculed everyone who believed in God. Part of his routine was to take out his pocket watch, open it, and say, "Almighty God, I'll give you five minutes to strike me dead for everything I've said." Then for three hundred seconds, he would wait for God to do something to him as he stared at the watch. When the time expired, he would say, "That proves there is no God," and he'd put away his timepiece.

When an evangelist by the name of Joseph Parker heard about it, he asked, "Did the gentleman believe that he could exhaust the patience of an eternal God in five minutes?"[26]

Abraham must have wondered when God was finally going to send the child that was promised, one who would be the firstborn of a new nation; God kept his promise in the fullness of time. David, hiding in caves for a decade, must have wondered when God would finally fulfill His promise, given in David's boyhood, to put the shepherd on the throne. God came through in due time. And the disciples must have wondered when God was going to reach down into the machinery of Roman cruelty and rescue Jesus from the torture, mockery, and execution that befell Him. When Jesus died on that cross, God seemed to be out of time. On Sunday morning, in the fullness of time, God carried out the plan He'd conceived before the foundations of the earth. Is there any reason to be impatient with our God?

I pray for things, not knowing when He will answer. I long for His coming, having no inside knowledge of when He will appear. I want to see the end of our local drought, the recovery of our economy, or any number of other things that may seem delayed. But I know this: *delay* is not a word found in God's vocabulary. Never yet has He been too late or too early by even the flicker of an eyelash. He is not slack regarding His promises, and we'll understand it better by and by. It's the divine prerogative to schedule and the human prerogative to wait in faithful patience.

The Implications of Patience

Finally, we explore the implications of patience. In James 5:8, we learn that we are to "establish our hearts." What exactly is an established heart?

The phrase here means "make your heart firm." One New Testament paraphrase says, "You must put iron into your hearts" (Charles Bray Williams). The New English Bible calls upon us to be "stouthearted."

James is talking about taking the initiative to strengthen ourselves from the inside—to gird up the soul. In other words, we are to develop confidence as we wait. His imagery is all about bracing some object of support so that it will not give way, like checking the load-bearing pillars to make sure they'll support the roof. We don't want our faith to weaken as God tarries, or to give in to those mockers who are described by Peter. When faith is challenged, it needs to be buttressed. Therefore James is saying, "Don't just sit there—pump up your faith, so that you can stand firm."

Linda Derby of Tulsa, Oklahoma, learned that her daughter-in-law, a young missionary wife with twin boys, had been diagnosed with breast cancer. Linda waited breathlessly for every bit of news—first, the good news that would send her spirits soaring, then the bad, which would send her into the depths of depression. It felt terrible to be so helplessly concerned for her daughter-in-law. Finally Linda realized that she couldn't sustain the emotional roller coaster. She retreated to the confines of her own room, where she spent time in serious prayer. Linda told God she was going to let Him be God. She needed to acknowledge that He was in control of everything, even during a season of fear and anxiety.[27] From the moment she committed it all to His sovereign purpose, her anxiety began to melt away.

Linda's example is a model for the attitude that we should accept. It's not that we should settle for a sad and passive resignation to destiny. God doesn't want us shrugging complacently and saying, "It is what it is." I'm talking about real hope in the face of uncertainty. The patience God wants to build in us is dynamic and vibrant, not a bland and apathetic submission. We base our perspective on the fact that a loving God is in charge of this, His universe, and patience means being steadfast in our faith even when life is difficult. In Him we can have confident patience, strength, and endurance.

It's been said that patience is "doing something else in the meantime." And that "something else" we do is to find how to profit from the very trials we're waiting through.[28]

How many blessings are never received because we lack patience? Quite often we fail to see that trials are opportunities in disguise. We are to "establish our hearts" by claiming the promises of Scripture and waiting for Christ to either return or to redeem our faith through fruitfulness.

When the Son Sets You Free

Novelist Herman Wouk has written of a meeting he had with David Ben-Gurion, Israel's first president. Ben-Gurion urged him to move to the newly established nation. This was 1955, and *fedayeen* terrorists were still bringing regular bloodshed to the countryside. Ben-Gurion had left office and had begun his memoirs by this time. He invited Wouk and his wife for a visit to his home, where they talked for hours. At the end of the visit, he renewed his invitation to come live in Israel. "Here you will be free," he said.

The Wouks had arrived with an escort manning a mounted machine-gun, on the alert for terrorists. "Free?" Wouk asked. "With your roads impassable after sundown?"

"I did not say safe," replied the old man. "I said *free*."[29]

What we want is courage dependent on earthly security; what we need is courage based on heavenly security. We want comfort, but He gives something better: *freedom*. Because our destiny is settled, because this world is in the hands of God, we can be free from anxiety if we only have the faith. We can be free from the emotional tyranny of circumstances. Present discomfort that yields eternal joy is a formula we can receive with hearts of gratitude.

I've mentioned my inability to avoid getting lost en route to anywhere you can name. Naturally I had a GPS system installed in my car. Great—that solved half the problem. You have to promise not to program the system while driving, and that's good because I can't get myself further lost while I'm parked and staring at the dashboard. But now I have to know how to put the addresses into the system—which is even harder than finding where I want to go. Where do I get a GPS to help me from getting lost in the instructions to my GPS? All right, go ahead and laugh, I'm technologically challenged too. But there's hope. My new leased car came with OnStar. I had no idea that this was a good thing until the day when I pushed the little OnStar button. Immediately I heard a nice, clear, female voice—and she knew my name! "Good morning, Dr. Jeremiah. How can I help you?"

Well, I wanted to get to a football game to see my grandson play. I'd been to that field before, but it was when his father was playing there. I gave the location and the kind voice said, "Just a moment." It was less than a moment before I was hearing, "I have downloaded the directions into your GPS system, and you'll be verbally guided from where you are to where you're headed." Then a second clear feminine voice began telling me *exactly* where to turn. Not only that, but exactly *when*—as if she were in the car with me! She'd say, "Take that right turn in fifty feet."

I know you've probably been there and done that, and it's no big deal for you. But my jaw was dropping. I felt this was a miracle on the level of Moses and the burning bush. I was driving through neighborhoods that were foreign to me, and I was cruising, confidently courageous! My anxiety was completely gone because I knew I could trust the voice to lead me to my destination.

Don't you wish there was a GPS for life? In a way, there is. God not only knows where you are with better-than-satellite precision, but He knows the trials ahead on your path. He knows the turns that will bless your life and those turns that will cause you heartache. Growing in Christ is the increasing ability to receive that signal—to know His still, small voice that is clear enough to those who trust Him. When you realize He is leading you, the anxiety just drains out of your life. It is replaced by the kind of patience that all these Bible writers describe. Then, what will you do with all that extra energy that you used to put into nail-biting and fretting? You'll find yourself using it to minister to others.

It's really a simple matter of obedience. I realize that we all have friends and family who are "fainting through unbelief or fretting through impatience," who are jobless, who aren't sure what is happening in the world. You can be the GPS for those people who are moving through strange new places in their lives. You can come alongside them and say, "Let me walk with you. Let me be a kind voice in your life." Can't you see how a time like this can be a wonderful opportunity for those of us who know and love the Lord?

For me, the Bible is the best GPS for my life. I thumb through its pages and hear a chorus of voices offering affirmation even though these people have been through far more anxiety than I could imagine. From the Old Testament book of Deuteronomy comes the word of Moses, who has endured forty years of wilderness, with whining in surround-sound. Moses says: "Be strong and of good courage, do not fear nor be afraid of them; for the Lord your God, He is the One who goes with you. He will not leave you nor forsake you" (Deuteronomy 31:6).

David, who has dealt with the darker nights of the soul, confides, "I would have lost heart unless I had believed that I would see the goodness of the LORD in the land of the living. Wait on the LORD; be of good courage, and He shall strengthen your heart; wait, I say, on the Lord!" (Psalm 27:13–14).

Isaiah, having wept for a wayward nation, adds, "The work of righteousness will be peace, and the effect of righteousness, quietness and assurance forever" (Isaiah 32:17).

Paul is quick to contribute: "We have such trust through Christ toward God" (2 Corinthians 3:4). He adds, "our sufficiency is from God." (v.5). Our confidence comes from Him!

From Hebrews we hear directions for the most important turn: "Therefore do not cast away your confidence, which has great reward" (Hebrews 10:35).

When the whole world is hanging by a thread—and when you yourself wonder if you're near the end of your rope—hold on to the confidence of the Lord, don't cast it away in the time of trial. Confidence is a longer word for faith, and that is the quiet spirit of the soul in a child of God. We will not despair. We will not give in to anger, and we will not cut the corners on our faithful obedience. When the going gets tough, the tough just pray harder—harder still as they see the day approaching.

TEN

Stay Convinced

I'VE THOUGHT LONG AND HARD ABOUT WORLD CONDITIONS, BUT I was still taken back by the headline of a recent opinion column by the Israeli journalist, Eitan Haber. It blared: *World War III has started!* Haber was writing about the success of North Korea's nuclear program, and he warned that the test missile fired recently by the North Koreans landed squarely in the prime minister's office in Jerusalem.[1]

The world is quickly reaching a point of no return, Haber suggested, especially when it comes to the Middle East. Experts believe the Iran–North Korean nuclear axis is now even stronger than when it was when it was formed in 2007. North Korea appears ready to supply nuclear weapons in exchange for subsidized oil from a nuclearizing Iran that is threatening to destroy Israel.[2]

With rogue states like Iran and North Korea grabbing the headlines, it's easy to forget that somewhere in the world right now there's a nuclear weapon already waiting to go off: maybe in a bunker in Pakistan, an armory in India, a silo in Israel, or stashed away in an Afghan cave. Perhaps below ground in Russia or on a firing range in

China. God forbid it's sitting in a suitcase on the docks of New York City.

Depending on who you believe, about twenty-five thousand nukes are scattered around the world.[3] The top Russian defense expert under Yeltsin revealed that nearly 40 percent of so-called suitcase bombs were unaccounted for.[4] Israel itself is believed to possess numerous nuclear weapons.

Elizabeth Zolotukhina, editor of the Case Studies Working Group with the Project on National Security Reform, recently warned that purveyors of nuclear materials are communicating with customers using sophisticated new methods not readily apparent to Western intelligent officials. The nuclear black market, she warned, is becoming more professional by the day, and is surprisingly strong and resilient.[5]

National Defense Magazine recently ran a chilling article entitled, "7 Deadly Myths About Weapons of Terror," warning that smuggled nukes cannot be easily detected at US ports. Our ability to spot small amounts of nuclear components is "over-hyped," said the report.[6]

All it takes is one explosion, and history will never recover.

It's a horrific thought, but what if a nuclear explosion occurred somewhere in the world tomorrow? What would people do? Where would people turn? What if a gathering of world leaders were attacked by terrorists? These are apocalyptic questions, but we're living in apocalyptic times. I'm not an alarmist, but sometimes I do feel alarmed.

And then I remember Romans 13:11, a verse with a clarion call from the Lord to be ready for the return of Christ. Here we find a clear strategy for living proactively as appalling things transpire around us. No weapon on earth can blast this verse out of the Bible; rather, these words tell us how to respond internally and intentionally to the times in which we're living.

Let me express to you the importance of this verse to me. The volume preceding this one, *What in the World Is Going On?*, has been the best-selling title of all my books. I've been asked to sign many copies, and on every occasion, after signing my name, I've written *Romans 13:11* on the flyleaf in hopes that the book's owner will turn to that verse and be compelled by its truth.

In this book, you'll notice that the conversation, like a boomerang, always comes back around to Christ's return. Now we have a chapter in which that subject is fully front and center. As I was deep in God's Word, researching the topic of what in the world we should do, I found that the Bible itself comes back to this topic over and over. In good times or bad times, God wants us to be alert concerning this issue, and never to fall asleep like negligent sentries on the tower of the fort. As we see our culture in decline, we know we are at war with the enemy; we need to be more vigilant than ever.

Read and reflect on Paul's words for us:

And do this, knowing the time, that now it is high time to awaken out of sleep; for now our salvation is nearer than when we first believed. The night is far spent, the day is at hand. Therefore let us cast off the works of darkness, and let us put on the armor of light. Let us walk properly, as in the day, not in revelry and drunkenness, not in lewdness and lust, not in strife and envy. But put on the Lord Jesus Christ, and make no provision for the flesh, to fulfill its lusts. (Romans 13:11–14)

In words terse and blunt, you might say that Paul's message is, *Live like you were dying.* That phrase was Tim McGraw's choice from the title song of one of his albums. In part, the lyrics are:

I loved deeper, and I spoke sweeter,
I gave forgiveness I'd been denying.
Someday I hope you get to live
Like you were dying.[7]

Meanwhile, Carnegie Mellon University Professor Randy Pausch was invited to be a speaker in an ongoing series asking thoughtful lecturers to assume they were giving their last presentation—to lecture as if they were dying. As it turned out, this was really the case with Pausch, who would be a victim of pancreatic cancer at forty-seven. He delivered an unforgettable talk that became a book with more than ten million readers, *The Last Lecture*.[8]

The country singer and the university professor hit a common chord: the importance of living on purpose, of moving through life with a sense of urgency based on something higher than the pursuit of pleasure. How much more should this apply to those of us who follow Christ?

If the church seems to be snoring through the fire alarm, it's not the first time. Listen to a few critical blasts from the past:

- "It has been a year of very limited spiritual fruitage, and great destitution; the church has fallen asleep."—Charles Brown, Midwestern evangelist[9]
- "I am sure I need not unroll a page of history and ask you to glance your eye down it except for a second; for again and again you will see it has occurred that the church has fallen asleep, and her ministers have become . . . destitute of zeal, having no ardent passion."—Charles Haddon Spurgeon[10]
- "It is not correct to say that the Church 'fell asleep' in

the last century, simply because it had never been awake."
—Henry Richard[11]

• "What is the present condition of the evangelical church? The bulk of Christians are asleep. I do not mean that the bulk of Christians who come to evangelical churches are not converted because if I meant that I would say they were dead and never had been born again. But I say they are asleep. It is possible to be morally asleep yet mentally, intellectually, physically and theologically alert. The present condition is that we are asleep."—A. W. Tozer[12]

In my last book, I quoted an observation by Vance Havner that bears repeating: "The devil has chloroformed the atmosphere of this age . . . we need to take down our 'Do not disturb' signs, snap out of our stupor, come out of our coma, and awake from our apathy."[13]

Tozer again: "God's alarm has been going off for years. Are we listening? Let's wake up—you and me!"[14] From the pages of Scripture, written so long ago, that alarm has never ceased. It calls us to snap out of the reverie of what to watch on TV tonight, where to find a good pizza. We can almost hear the voice of Jesus in the garden at night, imploring His disciples, "Watch and pray, lest you enter into temptation . . . Behold, the hour is at hand" (Matthew 26:40, 45).

Romans 13 offers four keys to resisting the seductiveness of this world.

We Are to Watch Vigilantly

First, Paul tells us that "now it is high time to awake out of sleep; for now our salvation is nearer than when we first believed" (Romans

13:11). In the golden days of radio, the thriller program called *Lights Out* always began with a voice intoning, "It . . . is . . . *later* . . . *than* . . . *you* . . . *think*," pronouncing each word in synchronization with the chimes of a clock.

In a less sensationalistic manner, Paul is saying just that. The word for *time* here is *kairos*, which refers to the kind or quality of time; a season or an opportunity. This is not the same as *chronos*, which is actual, chronological time. Time is the theme of this passage, as evidenced by five references to the subject.

Throughout the Bible we are admonished to know the times and the seasons. In the Old Testament, a group was appointed for the specific purpose of discerning the times: "the sons of Issachar who had understanding of the times, to know what Israel ought to do" (1 Chronicles 12:32).

That crucial task, "understanding the present time," is Paul's theme here. The present time is the age of salvation that has come in the person of Jesus Christ. Paul consistently sets a dividing point between this age, which began with Christ's first coming, and the age to come, which will be ushered in when He comes again (1 Corinthians 1:20; 2:6, 8; 3:18; 2 Corinthians 4:4; Galatians 1:4, 14; Ephesians 1:21; 1 Timothy 6:19; Titus 2:12; Matthew 12:32; and Hebrews 6:5).

Reckoning with the future is always a part of wisdom. Many of us hire financial planners to help us prepare for the future and manage our money in a way that will provide security and (if we are believers) glorify God through our giving. In any time or season, it's always wise to factor the future into our plans. But now, all the wires have been tripped in God's warning system and we're on red alert. We must increase our watchfulness.

On one occasion Jesus scolded His critics: "You know how to

discern the face of the sky, but you cannot discern the signs of the times" (Matthew 16:3). In other words, they watched for rain or for the setting sun, but not for spiritual signals. Today's technology lets us consult seven-day weather forecasts with reasonable accuracy. Doctors can predict that certain diseases may occur, even before they are manifest. Some even spend their lives compiling data on stars many light years distant, and forecast the life cycle of those stars. But all the while, we are remarkably blind to the workings of the Holy Spirit in our very lives. We are hypnotized by the rhythm of life and culture, as if this moment has no bearing on eternal reality.

Some laugh at the very suggestion of spiritual barometric readings. As we have seen, Peter encountered these mockers: "Scoffers will come in the last days, walking according to their own lusts, and saying, 'Where is the promise of His coming? For since the fathers fell asleep, all things continue as they were from the beginning of creation'" (2 Peter 3:3–4).

You've heard this just as I have. With more than a little smugness, the skeptics smile and say, "That hysteria has always been with us. Every decade someone opens his Bible and declares that the End Times are upon us. Funny how those same prophecies are so flexible they work in every generation. And still no Rapture."

The same kind of skepticism was expressed on the eve of the stock market and mortgage meltdowns. To be sure, there were voices telling us there would be terrible economic consequences to the way we were conducting our business. But they were laughed off as "economic doom prophets." Talk to the Wall Street gurus today and you'll see them wince a bit before quoting, "Past performance . . . is not a predictor of future performance."[15] Some lessons have to be learned the hard way.

The Imminence of Our Lord's Return

When we speak of the imminence of Christ's return, we're using the idea of time that Paul does—not chronological, but seasonal. We're not setting a date. We're speaking of the fact that all is in readiness, and there's no reason it couldn't happen today. Snow could be in the weather forecast, but no meteorologist would be able to tell you it would start falling on your yard at 3:15 in the afternoon. He could only tell you that it was imminent because all of the necessary conditions were in play for snow to arrive. With Christ, we're talking about prerequisites rather than precision.

I can identify with the frustration of Dr. Paul Kintner of Cornell University. He says his students "show a deep indifference" when he lectures about an event he and other reputable scientists at the US National Academy of Sciences deem imminent—a violent storm on the surface of the sun that "could conceivably be the worst natural disaster possible" on Earth—worse than even Hurricane Katrina. He adds, "It is terribly difficult to inspire people to prepare for a potential crisis that has never happened before and may not happen for decades to come."[16] Just because a highly probable event has not yet occurred is no guarantee that it will never happen.

Since NASA scientists are a pretty conservative group, if they are warning of a probable catastrophic geomagnetic storm occurring soon and without warning, there must be reason for concern.

One such solar storm, known as the Carrington Event, occurred in 1850, and it provides a cautionary note for us today. Just before daybreak on September 2 of that year, brilliant red, green, and purple auroras burst throughout the skies as far south as the tropics, which "produced enough light to rival the brightness of the sun itself."

Visually, the effect was awe-inspiring; pragmatically, there was chaos. The electric grid, such as it was at that time, was fried. Telegraph was the state of communication art at the time, and telegraph operators were shocked by flying sparks. Paper was set on fire and messages were sent even after machines were unplugged.

Scientists aren't comfortable with the implications of something like that happening in the context of today's technology. Everything from drinking water, fuel delivery, and ambient environmental controls like heating and cooling would be severely impacted. It is possible for sun storms to cause devastating results on Earth. NASA watches the skies for signs of supersolar flares that could create havoc throughout the world.[17]

Paul urges us to watch the skies for entirely different reasons. His idea of salvation, compared to our typical conception today, is like a widescreen HDTV picture compared to a wavy black-and-white one on a 1950s picture tube. We tend to simplistically think of salvation as a passing moment, the one when we accept Christ. Even then, we consider it to be a simple intellectual decision that affiliates us with a religion and serves as a simple ticket to heaven's gate—something to tuck away and forget about, like that life insurance policy or birth certificate.

Paul, on the other hand, uses a dynamic word for salvation that comes in three tenses—three dramatic dimensions. Past salvation is the moment when we say yes to Christ, are sealed by the Holy Spirit, and have our sins washed by the blood of Christ, with that debt declared paid in full, so that we are seated with Him in the heavenly places. And that's just the past part.

Present salvation is an ongoing growth process, as spiritual molecule by spiritual molecule we are conformed to the image of Christ through the redeeming work of the Holy Spirit. Through prayer and the Word, we learn to experience victory in Christ, issue by issue.

Then, most thrilling of all, there is a future salvation. That is the event Paul is describing in Romans 13 and elsewhere. There will be a day when we are finally freed from the presence of sin. As there can be no sin in heaven, no impurity in God's holy presence, it must finally be eliminated for good. We will see that happen, and I can't imagine how wonderful it will be.

This is threefold salvation. It began when I trusted Christ, and the penalty was removed. It continued as I began walking with the Lord, and more and more I learned how to be victorious over temptation and in trials. Salvation will be complete when Jesus takes me unto Himself in the future, when sin is judged and destroyed, and eternal life begins for us. And that day, Paul tells us, "is nearer than when we first believed."

No one could have a more prophetic name than me: *David Paul Jeremiah*. But I'm not a biblical prophet. Even so, reading this verse gets us all involved in prophecy. We are included in the whispers of heaven, telling us to stand by, something wonderful is in the wings . . . and objects in the biblical mirror are closer than they may appear.

The Incentive of Our Lord's Return

Our love for Christ is incentive enough for us to await His return. But Paul gives us more. He tells us that in light of these expectations, we have work to do: "Knowing the time, that now it is high time to awake out of sleep" (Romans 13:11).

We define sleep as the suspension of consciousness. It can also mean allowing one's alertness, vigilance, or attentiveness to lie dormant—the human body doing absolutely nothing. We could use some of the same language to describe today's church—the Christian body doing absolutely nothing. At least this is true concerning the matter of His return. The catastrophic events in our present day world seem to have little or no impact on our individual or collective sense of urgency.

Charles Spurgeon preached to Victorian England about the same problem: "You can sleep, but you cannot induce the devil to close his eyes . . . The prince of the power of the air keeps his servants well up to their work . . . if we could, with a glance, see the activities of the servants of Satan, we would be astonished at our own sluggishness."[18]

Paul wants to astonish us out of our sluggishness with his words of urgency. And once he has our attention, he tells us what to do: "Owe no one anything except to love one another, for he who loves another has fulfilled the law" (Romans 13:8). He follows with a summary of the Ten Commandments (Exodus 20). You may remember that the first four commandments tell us how to love God; the final six tell us how to love people. Here in Romans, Paul is emphasizing the final commandments—the relational ones. He concludes, as Christ does in the gospels, that love is the grand summation of them all.

Love, in other words, takes care of the bill. If you have it, you will owe none of those debts Paul says to avoid because if you love your neighbor, you won't steal from him or lie to him. Love is the grand shortcut to fulfilling God's commandments. The Old Testament system works on the basis of detailed restrictions: *Thou shalt not.* The gospel, however, offers a streamlined and proactive way to live. We don't have to worry so much about what we should *not* do because we are busy with what we *should*, which is one simple thing: love those we would ordinarily not love. Simple, yes, but radical and foreign to this world. As the Scottish preacher Alexander Maclaren puts it, we become "a new thing . . . a community held together by love and not by geographical accidents or linguistic affinities, or the iron fetters of the conqueror."[19]

What does this have to do with the second coming of Christ? Love is an incentive for making right choices under duress. The next time you're stuck in traffic, think, *Do I want to be honking my horn and shaking my fist at the instant I'm suddenly looking into the eyes of my Lord?* Paul is saying, "Get your relationships in order. He could be here before you finish reading this sentence." One writer stated it well: With every passing day, we "pitch our moving tent a day's march nearer home."[20]

We Are to War Valiantly

What else can we do? "The night is far spent, the day is at hand. Therefore let us cast off the works of darkness, and let us put on the armor of light" (Romans 13:12). Paul is about to make a rather aggressive point about the way you and I are to live our lives.

Put Off Darkness. When Paul tells us to *cast off* darkness, he chooses a decisive verb. It means to deliberately, purposefully, significantly, and permanently put aside the things of darkness. But what kind of darkness? He refers to the residue of the old, pre-Christian life; the difference between a child of God and the natural man, who is still walking in the shadow. By rights the old man should have no hold on us, but just the same, we fall into his patterns. We speak harsh words. We tell lies. We judge each other. We cannot stand each other's successes, and we often act like it is our duty to keep others in their place.

Paul is warning us that while Christ is accepted in a moment, sin remains our foe for a lifetime. We give in to the "little" temptations; we make a concession here, an exception there, and before we know it, we've conceded a great deal of authority to sin. We must put off darkness deliberately and purposefully, and do the same tomorrow and each day. Every victory of the redeemed will make us stronger while every concession draws us deeper into the slavery of sin.

Therefore, just as we are vigilant in watching for the return of Christ, like a guard on the wall, so must we be on constant guard against the encroachment of the old ways. We can't allow the devil to get his little toe into the door. The good news is that "the night is spent," as Paul poetically expresses it. "The day is at hand." The devil has played all his cards, and we have the victory of Christ on our side. As good soldiers, then, we buckle on the "armor of light" and prepare to make our stand.

Put on the Light. How do you put off the darkness of a room? That's easy—you flip a switch, and light makes darkness flee. There was no electricity in Paul's time, so he uses military language: "Put on the armor of light." This is the New Testament picture for walking in fellowship with God. "If we walk in the light as He is in the light, we have fellowship with one another" (1 John 1:7). Because we are saved, and indwelt by the Holy Spirit, we push back the assault of the rulers of darkness with the decisiveness of a great soldier.[21] In chaotic times, the battle rages wildly. More than ever we need to strap on that armor; more than ever we need to know our allies from our enemies. A soldier may stand on the wall, but he never sits on the fence.

About sitting on the fence: a new Barna research report suggests that three quarters of American Christians believe God is the "all powerful, all-knowing Creator of the Universe who rules the world today." So far, so good. The problems come when the subject turns to Jesus, Satan, and the Holy Spirit. Thirty-nine percent believe Jesus sinned during His time on earth, and 58 percent of Christians do not believe that the Holy Spirit is a living being. Strangely, nearly 60 percent don't believe Satan is real, while 64 percent believe that demons can affect us. Apparently demons are more believable to some people than the work of the living, indwelling Holy Spirit.

Consider also that one out of every three Christians believes the Bible and the Koran teach the same truths. We have to conclude that most of these have read neither book. Do you see now why we speak of the need for believers to wake up?[22]

I would say that the poll results suggest that we're not sitting on the fence at this point; we're helping the enemy tear down the fence entirely. Barna has concluded that American Christians tend to stretch the Bible to fit their everyday experiences. What we are called to do is to face our everyday experiences with the undiluted, uncompromised wisdom of the Word of God. We are soldiers, not defectors.

We Are to Walk Virtuously

Now we are ready for Paul's third admonition as we watch vigilantly and war valiantly; we must also walk virtuously. "Let us walk properly, as in the day, not in revelry and drunkenness, not in lewdness and lust, not in strife and envy" (Romans 13:13). Paul often lists traits, good and bad. Again, this list is not an exhaustive one. But it's enough to give a good indication of someone who is not walking in the light. We have two checkpoints here:

- *We are to reject public sins of the night.* "Drunkenness and revelry" is Paul's first category, and it's not difficult to understand what kind of sin he means: disorderly social behavior. Thinking of warfare again, Paul may have envisioned the soldier who goes into the city on leave and abuses alcohol. The next day, he is worthless to the army. Paul's message: "You're in the army now. Don't disgrace the uniform."

- *We are to renounce private sins.* What about who we are when no one is looking? Paul warns us against "lewdness and lust, strife and envy." These are usually the most dangerous sins of all because they hide in the human heart. We can't be held accountable by others for what they can't see, but we can become useless to God. The self-centered person becomes concerned with ego more than Christ, and ego can be defined as Edging God Out. Paul wants us to be aware of sin in its daily and nightly manifestations, its assaults from the inside and the outside.

We Are to Wait Victoriously

So far we've encountered a lot of soldierly discipline. Here's the payoff. All these things that Paul asks us to do are possible and positive. The strength and the strategy are both available to us—the strength through the Spirit, the strategy through the Word. Once we determine to live this way, we are happier, healthier, and far more productive.

But how do we get from where we are to where we want to be? Many Christians live in quiet defeat every day. Perhaps you would include yourself in that category. So many good people love the Lord, attend church regularly, and try to pray, all the while having a sense that there *must be more.* A. W. Tozer wrote about the spiritual craving people were feeling even in his time: "The hungry sheep look up, and are not fed. It is a solemn thing, and no small scandal in the Kingdom, to see God's children starving while actually seated at the Father's table."[23]

Maybe you're reading some of the chapters of this book while thinking, *Of course I would love to experience more of God, but I just don't ever seem to get there. My days are a series of small defeats, clusters of sin I can't overcome, and prayers that seem to bounce off the ceiling. Is there a way to get past the obstacles and live the kind of life you're describing?*

And the answer, as you might expect, is yes. Nobody has to live a disappointing Christian life. If you'll think about it, there are people we observe who are living in victory. We know it can be done because we've seen it—and we know that God is not partial in His dealings with men. This next section of Romans 13 gives us a genuine, hands-on strategy to live the kind of life we'd like to be living when Christ returns. Romans 13:14 has two calls to action. Read the verse again, and you'll see what they are: "Put on the Lord Jesus Christ, and make no provision for the flesh, to fulfill its lusts."

Yes, it's true that these steps are easier to talk through than walk through. How do you "put on Christ," and how do you "make no provision for the flesh"? Let's take them one at a time, and let me offer you an outlook that has helped me.

- *Putting on Christ.* Ray Stedman suggests this approach: "When I get up in the morning, I put on my clothes, intending them to be part of me all day, to go where I go and do what I do. They cover me and make me presentable to others. That is the purpose of clothes. In the same way, the apostle is saying to us, 'Put on Jesus Christ when you get up in the morning. Make Him a part of your life that day. Intend that he go with you everywhere you go, and that he act through you in everything you do. Call upon his resources. Live your life IN CHRIST.'"[24]

- *No Provision for Flesh.* What about the second warning? It concerns avoiding any temptation to gratify the desires of the flesh.

Harry Truman's biographer, David McCullough, recounts an example from Truman's life. The president was in the midst of talks with the USSR and Great Britain. The question at hand was what to do with postwar Germany, and there was great deal of anxiety and stress. After one really tough day, according to a Secret Service agent, Truman was ready to head back to his quarters. An Army public relations officer jauntily asked him for a ride. Truman, always the down-to-earth type, gave him a seat in the car. As a thank-you gesture, the stranger offered to get Truman anything he wanted from the city's thriving black market. He suggested a few of the products he dealt in: cigarettes, watches, whiskey, women—with a leering emphasis on that final one.

The smile was gone from President Truman's face. He replied, "Listen, son, I married my sweetheart. She doesn't run around on me, and I don't run around on her. I want that understood. Don't ever mention that kind of stuff to me again."

When they arrived at the yellow stucco house assigned for his use at the conference, Truman left the car with no further word to the now humbled officer.[25]

There's an old Native American saying that goes like this: "Call on God, but row away from the rocks." The idea is to put yourself in the best situation to succeed, and as far away as possible from the place of failure. Some people need to erase a few streets from their maps. Still others need to install software to protect their eyes from certain Internet destinations. When you're on a diet, you don't loiter at the ice cream parlor. That's what Paul means by making no provision for the flesh.

According to a *National Review Online* article, Americans rent eight hundred million pornographic videos and DVDs every year. A *vast majority* of men between the ages of eighteen to thirty-four frequent pornographic Web sites monthly. Among those addicted to pornography are a great number of people professing to be followers of Jesus Christ. We can only wonder if they've received the information that, according to research, pornography actually produces changes in the brains of users—changes that affect one's ability to give or receive genuine love.[26]

I find these facts extremely disheartening, even tragic. Don't you? So many children of God, blessed benefactors of the blood of Christ and the surpassing love of God, are choosing to hand themselves over to a new kind of slavery. We have the opportunity to walk in the light, but we wander off into dark alleys. We damage the precious minds God has given us, the very temples in which the Holy Spirit dwells.

The Bible tells us to run from four things: idolatry (1 Corinthians 10:14); youthful lusts (2 Timothy 2:22); materialism (1 Timothy 6:17) and sexual immorality: "Flee from sexual immorality. All other sins a man commits are outside his body, but he who sins sexually sins against his own body. Do you not know that your body is a temple of the Holy Spirit, who is in you, whom you have received from God? You are not your own; you were bought at a price. Therefore honor God with your body" (1 Corinthians 6:18–20 NIV).

Ray Stedman spells it out in language no one can misinterpret:

"'Flee immorality'—that is the advice everywhere in the Bible. Do not try to fight with it; do not try to overcome it; do not try to suppress it. Get away! These are subtle, powerful forces, and the widespread destruction we see in lives around us is simple testimony to the subtlety with which they can conquer us."[27]

The devil has a broad arsenal of weapons. But we are not helpless. We can strap on the armor of light (Ephesians 6), and Satan will flee. We can take simple steps to avoid the relentless temptations that are bearing down on us. Most of all, we can ask God to help us. The power of the cross is the most awesome force in the universe. Paul writes, "I have been crucified with Christ; it is no longer I who live, but Christ lives in me; and the life which I now live in the flesh I live by faith in the Son of God, who loved me and gave Himself for me" (Galatians 2:20).

Just knowing—*really* knowing—that Christ lives in you is half the battle. You can experience that power every single day. I'll never forget the first time I saw the film *The Passion of the Christ*. A group from our staff attended a premiere in Dallas. Like most people at that time, we had heard publicity and controversy about the film, and we had no idea what to expect. It was, of course, just a movie, and we'd seen any number of other movies about Jesus. In short, we were totally unprepared for the cinematic experience that was ours in that darkened church. I've spent much of my life studying the gospels, reading and praying and reflecting on the meaning of the Cross. But I had never seen it like this—not even close. We sat and watched a bloody, gory, graphic depiction of what the Lord endured for our sake.

Yes, we knew it was only a movie. We knew the blood was not real. None of that made any difference at all. God spoke to us in the very deep corners of our souls—places that hadn't before been touched in such an emotional way. It wasn't just the crucifixion, but the beatings, the spitting, and the pathetic mockery of Jesus. We were hearing the words in true Aramaic, as they were spoken two thousand years ago. I would never have thought any film could affect me so powerfully.

You may remember what movie theaters were like, all across our country, as the lights came on after that film—awed silence; stifled sobs. As we returned to California on the airplane, there was silence among us. We were each left to our private thoughts and reflections, processing what we had seen; talking to God about it. My own prayer was, "Lord, help me to live my life from this moment onward in such a way that I never do anything to hurt You or to break Your heart. Not after what You have done for me."

That's the power of the Cross, isn't it? It stands on that rock at Calvary, even today, casting its shadow across an entire planet, and across twenty centuries until it engulfs every one of us with its unquenchable power. To let ourselves experience that cross—to stand weeping before it with Mary and John and the centurion and millions of Christians through the ages—is to be radically and entirely changed from the inside out. To catch, even through a glass darkly, a fleeting glimpse of Christ and His incredible love for us, is to devote ourselves wholeheartedly to giving Him our lives in return.

In another movie from a few years ago, we cover a span of fifty years through a series of flashbacks. The four Ryan brothers have all bravely gone off to fight in World War II. When information surfaced that the other three brothers had died within days of one another, a senior official in Washington DC orders a special mission to bring Private James Ryan home from the front. Because Ryan's unit is listed as missing in action, it becomes a search mission, as well. Captain Miller assembles a seven-man rescue squad that succeeds in locating Ryan who refuses to leave his unit, despite the news of the death of his brothers. Most of the men on that mission lose their lives in the effort to save Ryan or in a subsequent battle between Ryan's unit and the enemy forces. As if holding Ryan responsible for the great sacrifice made on his behalf, the mortally wounded Captain Miller pulls the stunned private toward him and with his final breath says, "*James, earn* this—*earn* it!"

Then the scene flashes forward to the present where James Francis Ryan, now in his eighties, is seen paying homage at Captain Miller's grave at Omaha Beach in Normandy, France. Overcome with emotion and perhaps some guilt, he says to the grave marker, as if to Miller and the rest: "I hope . . . I've earned what all of you have done for me."[28]

We all know that no one could ever merit such a great sacrifice; no one could ever do enough to earn the incredible price of the gift of a rescued life. No gift is ever earned, especially the gift of life.

That is the truth about salvation as well; we can never earn it. There is zero mathematical possibility that a sinful life can ever, under any circumstances, make a good exchange for the one perfect and holy life that was ever lived; no way human blood can equate to the blood of God's Son. We can't earn it. But what we can do is to know what Christ has done in the past, to know He is with us right now, and to know that He is physically coming back soon. We know those things with our minds. But do we know them with our hearts? Or are we dozing?

A recent headline called the recent nuclear developments by North Korea and Iran a wake-up call to the world. Well, the world has had an endless series of wake-up calls over the past decade.

If we're not out of bed by now, we may be unconscious.

I believe Christians all over the world are wide awake and more aware of the times than we've ever been. As followers of Christ, we must be alert, watchful, and vigilant, with one eye on the headlines and the other on the eastern skies.

That's what Paul is shouting: "Awake! Awake! He's coming! Live every single moment for Him as if you knew this would be your last on earth and the sweet moment of reunion. Do nothing you wouldn't want to be doing when the Lord of the universe comes to claim His bride. The victory will be overwhelming—let's put on the armor of light and take our stand."

One More Thing

Now that we've finished our journey through these chapters, I would ask you to consider two conditions, and whether either has changed.

1. The condition of the world. How has it changed?
2. The condition of your spirit. How has it changed?

During my writing and your reading, our country may have completely turned itself around. There might be peace on earth, a thriving business climate, and a fresh housing boom. Somehow I doubt it—but I won't say it's impossible. We can agree, at least, that it's a big world in the hands of a big God. Who knows what He has in store?

You—on the other hand—now that's a different question. If you have seriously interacted with the biblical truths in this book, I really believe that you have become a different person. My prayer would be that you are more hopeful, realizing that our Lord's return is certain, and I believe, very soon. I would also hope you would be more eager to dig in at church and begin encouraging people; to approach God in prayer with a revitalized eagerness to know His touch; and to let your joy in Christ shine as a light during a time of so much darkness.

These are the most challenging days I've seen in the span of my life, and I would guess it's the same for you. But my faith has not been shaken by so much as a molecule of a mustard seed. I love and trust the Lord of this universe more than ever. The more wayward our society becomes, the darker our culture grows, the more attractive to me is the life and love of Jesus. More than anything in this world, I want others to see in Him what I see. Don't you agree with me? Never before have I felt such an urgency to get the Word out and to see spiritual revival among us.

If we're agreed on that point, let's cast aside our fear of the world out there and get to work. Let's go *light it up.* We need to walk through its streets, find the lonely and the frightened and the downtrodden, and tell them the good news their souls are yearning to hear. You ask what on earth should we do? Along with the ten specific action points I've suggested, I want to remind you of this absolutely critical one: *Share your faith.* There is such a hunger for it out there that you're going to be shocked to see that the world is more prepared than ever to hear about a God of hope.

Imagine the following scenario coming to pass: There is a great commotion in the streets of the city. From the heavens comes a sound of a thunderous fanfare, a blinding light envelops everything, and Christ is revealed in all His glory as the King of creation. He gathers all His children to His side, and when He comes to you, your hands are interlocked with those of a brand-new believer you've just that moment led to the Lord. In the absolute final second of this epoch, your friend's eternal destination has been sealed—not a half-second too soon. And imagine that this friend is one of many you've arranged to take with you to the home that Jesus has been preparing for us.

Let's make it happen just like that. We need only decide that we love Christ that much. Are you ready to get to work? Where on earth should we start?

What About *After* Earth?

What on earth should we do to live confidently in these chaotic days? In this book we've answered that question. We must be about our Father's business. As the day approaches, that business is more urgent than ever.

But let me propose another question; this one is personal. Actually, it's the same question I asked the listeners of our radio program *Turning Point* the day Chaplain Brad Borders heard it. *What's going to happen on the day you die? Have you made any plans for life after your life on earth is done?* God has certainly made plans for you, and He has sent you an engraved invitation. That invitation came in human form, as His only begotten Son, Jesus Christ. I hope and pray that you've accepted the invitation, that you've made Christ your Savior for eternity and your master for right now. But I want you to be certain about this issue.

You see, one of the symptoms of our troubled times is a tangled mess of confusion and misinformation on the things that really matter. People have a lot of ideas about heaven and salvation, and many of these ideas don't come from God's inspired Word. Therefore let's take a careful look at what's involved in identifying with Christ and having the assurance of salvation.

The Bible tells us that every one of us is a sinner. What that means is that all of us "miss the mark" of the perfection that God requires.

Every day, in many ways, we fail to live up to God's standard. Since He is holy and perfect, there can be no sin in His presence. Therefore, when it comes to being in heaven—the spiritual domain of His presence—we have a big problem. Our sin would make us ineligible to go there. Not only that, but we would have earned the penalty of death, which sin assures.

Our sin creates a barrier between God and His children. It would be insurmountable if God hadn't acted out of His love and compassion for our predicament. He sent His perfect Son, Jesus Christ, to this world. Jesus lived a life that showed us exactly how we should be living. Then, though He was completely without sin, He died on the cross, taking the punishment we had earned. You see, as He suffered and died, He voluntarily took all of our sin upon Himself. A perfect man took the punishment that sinful people had earned so that those people could be declared sinless and worthy to stand in God's presence someday.

That forgiveness begins immediately, on the sole condition that you accept His gift through faith. There is nothing you can do to earn that salvation; only accept it and identify with Christ. Then there is nothing you can do to lose it. The second you say yes to Christ, your sins are fully forgiven. The Holy Spirit enters your life, and from that moment on, He serves as your counselor and encourager. He will help to mold you to be more like Christ.

What, then, must you do to be saved? Simply pray to God and ask Him to forgive you of all your sins. Ask Christ to become your Lord and master, and then make a commitment to serve Him for the rest of your life. When you pray, you can use your own words—God knows your heart and simply asks you to be sincere. But you might say something like this: "Lord, I am a sinner. I own up to the fact that

I can never please You through my own efforts. Every day of my life I miss the mark. But I know that Your Son, Jesus Christ, died for me, in all His perfection, to pay the price of my sins. I accept His gift. I acknowledge His sacrifice on my behalf. And from this moment on, I identify with Him and will follow Him wholeheartedly, finding and doing His will for my life."

What will it feel like? Perhaps not much at all—not at first. This isn't about emotions, but about an act of your will. Though the moment may be very quiet, heaven will be rejoicing, and God will see you clothed in the perfection of Christ. You will be His child. Then, as you begin to read your Bible every day (the gospel of John is a great place to start), you will grow as a believer. Spend daily time in prayer, and find a church where the gospel is preached, the Bible is believed, and where the people are kind and caring.

We also want to be certain that you get off to the best possible start in following your Lord and Savior. If you need guidance or have questions, let us know at *Turning Point Ministries*:

P.O. Box 3838
San Diego, CA 92163

If you prayed to accept Christ, welcome to the family! You have begun a joyful life that will culminate in the wonderful reunion we've been describing, when Christ comes to take His children home. What a day of rejoicing that will be.

Notes

Introduction: Knowing the Signs

1. Fred R. Shapiro, ed., *Yale Book of Quotations* (New Haven, CT: Yale University Press, 2006), 206.
2. Renae Merle, "Wall Street's Final '08 Toll: $6.9 Trillion Wiped Out," *Washington Post*, 1 January 2009, www.washingtonpost.com/wp-dyn/content/article/2008/12/31/AR2008123101083.html (accessed 26 June 2009).
3. Luisa Kroll, Matthew Miller and Tatiana Serafin, "The World's Billionaires," *Forbes*, 11 March 2009, www.forbes.com/2009/03/11/worlds-richest-people-billionaires-2009-billionaires-intro.html (accessed 26 June 2009).
4. Emily Kaiser, "Update 2- US 2008 household wealth fell $11.2 trillion," *Reuters*, 12 March 2009, www.reutcrs.com/article/marketsNews/idUSN1237085520090312 (accessed 26 June 2009).
5. "Economic News Release," *Bureau of Labor Statistics*, 5 June 2009, Al Jazeera, www.bls.gov/news.release/empsit.nr0.htm (accessed 26 June 2009).
6. Dan Levy, "Foreclosure Filings in U.S. Jumped 30% in February" (Update 3), *Bloomberg.com*, 12 March 2009, www.bloomberg.com/apps/news?pid=20601103&sid=aUzNMbJ3CIII&refer=news (accessed 27 June 2009).
7. Jeannine Aversa, "Forecasters see higher U.S. unemployment this year; Canadian jobless rate set to rise," Associated Press, 23 February 2009, humantimes.com/articleaction/printnow/59007 (accessed 27 June 2009).

8. "A look at economic developments around the globe," Associated Press Archives, 12 March 2009. The complete article can be purchased via e-mail at ap@newsbank.com.

9. Simon Hooper, "Putin: Financial crisis is 'perfect storm,'" *CNN. com/world business*, 28 January 2009, cnn.com/2009/ BUSINESS/01/28/davos.wef.wedsnesday.wrap/index.html (27 June 2009).

10. "U.S. protests harassing of Navy ship by Chinese," Associated Press, *MSMBC.com*, 11 June 2009; www.msnbc.msn.com/ id/29596179 (accessed 11 June 2009); and "North Korea warned over nuclear move," One-Minute World News, *BBC.com*, 24 September 2008, news.bbc.co.uk/2/hi/asia-pacific/7634190.stm (accessed 27 June 2009).

11. Eric Talmadge and Anne Gearan, "US officials: North Korea may launch new missiles," Associated Press, 29 May 2009, www.google. com/hostednews/ap/article/ ALeqM5iURO8fOyWVOA0ytFlaAGuC9F7R9wD98G52L00 (accessed 27 June 2009).

12. Ibid., Hooper.

13. "Recent Earthquakes in California and Nevada: Index Map of Recent Earthquakes in California-Nevada," 18 May 2009, quake. usgs.gov/recenteqs (accessed 17 June 2009).

14. "Earthquake Fact and Statistics: Number of Earthquakes Worldwide for 2000–2009," neic.usgs.gov/neis/eqlists/eqstats.html (accessed 2 July 2009).

Chapter 1: Stay Calm

1. Based on personal conversations with friends in Beijing (RJM).

2. Marianne Bray, "Beijing to Shoot Down Olympic Rain," *CNN*, 9 June 2006, www.cnn.com/2006/WORLD/asiapcf/06/05/china.rain/ index.html (accessed 27 June 2009).

3. Leonard David, "U.S. Military Wants to Own the Weather," Space. com, 31 October 2005;www.Space.com/scienceastronomy/051031_ Mystery_Monday.html (accessed 1 July 2009).

4. Quoted in *Weather Warfare: the Military's Plan to Draft Mother*

Nature by Jerry E. Smith (Kempton, IL: Adventures Unlimited Press, 2006), i.

5. Michel Chossedovsky, "Weather Warfare," *The Ecologist,* 22 May 2008, globalresearch.ca/articles/haarpecologist.pdf (accessed 27 June 2009).

6. Pam Belluck, "Recession Anxiety Seeps Into Everyday Lives," *New York Times,* 9 April 2009, page A1; Steven Reinberg, "Anti-Anxiety Medications Online," *Anti-anxiety Medications.org,* 10 June 2008, www.antianxietymedications.org/15-million-americans-suffer-from-social-anxiety-disorder.html (accessed 27 June 2009).

7. Paul Tournier, *A Place for You,* (New York: Harper and Row, 1968), 9.

8. Hyde Flippo, "Ludwig II: The Swan King and His Castles," *The German Way & More.com,* www.german-way.com/ludwig.html (accessed 27 June 2009).

9. C. S. Lewis, *The Problem of Pain,* The Complete C.S. Lewis Signature Classics (New York: HarperOne, 2002), 639–640.

10. "Part 2: Down but Not Out," *Time,* 2 December 1991, www.time.com/time/magazine/article/0,9171,974392,00.html?iid=chix-sphere (accessed 27 June 2009).

11. *General MacArthur Speeches and Reports 1908-1964,* Edward T. Imparato, ed. (Nashville, TN: Turner Publishing Company, 2000), 126.

12. William Barclay, *The Gospel of John, Vol. 2,* (Philadelphia, PA: Westminster Press, 1975), 157.

13. "Summary of Key Findings and Statistics on Religion in America," *Report 1: Religious Alliliation, Pew Research Center Publications,* 23 June 2008, religions.pewforum.org/reports (accessed 16 June 2009), and "Many Americans Say Other Faiths Can Lead to Eternal Life," *Pew Research Center Publications,* 18 December 2008, pewresearch.org/pubs/1062/many-americans-say-other-faiths-can-lead-to-eternal-life (accessed 27 June 2009).

14. Christianity Today Poll, 27 March 2009, www.christianitytoday.com/ct/features/poll.html (accessed 27 March 2009).

15. Ruthanna Metzger, "It's Not in the Book!" *Eternal Perspective Ministries,* www.epm.org/artman2/publish/salvation/It_s_Not_in_the_Book.shtml (accessed 27 June 2009).

16. Mark Twain, editorial in *Hartford Courant*, 1897. See also Ralph Keyes, *The Quote Verifier* (New York: Macmillan, 2006), 243.

Chapter 2: Stay Compassionate

1. "An All-Star True Story, The Ami Ortiz 'Uvdah Interview' Channel 8 (Israel)," 2 March 2009. Transcript at www.amiortiz.com/ (accessed 9 June 2009).

2. Ibid., Ami Ortiz.com, "Leah's Updates."

3. "Starbucks Customers Pay It Forward 109 Times," *KCRA.com*, Sacramento, CA, 24 November 2008, www.kcra.com/cnn-news/18052349/detail.html (accessed 28 June 2009).

4. "To Benjamin Webb," *The Writings of Benjamin Franklin*: 1783–1788, ed., Albert Henry Smyth (New York: The Macmillan Company, 1907), 197.

5. Philip Yancey, "A Surefire Investment," *Christianity Today.com*, 3 February 2009, www.christianitytoday.com/ct/2009/january/29.80.html (accessed 28 June 2009).

6. Shannon Ethridge, "Why Didn't He Hate Me?" *Campus Life IGNITE*, February 2008, www.christianitytoday.com/cl/2008/001/10.44.html (accessed 27 June 2009).

7. Henry Wadsworth Longfellow, *The Prose Works of Henry Wadsworth Longfellow* (New York: Houghton, Mifflin and Company, 1890), 405.

8. Henri J. M. Nouwen, *The Way of the Heart* (New York: Harper One, 1991), 34.

9. Paul L. Maier, *Eusebius: The Church History* (Grand Rapids: Kregel, 1999), 269.

10. C. S. Lewis, *Mere Christianity* in The Complete C.S. Lewis Signature Classics (New York: HarperOne, 2002), 110-111.

11. From Joel C. Rosenberg, *Inside the Revolution* (Carol Stream, IL: Tyndale, 2009), 363–368.

12. *Christian History & Biography Magazine*, Issue 82, Spring 2004, 13.

13. Roy Anthony Borges, "Love Your Enemies: One Prisoner's Story of Risky Obedience," *Discipleship Journal*, Issue 107, 42–43.

Chapter 3: Stay Constructive

1. Cathy Lynn Crossman, "An inaugural first: Obama acknowledges 'non-believers,'" *USA Today*, 22 January 2009, www.usatoday.com/news/religion/2009-01-20-obama-non-believers_N.htm (accessed 27 June 2009).

2. Stephen Ambrose, *Citizen Soldiers: The U. S. Army from the Normandy Beaches to the Bulge to the Surrender of Germany* (New York: Simon & Schuster, 1998), 471–472.

3. Eugene H. Peterson, *The Message: The New Testament in Contemporary Language* (Colorado Springs, CO: Navpress, 1993), 2171.

4. "Kurt Vonnegut's Rules for Writing a Poem." *Improv Encyclopedia. org*, improvencyclopedia.org/references/Kurt_Vonnegut's_Rules_for_Writing_a_Poem.html (accessed 28 June 2009).

5. Erwin Raphael McManus, *An Unstoppable Force: Daring to Become the Church God Had in Mind* (Loveland, CO: Group Publishing, 2000), 29–31.

6. Nicole Johnson, *The Invisible Woman: When Only God Sees* (Thomas Nelson, 2005), 31, 41, passim.

7. Jonathan Edwards, *The Works of Jonathan Edwards, Vol. I*, www.*ccel.org*/ccel/edwards/works1.ix.iv.html?highlight=mysticism#highl ight (accessed 28 June 2009).

8. "Survey Describes the Spiritual Gifts That Christians Say They Have," *Barna.org*, 9 February 2009, www.barna.org/barna-update/article/12-faithspirituality/211-survey-describes-the-spiritual-gifts-that-christians-say-they-have (accessed 28 June 2009).

9. Dr. Robert McNeish, "Lessons from Geese," Northminster Presbyterian Church, Reisterstown, MD, 1972, suewidemark.com/lessonsgeese.htm (accessed 28 June 2009).

Chapter 4: Stay Challenged

1. Compiled from www.vt.edu/remember/biographies/liviu_librescu.html and "Holocaust survivor sacrificed himself to save students," www.abc.net.au/news/newsitems/200704/s1899900.htm (accessed 28 June 2009).

2. Geoffrey T. Bull, *When Iron Gates Yield* (London: Pickering & Inglis, 1976), 199–223.

3. Madeleine Brand and Howard Berkes, "China Celebrates Opening of Summer Olympics," *NPR.org*, 8 August 2008, www.npr.org/templates/story/story.php?storyId=93420251 (accessed 28 June 2009).

4. R. C. Sproul, *Knowing Scripture* (Downers Grove, IL: InterVarsity Press, 2009), 31.

5. Louis A. Barbieri, Jr., *First and Second Peter* (Chicago, IL: Moody Press, 1998), 97.

6. Sabina Wurmbrand, transcribed by her granddaughter, Andrea Wurmbrand, "In God's Beauty Parlor," transcript members.cox.net/wurmbrand/godsbeautyparlor.html (accessed 28 June 2009). See also Todd Nettleton, "Sabina Wurmbrand," *Banner of Truth Trust*, "In The News," www.banneroftruth.org/pages/news/2000/08/sabina_wurmbrand.php (accessed 28 June 2009).

Chapter 5: Stay Connected

1. "Google search finds missing child,"*BBC.Com*/News, 9 January 2009, news.bbc.co.uk/2/hi/technology/7820984.stm (accessed 28 June 2009). See also George Barnes and Danielle Williamson, "Athol woman and granddaughter found in Virginia," *Telegram & Gazette Staff* (Worcester, MA), 7 January 2009, www.telegram.com/article/20090107/NEWS/901070289/1116 (accessed 28 June 2009).

2. Steven Johnson, "How Twitter Will Change the Way We Live," *Time*, 5 June 2009, www.time.com/time/business/article/0,8599,1902604,00.html (accessed 28 June 2009).

3. Ibid., Schaffner.

4. Michael Paulson, "Here's the church, but where are the people?" *The Boston Globe*, boston.com, 15 June 2008, www.boston.com/news/local/articles/2008/06/15/heres_the_church_but_where_are_the_people/ (accessed 28 June 2009).

5. "Southern Baptists and Catholics join US church decline trend," *Ekklesia, News Brief*, 2 March 2009, www.ekklesia.co.uk/node/8828 (accessed 28 June 2009).

6. Robert D. Putnam, *Bowling Alone: The Collapse and Revival of American Community* (New York: Simon and Schuster, 2001), 72.

7. Charles Colson, *Being the Body* (Nashville: Thomas Nelson, 2003), 19.

8. Paul Vitello, "Bad Times Draw Bigger Crowds to Churches," *New York Times.com*, 14 December 2008, www.nytimes.com/2008/12/14/nyregion/14churches.html (accessed 28 June 2009).

9. Leonard Sweet, *11: Indispensable Relationships You Can't Be Without*, (Colorado Springs, CO: David C. Cook, 2008), 23.

10. Ed Bahler and Bill Coucenour, "Created to Connect," *Your Church*, January/February 2009, 56.

11. Personal Lecture Notes: "The Trinity," Dr. Russell Moore, Southern Seminary.

12. Nina Ellison, *Mama John: The Lifelong Missionary Service of Mary Saunders* (Birmingham, AL: New Hope, 1996), 8.

13. Joel C. Rosenberg, *Inside the Revolution* (Carol Stream, IL: Tyndale House, 2009), 417.

14. Dave Anderson, "At Last, Jackson Is 'The Straw That Stirs the Drink,'" *New York Times on the Web*, 30 June 1980, www.nytimes.com/specials/baseball/yankees/nyy-rotb-jackson.html (accessed 28 June 2009).

15. Alvin J. Schmidt, *How Christianity Changed the World* (Grand Rapids: Zondervan, 2001, 2004), 157–158.

16. Phillip Yancey, *Reaching for the Invisible God*, (Grand Rapids, MI: Zondervan Publishing, 2000), 170.

17. Ted W. Engstrom, *The Fine Art of Friendship* (Nashville: Thomas Nelson, 1985), 131–132.

18. Clive Anderson, *Travel with CH Spurgeon: In the Footsteps of the Prince of Preachers* (Epson, Surry UK: Day One Publications, 2002), 16.

19. Robert J. Morgan, *Nelson's Complete Book of Stories, Illustrations and Quotes* (Nashville: Thomas Nelson, 2000), 127.

20. "Go to Church," *The Lutheran Pioneer*, May 1907, (St. Louis: Evangelical Lutheran Synodical Conference, May 1907.

Chapter 6: Stay Centered

1. Raja Abdulrahim and Jessica Garrison, "Friends speak up for L.A. journalists held by N. Korea," *Los Angeles Times*, 11 June 2009, www.latimes.com/news/local/la-me-korea-ling-lee11-2009jun11,0,7875895.story (accessed 28 June 2009).

2. Jae-Soon Chang and Kwang-tae Kim, "NKorea steps up rhetoric amid nuclear crisis," Associated Press, Yahoo! News, 9 June 2009, www.news.yahoo.com/s/ap/20090609/ap_on_re_as/as_koreas_nuclear (accessed 1 July 2009).

3. "Fax Threaten VOM Project," *PersecutionBlog.com*, 11 June 2009, www.persecutionblog.com/ (accessed 28 June 2009).

4. "World Watch 2009," *Open Doors.org.*, January 2009, www.opendoorsusa.org/content/view/432/ (accessed 28 June 2009).

5. "North Korean Christians Question Regime's Claims," *ReligionNewsBlog.com*, 27 April 2009, www.religionnewsblog.com/23425 (accessed 28 June 2009).

6. Ibid.

7. James Hill and Jaime Hennessey, "Kevin Everett: 'He Is a Tiger,'" *ABC News.com*, 31 January 2008, abcnews.go.com/Health/story?id=4216671&page=1 (accessed 28 June 2009).

8. R. G. Bratcher and E. A. Nida, *A Handbook on Paul's Letters to the Colossians and to Philemon*. Originally published as *A Translator's Handbook on Paul's Letters to the Colossians and to Philemon: Helps for Translators*. UBS handbook series (74) (New York: United Bible Societies, 1977).

9. John Phillips, *Exploring Colossians and Philemon: An Expository Commentary* (Grand Rapids: Kregel Publications, 2002),159, 163.

10. Vance Havner, *Vance Havner Quotebook*, Denis J. Hester, comp. (Grand Rapids: Baker Book House, 1986), 29.

11. *The Ante Nicene Fathers, Volume 1: Apostolic Fathers*, "The Epistle of Mathetes to Diognetus," chapter 2.

12. "Oath of Allegiance for Naturalized Citizens," *About.com*, immigration.about.com/od/uscitizenship/a/AllegianceOath.htm (accessed 28 June 2009).

13. Ibid., Bratcher.

14. Bob Laurent, *Watchman Nee: Man of Suffering* (Uhrichsville, OH: Barbour Publishing, Inc, u.d.), 67–68.

15. Charles Spurgeon, "Death and Its Sentence Abolished," 15 January 1899, www.spurgeon.org/sermons/2605.htm (accessed 28 June 2009).

16. Charles Swindoll, *The Tale of the Tardy Oxcart* (Nashville, TN: Word, 1998), 77.

17. John Ortberg, *Faith and Doubt* (Grand Rapids, MI: Zondervan, 2008), 84–85.

18. Robert J. Morgan, *From This Verse* (Nashville: Thomas Nelson, 1998), installment for July 4. See also Richard S. Greene, "Where Will the Money Come From?" *Decision Magazine*, May 1997, 32–33.

19. Geoffrey Thomas, *Reading the Bible* (Carlisle, PA: The Banner of Truth Trust, 1995), 10.

20. Rebecca K. Grosenbach, "A Holy Pursuit," *Inside Story*, Navigators. org, March 2009, www.navigators.org/us/view/one-to-one_mr/2009/mar09/items/inside-story (accessed 28 June2009).

21. Jerry Bridges, *Trusting God* (Colorado Springs, CO: NavPress, 2008) 7, 14, 16.

22. Helen H. Lemmel, "Turn Your Eyes upon Jesus,"1922, *Cyberhymnal.org*, www.cyberhymnal.org/htm/t/u/turnyour.htm (accessed 28 June 2009).

23. Randy Alcorn, *The Treasure Principle* (Sisters, OR: Multnomah Press, 2001), 42–43.

24. Ibid.

25. Viktor E. Frankl, *Man's Searching for Meaning* (Boston: Beacon Press, 1992), 48–52.

26. G. Campbell Morgan, "The Fixed Heart in the Day of Frightfulness" in *The Shadow of Grace—The Life and Meditations of G. Campbell Morgan*, Richard Morgan, Howard Morgan and John Morgan, comp. and ed. (Grand Rapids, MI: Baker Books, 2007), 76.

Chapter 7: Stay Confident

1. See video of the 29 September 2008 interview www.youtube.com/watch?v=PHH2JItePlc&feature=PlayList&p=0AD448945A54A8B9&

playnext=1&playnext_from=PL&index=9. Transcribed by the author (accessed 28 June 2009).

2. Stephen Thompson, "Is There A God?" *A. V. Club.com*, 9 October 2002, www.avclub.com/articles/is-there-a-god,1413/ (accessed 28 June 2009).

3. Dan Gilgoff, "Bobby Jindal's Come-to-Jesus Writings," *U.S. News. com*, 24 February 2009, www.usnews.com/blogs/god-and-country/2009/2/24/bobby-jindals-come-to-jesus-writings.html (accessed 28 June 2009).

4. Winne Hu, "In a New Generation of College Students, Many Opt for the Life Examined," *New York Times*, 6 April 2008, www.nytimes.com/2008/04/06/education/06philosophy.html (accessed 28 June 2009).

5. Beth Moore, *Voice of the Faithful* (Nashville, TN: Thomas Nelson, 2005), 39–40.

6. "Titanic Memorandum", National Archives and Record Administration: American Originals, www.archives.gov/exhibits/american_originals/titanic.html (accessed 28 June 2009).

7. Thomas Watson, "A Body of Divinity," *Puritanism Today*, puritanismtoday.wordpress.com/theologians-preaching-and%20-%20preachers/ (accessed 28 June 2009).

8. Told by M. R. De Haan, MD, quoted at www.preceptaustin. org/2_timothy_42.htm (accessed 28 June 2009).

9. Rob Suggs, *It Came from Beneath the Pew* (Downers Grove, IL: InterVarsity Press, 1989).

10. J. Sidlow Baxter, *The Master Theme of the Bible, Part One: The Doctrine of the Lamb* (Wheaton: Tyndale House Publishers, Inc., 1985), 19.

11. Arthur T. Pierson, *Many Infallible Proofs: The Evidences of Christianity, Volume One* (Grand Rapids: Zondervan Publishing House, 1886), 90.

12. Jill Morgan, *A Man of the Word: Life of G. Campbell Morgan* (Grand Rapids: Baker, 1972), 38–41.

13. Henry F. Schaefer III, *Science and Christianity: Conflict or Coherence?* (Athens, GA: The University of Georgia Press, 2003), passim.

14. John Steinbeck, *Travels with Charley* (New York: Penguin Classics, 1997), 60–61.
15. R. Kent Hughes, *Luke* (Wheaton, IL: Crossway Books, 1998), 145–149.
16. Amy Carmichael, *Edges of His Ways* (Fort Washington, PA: Christian Literature Crusade, 1998), 41.
17. Corrie Ten Boom with Elizabeth and John Sherrill, *The Hiding Place* (New York: Bantam Books, 1974), 130, 134–135.
18. Ibid., 194.

Chapter 8: Stay Consistent

1. "Couple: County Trying to Stop Home Bible Studies," *10 News.com*: San Diego News, www.10news.com/news/19562217/detail.html (accessed 28 June 2009).
2. Rob Suggs, *Top Dawg: Mark Richt and the Revival of Georgia Football* (Nashville: Thomas Nelson, 2008), 5.
3. V. Raymond Edman, *They Found the Secret* (Grand Rapids: Zondervan, 1960), Chapter 1.
4. Eugene Peterson, *A Long Obedience in the Same Direction: Discipleship in an Instant Society* (Downers Grove, IL: InterVarsity Press, 1980).
5. Cartoonist Rob Portlock in *Leadership*, Vol. 13, no. 3.
6. Marjorie Howard, "Consistently Caring," *Tufts Journal,* January 2008, tuftsjournal.tufts.edu/archive/2008/january/corner/index.shtml (accessed 1 July 2009).
7. Danielle Bean, "Amazing Adoption Story," *Faith and Family Live!* 13 November 2008, view video at www.faithandfamilylive.com/blog/amazing_adoption_story (accessed 28 June 2009).
8. Omar El Akkad, "This Is Your Brain on Religion," (Toronto) *Globe and Mail,* 5 March 2009. The complete article may be purchased at GlobeandMail.com. See also Jenny Green, "Religious brains more calm in face of anxiety: study," *Calgary Herald.com*, Canwest News Service, 4 March 2009, www.calgaryherald.com/Life/Religious+brains+more+calm+face+anxiety+study/1354346/story.html (accessed 28 June 2009).

9. Dorothy Fields, "Pick Yourself Up," (© 1936) at lyricsplayground. com/alpha/songs/p/pickyourselfup.shtml (accessed 1 July 2009).

10. Frank Houghton, *Amy Carmichael of Dohnavur* (London: S.P.C.K. 1959, distributed by Christian Literature Crusade, Fort Washington, PA, 1959), 115, 357, and passim.

11. Charles Swindoll, *Rise and Shine* (Portland, OR: Multnomah Press, 1989), 169. See also Martin Hodgson, "Christian driver refuses to board bus carrying atheist slogan," The Guardian, 17 January 2009, www.guardian.co.uk/world/2009/jan/17/atheist-bus-campaign (accessed 29 June 2009).

12. "Man refuses to drive 'no God' bus," *BBC News/UK*, 16 January 2009, news.bbc.co.uk/2/hi/uk_news/england/hampshire/7832647. stm (accessed 28 June 2009).

Chapter 9: Stay Committed

1. Duncan Greenberg and Tatiana Serafin, "Up in Smoke," *Forbes. com*, 30 March 2009, www.forbes.com/forbes/2009/0330/076-up-in-smoke.html (accessed 28 June 2009).

2. Ibid.

3. Carter Doughtery, "Town Mourns Typical Businessman Who Took Atypical Risks," *New York Times.com*: World Business, www. nytimes.com/2009/01/13/business/worldbusiness/13merckle. html?_r=1&ref=business (accessed 28 June 2009).

4. William Boston, "Financial Casualty: Why Merckle Killed Himself," *Time*, 6 January 2009, www.time.com/time/business/ article/0,8599,1870007,00.html (accessed 28 June 2009).

5. Ibid., Doughtery.

6. Timothy Martin and Kevin Helliker, "Real-Estate Executive Found Dead in Apparent Suicide," *Wall Street Journal*, 7 January 2009, online.wsj.com/article/SB123127267562558295.html (accessed 28 June 2009).

7. "Sale ordered of Marcus Schrenker's home, plane," Associated Press, Noblesville, Indiana, *The Herald Bulletin*, 2 June 2009, www. theheraldbulletin.com/local/local_story_153205807.html/ resources_printstory (accessed 28 June 2009).

8. Mike Whitney, "Financial Markets and Economic Crash, the Next Leg Down Will Be Worse," *Market Oracle.com*, 26 May 2009, www.marketoracle.co.uk/index.php?name=News&file=article&sid=10904 (accessed 28 June 2009).

9. John Horgan, "The California dream is on life support," *San Mateo County Times*, 26 May 2009, Inside Bay Area.com, www.insidebayarea.com/sanmateocountytimes/localnews/ci_12453299 (accessed 28 June 2009).

10. Karen Garloch, "Economic hard times may be fueling rise in suicide attempts," *Charlotte Observer*, 27 May 2009, www.charlotteobserver.com/597/story/747127.html?storylink=omni_popular (accessed 28 June 2009).

11. "Buffett Says Five Years for Economy to Recover," *Sydney Morning Herald*, 19 March 2009, www.midasletter.com/news/09031906_Buffett-says-five-years-for-economy-to-recover.php (accessed 28 June 2009).

12. Steven Erlanger and Stephen Castle, "European Leader Assails American Stimulus Plan," *New York Times.com*, 25 March 2009, www.nytimes.com/2009/03/26/world/europe/26czech.html (accessed 28 June 2009).

13. Robert J. Morgan, *Nelson's Complete Book of Stories, Illustrations & Quotes* (Nashville, TN: Thomas Nelson, 2000), 600_601.

14. "William Carey: Father of modern Protestant missions," *Christianity Today.com*, Christian History, 8 August 2008, www.christianitytoday.com/ch/131christians/missionaries/carey.html (accessed 28 June 2009).

15. Eugene Myers Harrison, "Adoniram Judson," www.reformedreader.org/rbb/judson/ajbio.htm (accessed 28 June 2009).

16. Robert Stuart MacArthur, *Quick Truths in Quaint Texts: Second Series* (Philadelphia: American Baptist Publication Society, 1870), 172.

17. Don Aycock, *Living by the Fruit of the Spirit* (Grand Rapids, MI: Kregel Publications, 1999), 54.

18. Hamilton Smith, ed., *Gleanings from the Past, Vol.3* (London: Central Bible Truth Depot, 1915), www.stempublishing.com/authors/smith/WATSON.html (accessed 28 June 2009).

19. Robert J. Morgan, *Moments for Families with Prodigals* (Colorado Springs: NavPress, 2003), 101.

20. "When Will Jesus Return?" *Pew Research Center Publications*, 9 April 2009, pewresearch.org/pubs/1187/poll-christians-jesus-second-coming-timing (accessed 28 June 2009).

21. Charles Wentworth Upham, *George Washington, The Life of General Washington: First President of the United States, Vol. II*, (London: National Illustrated Library, 1852), 181.

22. "Seed Germination," *Washington State University*, gardening.wsu.edu/library/vege004/vege004.htm (accessed 28 June 2009).

23. Alfred Edersheim, *The Life and Times of Jesus the Messiah* (Hendrickson Publishers, Inc., 1993) 119–120.

24. Kevin Miller, "The End of the World As We Know It," *Preaching Today*, www.preachingtoday.com/sermons/sermons/endoftheworldasweknowit.html (accessed 28 June 2009).

25. Stephen Charnock, *The Existence and Attributes of God* (Grand Rapids: Baker Books, 1996; originally published in 1853), 278, 279, 281.

26. David Dunlap, "Eternity of God," *Bible & Life Bible Teaching Newsletter*, 1 January 2000, www. peter.sff.home.insightbb.com/bibleandlife_2000_1.htm (accessed 1 July 2009).

27. Linda Derby, *Life's Sticky Wicks* (working title/unpublished manuscript), 20.

28. W. E. Sangster, *The Pure in Heart*, cited in William Sykes, ed., *The Eternal Vision—The Ultimate Collection of Spiritual Quotations* (Peabody, MA: Hendrickson Publishers, Inc., 2002), 315.

29. *Perfect Illustrations for Every Topic and Occasion, Preaching Today. com* (Wheaton, IL: Tyndale House Publishers, 2002), 97.

Chapter 10: Stay Convinced

1. Eiten Haber, "World War III has started," *Ynet News Opinion*, Ynetnews.com, 27 May 2009, www.ynetnews.com/articles/0,7340,L-3722339,00.html (accessed 28 June 2009).

2. Con Coughlin, "N. Korea helping Iran with nuclear testing," Telegraph.co.uk, 25 January 2007, www.telegraph.co.uk/news/

worldnews/1540429/N-Korea-helping-Iran-with-nuclear-testing. html (accessed 28 June 2009).

3. Sandra I. Erwin and Stew Magnuson, "7 Deadly Myths About Weapons of Terror," *National Defense Magazine,* June 2009, www. nationaldefensemagazine.org/ARCHIVE/2009/JUNE/ Pages/7Deadly.aspx (accessed 2 June 2009).

4. "Former Russian official says 100 portable bombs missing," AP, *Lubbock Avalanche-Journal,* 5 September 1997, www. lubbockonline.com/news/090597/LA0759.htm (accessed 2 June 2009). And Richard Miniter, *Disinformation* (Washington, DC: Regnery Publishing, 2005), especially "Myth #17: Suitcase Nukes are a Real Threat," 135ff.

5. Elizabeth Zolotukhini, "The Loose Russian Nukes,"GlobalSecurity. org, Sitrep Situation, 19 May 2009, sitrep.globalsecurity.org/articles/ 090519345-the-loose-russian-nukes.htm (accessed 28 June 2009).

6. Ibid., "7 Deadly Myths About Weapons of Terror."

7. "Live Like You Were Dying", words and music by James Timothy Nichols and Craig Michael Wiseman. © 2004 Warner-Tamerlane Publishing and Big Loud Shirt. ASCAP/BMI. All rights reserved.

8. *ABC News.go.com,* abcnews.go.com/GMA/LastLecture (accessed 28 June 2009).

9. "The Iowa Band," en.wikipedia.org/wiki/Iowa_Band (accessed 10 April 2009).

10. Charles Spurgeon, "A Bright Light in Deep Shades," *The Metropolitan Tabernacle Pulpit, Vol. XVIII* (London: Passmore & Alabaster, 1873), 270.

11. Henry Richard, *Letters and Essays on Wales* (1884) Internet Archive/Texts, www.archive.org/stream/lettersessaysonw00richiala/ lettersessaysonw00richiala_djvu.txt (accessed 28 June 2009).

12. A. W. Tozer (1897–1963), "Causes of a Dozing Church," *Tozer Devotional: Rut, Rot or Revival,* www.cmalliance.org/devotions/ tozer/tozer.jsp?id=328 (accessed 28 June 2009).

13. Vance Havner, *In Times Like These* (Old Tappan, NJ: Fleming H, Revell Company, 1969), 29, as quoted in David Jeremiah, *What in the World Is Going On?* (Nashville: Thomas Nelson, 2008), 232.

14. Ibid., Tozer.

15. Larry E. Swedroe, *What Wall Street Doesn't Want You to Know: How You Can Build Real Wealth* (New York: Macmillan, 2004), 11.

16. Michael Brooks, "Space storm alert: 90 seconds from catastrophe," *New Scientist.com*, 23 March 2009, www.newscientist.com/article/ mg20127001.300-space-storm-alert-90-seconds-from-catastrophe. html?full=true (accessed 28 June 2009).

17. "A Super Solar Flare," *NASA*, Science, NASA.gov, 6 May 2008, science.nasa.gov/headlines/y2008/06may_carringtonflare.htm (accessed 28 June 2009).

18. Charles Haddon Spurgeon, *The Metropolitan Tabernacle Pulpit: Sermons Preached and Revised, "Wake Up! Wake Up!"* (London: Passmore & Alabaster, 1879), 657.

19. Alexander Maclaren, *The Gospel According to St. John* (New York: A. C. Armstrong and Son, 1908), 228.

20. James Montgomery, "Forever with the Lord", *Poet's Portfolio*, 1835, Cyberhymnal.com. www.nethymnal.org/htm/f/w/fwithlor.htm (accessed 28 June 2009).

21. John Phillips, *Experiencing Romans,* (Chicago: Moody Press, 1969), 231.

22. "Most America Christians Do Not Believe that Satan or the Holy Spirit Exist," *Barna Research Group Update*, 13 April 2009, www. barna.org/barna-update/article/12-faithspirituality/260-most-american-christians-do-not-believe-that-satan-or-the-holy-spirit-exis (accessed 28 June 2009).

23. A. W. Tozer, *The Pursuit of the Holy* (Rockville, MD: 2008), front matter.

24. Ray Stedman, *From Guilt to Glory,* Volume 21 (Waco, TX: Word, 1978), 136.

25. David McCullough, *Truman* (New York: Simon & Schuster, 1992), 435.

26. Mona Charen, "'Tis the Season for Porn," *National Review Online*, 19 December 2008, article.nationalreview.com/?q=ZDkxN2NmO DI1NjE0OTNiZTI4MTNiMDRkZGY4MjI4Mzc= (accessed 28 June 2009).

27. Ray Stedman, *Expository Studies in I Corinthians: The Deep Things of God* (Waco, TX: Words Books, 1981), 130–131.

28. "Memorable Quotes for Saving Private Ryan," www.imdb.com/title/tt0120815/quotes (accessed 28 June 2009).

THREE
GREAT WAYS TO FURTHER YOUR STUDY

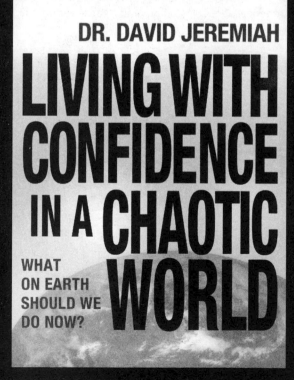

FROM THE *NEW YORK TIMES* BEST-SELLING AUTHOR OF
WHAT IN THE WORLD IS GOING ON?

DR. DAVID JEREMIAH

LIVING WITH CONFIDENCE IN A CHAOTIC WORLD

WHAT ON EARTH SHOULD WE DO NOW?

INCORPORATE THESE CORRELATING
STUDY MATERIALS
BY AUTHOR DR. DAVID JEREMIAH

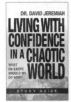

STUDY GUIDE

This 128-page study guide correlates with the *Living with Confidence in a Chaotic World* messages by Dr. David Jeremiah. Each lesson provides an outline, overview, and application study questions for each chapter.

AUDIO MESSAGE ALBUM
10 AUDIO MESSAGES

The material found in this book originated from messages preached by Dr. David Jeremiah at Shadow Mountain Community Church where he serves as Senior Pastor. These ten messages are conveniently packaged in one audio album.

DVD MESSAGE PRESENTATIONS
10 DVD MESSAGES

Watch Dr. Jeremiah deliver the ten *Living with Confidence in a Chaotic World* original messages in the special DVD collection.

SMALL GROUP STUDY CURRICULUM

The *Living with Confidence in a Chaotic World* DVD-Based Small Group Kit will take your small group or Sunday school class through ten weeks of Dr. Jeremiah's teaching for living with certain hope in our uncertain times.

ORDER THESE *LIVING WITH CONFIDENCE IN A CHAOTIC WORLD*
RESOURCE PRODUCTS FROM DAVIDJEREMIAH.ORG

THE NEW YORK TIMES BEST SELLER
THAT STARTED IT ALL!

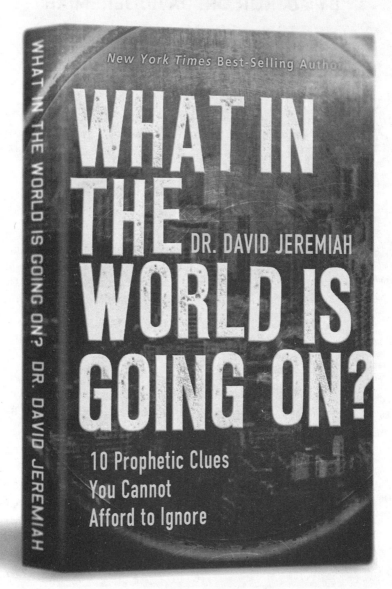

The Bible prophecy prequel to
Living with Confidence in a Chaotic World
by Dr. David Jeremiah

IS THE TURBULENT ECONOMIC & POLITICAL STATE OF THIS WORLD ACTUALLY PROPHESIED IN THE BIBLE?

If so, what are we to do about it? It is hard to piece together all this information in a way that gives a comprehensive picture of what the End Times will look like. That's why so many theories abound. And that's why Dr. David Jeremiah has written *What in the World Is Going On?*, a unique book that cuts through the hundreds of books and numerous theories to identify the ten essential biblical prophecies that are affecting our world today.

There is no other book like this. You'll find it is the ultimate study tool for understanding the future. You'll have a greater sense of comfort that, even in these turbulent times, God is indeed in control. If Bible prophecy has always been a mystery to you, Dr. Jeremiah's book will help you solve the mystery. At last, Bible prophecy can make sense, and make a difference. It's never been more important. *What in the World Is Going On?* is shocking and eye-opening but essential reading in these turbulent days.

WHAT IN THE WORLD IS GOING ON? BRINGS BIBLE PROPHECY TO LIGHT ON:

- The oil crisis
- The resurgence of Russia
- The new axis of evil
- The importance of Israel
- The new powers of the European Union

WHAT IN THE WORLD IS GOING ON?

is available in fine bookstores everywhere and through Turning Point where you will also find a correlating study guide, ten message CD album, DVD presentations, and small group curriculum of this book.

VISIT DAVIDJEREMIAH.ORG TO ORDER

OTHER TITLES
BY DR. DAVID JEREMIAH

CAPTURED BY GRACE   A *NEW YORK TIMES* BEST-SELLER!

By following the dramatic story of the "Amazing Grace" hymnwriter, John Newton, and the apostle Paul's own encounter with the God of grace, David Jeremiah helps readers understand the liberating power of permanent forgiveness and mercy.

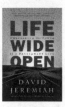

LIFE WIDE OPEN

In this energizing book, Dr. David Jeremiah opens our eyes to how we can live a life that exudes an attitude of hope and enthusiasm . . . a life of passion . . . a LIFE WIDE OPEN! *Life Wide Open* offers a vision, both spiritual and practical, of what our life can be when we allow the power of passion to permeate our souls.

SIGNS OF LIFE   A *NEW YORK TIMES* BEST-SELLER!

How does the world recognize us as God's ambassadors? In *Signs of Life* you will take a journey that will lead you to a fuller understanding of the marks that identify you as a Christian, signs that will advertise your faith and impact souls for eternity.

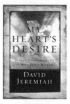

MY HEART'S DESIRE

How would you answer a pollster who appeared at your church asking for a definition of worship? Is it really a sin to worship without sacrifice? When you finish studying *My Heart's Desire*, you'll have not just an answer, but the biblical answer to that all-important question.

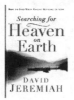

SEARCHING FOR HEAVEN ON EARTH
Join Dr. Jeremiah as he traces Solomon's path through the futility of:
• The search for wisdom and knowledge
• Wild living and the pursuit of pleasure
• Burying oneself in work
• Acquiring as much wealth as possible
Dr. Jeremiah takes readers on a discovery to find out what really matters in life, the secret to enjoying "heaven on earth."

WHEN YOUR WORLD FALLS APART
When Your World Falls Apart recounts Dr. Jeremiah's battle against cancer and the real-life stories of others who have struggled with tragedy. Highlighting ten Psalms of encouragement, each chapter is a beacon of light in those moments when life seems hopeless.

SLAYING THE GIANTS
Loneliness. Discouragement. Worry. Anger. Procrastination. Doubt. Fear. Guilt. Temptation. Resentment. Failure. Jealousy. Have these giants infiltrated your life? Do you need the tools to slay these daunting foes? With practical appeal and personal warmth, Dr. Jeremiah's book, *Slaying the Giants in Your Life* will become your very own giant-slaying manual.

TURNING POINTS & SANCTUARY
These 365-day devotionals by Dr. Jeremiah will equip you to live with God's perspective. These topically arranged devotionals enable you to relate biblical truths to the reality of everyday living—every day of the year. Perfect for yourself or your next gift-giving occasion, *Turning Points* and *Sanctuary* are beautifully packaged with a padded cover, original artwork throughout, and a ribbon page marker.

STAY CONNECTED
TO THE TEACHING OF DR. DAVID JEREMIAH

Take advantage of two great ways to let Dr. David Jeremiah give you
spiritual direction everyday! Both are absolutely FREE!

TURNING POINTS MAGAZINE AND DEVOTIONAL

Receive Dr. David Jeremiah's monthly
magazine, *Turning Points* each month:

- Monthly Study Focus
- 48 pages of life-changing reading
- Relevant Articles
- Special Features
- Humor Section
- Family Section
- Daily devotional readings for each
  day of the month
- Bible study resource offers
- Live Event Schedule
- Radio & Television Information

YOUR DAILY TURNING POINT E-DEVOTIONAL

Start your day off right! Find words of inspiration
and spiritual motivation waiting for you on your
computer every morning! You can receive a daily
e-devotion communication from David Jeremiah
that will strengthen your walk with God and
encourage you to live the authentic Christian life.

Sign up for these two **free** services by visiting
us online at www.DavidJeremiah.org and clicking
on MAGAZINE to sign up for your monthly copy
of *Turning Points* and your Daily Turning Point.

⬆ MAXIMUM CHURCH

READY! SET! GROWTH!
LET DR. JEREMIAH'S MAXIMUM CHURCH TAKE YOUR CHURCH THERE.

With a united vision to strengthen the Body of Christ and reach the community, your church can experience spiritual and fiscal growth through creative and compelling campaigns.

With over forty years of ministry experience, founder Dr. David Jeremiah now shares his passion for pulpit teaching and church leadership by offering solid Bible teaching campaigns designed to stimulate the spiritual and fiscal growth of local churches. Maximum Church campaigns are created for full-spectrum ministry including preaching, teaching, drama, small group Bible curriculum, and suggested Sunday school material—all supported by electronic, print, and audio visual files.

SIGNS OF LIFE

Lead your church to become one of Christ-like influence in your community as you take the five Life Signs discussed in this book and apply them to the lives of your congregation.

This campaign is based on Dr. David Jeremiah's best-selling book *Signs of Life*.

CAPTURED BY GRACE

Based on the best-selling book *Captured by Grace* by David Jeremiah, this ministry growth campaign will help your church and community discover the depths of God's unrelenting love and grace.

For more information on Maximum Church,
VISIT WWW.MAXIMUMCHURCH.COM